Miles — for once, probably
not music to your ears!

Back to the Drawing Board

Sir Sydney Chapman

With best wishes

Sydney

May 2011

Published in 2010 in association with
Absolute Design Solutions

ISBN 978-0-9552139-9-1

Cover and pages designed and typeset by
Rachel Jones
Absolute Design Solutions
www.absolutedesignsolutions.co.uk

Printed and bound in the UK by
Lightning Source

CONTENTS

INTRODUCTION

Four hundred years ago, a chapman had been described as:

> *"a paultrie pedlar who in a long packe or maund, which he carries for the most part open, and hanging from his neck before him, hath Almanacks, Bookes of News, or other trifling ware to sell."*

The word is almost defunct today but in longer dictionaries is described simply as a person who sells from door-to-door or in the street with a second meaning which refers to a person who tries to promote some cause.

I prefer the latter definition, though promoting my cause has led me to peddling my political prejudices from door-to-door in many streets over the more than fifty years that I have been a member of the Conservative Party.

Autobiographies are written by great men about great events, or perhaps by people who wish to promote their importance in the body politic. I prefer to call this offering a memoir as it is just a personal account of a mere backbencher who survived for thirty years at Westminster with six of them in the Government Whips' Office.

I retired from the House of Commons in 2005 but it was to be two years before I began the journey chronicling my life and another two to complete it. Much has happened since but I have not mentioned any later events, concentrating on my life as I saw things then.

When I left school, I trained as an architect and had no thoughts about reaching beyond the drawing board to the then hidden and uncertain depths of politics. But fate determined otherwise and this is my personal political odyssey.

If any part of it is not in accordance with the political correctness of our age, then I can only call in aid that it is written in the style and mores of my generation. For example, I was taught that 'he' includes 'she' or as I recall Margaret Thatcher putting it when Education Secretary: "in English usage, the man embraces the woman."

Readers will also realise that I cannot instinctively think or calculate in the metric system. Doubtless this is because my contemporaries were brought up to appreciate the virtues of imperial preference in weights and measures - as well as trade!

This septuagenarian has now lived through eighteen Parliaments which produced thirteen Prime Ministers, from Baldwin to Blair (and now Brown). Politics has truly been my life, but when a young constituent once asked me if I had been in politics all my life, I replied, a little too hastily, "not yet".

PROLOGUE

The majestic neo-classical Council House in Birmingham was playing host to the twelve parliamentary constituencies of Britain's second city as votes were being counted at the February 1974 General Election.

It was a biting cold and wet night and I was glad to have taken shelter in one of the large first floor reception rooms off the domed grand staircase after three weeks of campaigning for re-election as the MP for Handsworth.

I was not expected to win due to adverse boundary changes but three weeks is a sufficient time in politics to become deluded and even though the campaign had gone disastrously off-course for my party, I clung to the belief that things would turn out differently – at least in my bailiwick. In my mind, forlorn hope had been replaced with a fantasy of dramatic victory.

The counted votes are stacked in rows on a table and the comparative numbers cast for each candidate can be readily if somewhat roughly assessed. I was faltering from the start, but not too far behind to give up all hope of a late surge of support.

The Returning Officer, Marjorie Brown – the first woman Lord Mayor of Birmingham – called me over before she announced the inevitable. She consoled me by saying that although she was pleased to be declaring the third Conservative defeat in her city that night, she was personally sorry it was me. Later I realised that this subjective observation whispered to me was due to my being the only MP to have attended her Mayoral Ball a few months before. On that occasion she had proceeded in state, mace-bearer to the fore, from the top table to thank me publicly for coming.

The result was that my erstwhile majority of under 2000 had been turned into defeat by a similar margin. The winner speaks first and Mr John Lee stepped forward as the new Labour MP. He was no stranger to knife-edge recounts, victory or defeat, having just failed to represent Reading by 10 votes in 1964, winning the seat in 1966, and then losing it again in 1970. He modestly played down triumph but was shrewd enough not to thank me effusively as he correctly judged that another election would have to be held shortly.

My turn came to speak to the packed room. I said all the right and polite things and it was obvious that my opponents had no desire to rub my face in adversity. I was determined to concede defeat on an unusual note:

"And finally, my Lord Mayor, let me say that the only distinction I had in the last Parliament was to be the only architect in the House of Commons." The room fell silent with the assembled wondering what on earth I was talking about (not for the first or last time, I might add) "...And so I reckon that I'm the only failed politician tonight who can say with literal truth - ah well, back to the drawing board."

1

THE WORLD INTO
WHICH I CAME

Fourteen months after I was born, I had already lived under three monarchs. More than seventy years on I've lived under only four. I came into the world at lunchtime on an autumnal day in 1935 in the then family home, a largish house half way up Buxton Road on the east side of Macclesfield, an old silk town in Cheshire near the southern end of the Pennines.

My parents had moved from north-east England less than two years before. Father, named William after his grandfather and great grandfather, was better known as Billy. He was born in Ferryhill, County Durham in 1909 and educated at Barnard Castle before training as an architect and town planner at King's College Newcastle, then part of Durham University. His father, Sydney (b. 1880) was a builder who later moved to Whitley Bay on the coast outside Newcastle.

Father was the eldest of four children who were born over a time span of sixteen years and his younger brother Sydney, who showed every promise of becoming the black sheep of the family, died somewhat mysteriously aged eighteen jumping trains in Canada. I was named after him. The two other siblings were Mary (who I knew quite well in later life) and Joan (who died in her forties).

My mother, christened Edith Laura but known as Laurie, was born in the old town of Washington, County Durham in 1911. The family moved to Chester-le-Street when her father, Tom Wadge (b. 1874), became Sanitary Inspector of the old District Council, though mother's birth certificate describes him as an "Inspector of Nuisances."

Mother was the youngest of five children: Herbert, born in 1899 and just serving in World War I; Olive, Marie and Horace. Mother was studying at Durham University and played Hockey and Tennis for the County when she met my father. By all accounts, they quickly fell in love and married in 1933 without mother completing her degree course. They then moved to Macclesfield where my elder brother Michael was born ten months later. I do not know if it was a marriage made in Heaven but it certainly finished fifteen years later as a union dissolved in Hell.

Father had set up his practice in the middle of the town in Jordangate House, a Georgian building with a handsome façade. His first partner was Arthur Brookes, who became one of my godfathers and whose surname I bear as a middle name. The firm was called Dobson Chapman and Partners (Dobson being his middle name) and an architectural firm bearing this name still operated from there until recently. He had neat writing and was ambidextrous, having been naturally left-handed but forced to write with his other one at school.

An early commission was to design five houses in front of Butley Hall (a stone-facaded Georgian building) just outside Prestbury village, three miles north of Macclesfield. To build these homes in such a setting must have been controversial even in those days but the project proved successful, not least because it was a low density development covering three acres and the hall had already been converted into flats. He bought the plot immediately in front and built a four-bedroom house with a back garden large enough to include a tennis court. At the front of the house, but detached from it, he created a half-acre lawn and our home was grandly named Butley Hall Green. We moved in when I was fifteen-months-old and, shortly after, a sapling oak was planted by the Parish Council to commemorate the Coronation of King George VI.

It was in this pleasant environment that I was raised and spent the next fourteen years of my life. Prestbury ("the town of priests") is still a beautiful village dating from Saxon times – a Cross from the 10th century has been preserved in the churchyard, near a surviving Norman Chapel built in 1190. The present church was started thirty years later and today boasts a typical 15th century tower and, as with many other churches, an aisle was enlarged and other restoration work carried out, designed by the prolific Victorian architect Sir Gilbert Scott in the last quarter of the 19th century.

*   *   *

When I was born the world's population had just reached 2 billion with 46 million (less than 7 per cent over sixty-five) living on our small and already densely populated island. Since then, the earth's numbers have trebled while ours has passed 60 million (with nearly 17 per cent over sixty-five). I was among the 80 per cent who lived in a town or city when urban areas covered only 10 per cent of the UK's land area (today 20 per cent).

As soon as my birth was announced, Mao Tse-tung ended his Long March and Mussolini invaded Abyssinia. Shortly after, Hitler embarked on his extra-territorial ambitions and the Spanish Civil War began. My arrival was celebrated with the invention of nylon, George Gershwin's *Porgy and Bess*, T.S.Eliot's *Murder in the Cathedral* and Dimitri Shostakovich's *First Symphony*. Born in the same month as me were songsters-to-be as diverse as Luciano Pavarotti, Elvis Presley and Julie Andrews.

The World was beginning to shrink with flying becoming increasingly popular. Gatwick was about to be opened to relieve pressure on Croydon aerodrome and it was boasted that air traffic control would be able to handle six aircraft at a time. On land, Malcolm Campbell's car *Bluebird* broke through the 300mph barrier and the London & North Eastern Railway's *Silver Jubilee* set a record speed of 112mph.

At Westminster, Stanley Baldwin had become Prime Minister again in the continuing National Government, with his predecessor Ramsey MacDonald remaining in the ministerial team and being joined by his son, Malcolm – the first time in seventy years a father and son had both sat in the same Cabinet. However, Baldwin called an Election immediately after my birth and Ramsey (considered a traitor by some in his Party for forming the National Government in 1931) lost his seat to Manny Shinwell.

The result was another triumph for the Government dominated by the Tories who won 432 of the 615 seats, although they lost over 80 to Labour who trebled their numbers to 156, while the Liberals were reduced to 20. This political situation was reflected in two of the hit songs of the year: *Blue Moon* and *Red Sails in the Sunset*. Clement Attlee became the "stop-gap" leader of Labour (he went on to lead them for twenty years) and Anthony Eden became Foreign Secretary when Sir Samuel Hoare resigned following the storm of indignation aroused by the Anglo-French peace proposals for Abyssinia.

Britain's economy was beginning to revive with unemployment falling to under 2 million from the high of over 3 million three years before. However, there were only 10 million people employed. The pound bought nearly 5 US Dollars, 20 Deutschmarks, 25 Swiss Francs and 124 French Francs.

Average male earnings were £150 pa with women getting only £70. This blatant sex discrimination was accepted as the differential resulted in much more female employment. Agricultural workers earned less than £90 pa compared with miners getting £150 but the elite of the working class were train drivers who notched up over £250. The highest paid professional was a family doctor earning £1,000.

All these figures, of course, have to be set in the context of the living costs of the day. A 4lb loaf of bread cost 7.5d (just over 3p) and petrol only 1/6d a gallon (the equivalent of 1.6p per litre). The average house price was

£300 and new cars coming onto the market included the Ford V-8 at £225 and the SS Jaguar at £385.

Such has been inflation that today's £1 would have bought only 2.5p (sixpenny-piece or a "tanner" in pre-decimal coinage) worth of goods in 1935. However, male average earnings then would be the equivalent of only £6,000 pa today. All this begs the question of comparative standards of living. In those days the income of the average British family may have been appreciably less than one at the start of the third millennium, but their needs would have been fewer and the staples of life much cheaper.

We may look back and ask how the average family could have been comfortable without central heating, fitted carpets, the omnipresent TV, fridge or washing machine – only a scrubbing board with a mangle to put the sodden clothes through before hanging them out to dry. My mother's pride and joy was a Singer sewing machine.

All-in-all, my parents lived in an equally uncertain world as we do today but they inhabited a quieter, slower and less crowded environment in, perhaps, a more pleasant land.

*　　*　　*

My first memory was of being led with my brother Michael from the kitchen to the dining room and being shown a bunch of bananas in a bowl on the sideboard. Father said that it would be a long time before we saw any more of them. This, I have convinced myself, was on the day World War II broke out. My second earliest memory was being taken to see an old man living in a modest cottage in the village and being told that he had known someone who had fought at the Battle of Waterloo. This clearly impressed me but it was some time before I started making the age calculations.

That these earliest recollections were related to war was not a good omen but we were fortunate to be isolated from much of the misery of the new conflagration. My father was deemed to be in a 'reserved occupation' so was not conscripted into the armed forces. This must have been due to his town planning activities but very few of his contemporary professionals were spared the call of the military. The family was also fortunate in its location – a rural area well to the south of the Manchester conurbation. Only two bombs landed within five miles of our home and our air raid precautions involved no Anderson shelter, merely a metal shutter on a ground floor window. My mother's contribution to the War was to become an officer in the Girls Training Corps while father became a Macclesfield town councillor, returned unopposed following a vacancy.

My most evocative memory was regularly hearing the noise of dozens of Lancaster bombers flying overhead from Woodford aerodrome six miles away and praying for their safe return. Other sounds implanted in my mind were the noise of steam trains roaring past the village on a long and high embankment and the incessant chattering of rooks in old trees at the back of our garden. At an early age, I became fascinated with railways and soon became a keen train spotter, faithfully collecting and recording the names and numbers of the engines and learning by rote the times of all trains stopping at the station. My Uncle Herbert, headmaster of a secondary school in Sheffield, used to say of me that he did not know of another person with so much useless information. The railway had brought our village within 35 minutes of Manchester and the stationmaster, a Mr. Pritchard, constructed in timber a scaled down set of signals which was given to me one Christmas via Santa Claus. I derived many hours of pleasure setting them and was thrilled to be allowed into the actual station signal box to see the real ones being pulled and watching the express trains roar by. We had a dog – a black Labrador called Pax – who sometimes accompanied me on short walks to the village or station. One day she disappeared and I was told she had gone to stay with a friend of my father. It was only a long time later that I was told that she had been run over on the road behind our house.

As the war continued, and armed with the precautionary gas mask, I became more aware of the reasons for it and the various battles and other events which took place. These were heightened by the arrival of a thousand or more GIs who were billeted in the grounds of Mottram Hall (now a very up-market country hotel) two miles away. My father met a Lieutenant Norquist in our local pub 'The Admiral Rodney.' He hailed from Seattle and became a friend of the family in the few months leading up to the Normandy landings. For some time he sent food parcels to us but we were never able to find out where he was or what had happened to him.

This US visitation to our little corner of England sharpened my interest and I became absorbed in the battles for Europe, particularly recalling D-Day, the liberation of Paris and VE Day. I was nearly four years old when the war started and a mature nine-and-a half when it ended. The wireless played an important part in my early life, not only in providing information about the war but also entertainment. I can still hear the voice of Alvar Liddell reading the news bulletins and Tommy Handley's jokes on ITMA, the weekly comedy show which lampooned Hitler and introduced us to Mrs Mopp and her words: "Can I do you now, Sir." Later radio programmes I enjoyed varied from Richard Murdoch and Kenneth Horne's "Much Binding in the Marsh" to Alistair Cooke's weekly "Letter from America" which started just after the War ended and lasted until 2004. My first introduction to a BBC musical programme was probably Reginald Dixon playing the Wurlitzer organ at Blackpool Tower as well as George Formby strumming on his ukelele.

My education had begun at the age of three when I attended Prestbury High School, better known as Miss Tracey's Kindergarten, which occupied the ground floor of Butley Hall. As this school was directly opposite our house, I was not homesick and must have enjoyed my first academic encounter but I cannot in truth remember much about it. Later I became a regular reader of the two leading comics, the *Beano* and *Dandy* and avidly followed the escapades of such heroes as 'Desperate Dan' and 'Dennis the Menace.'

Before I was six, I became a day boy at Beech Hall, a preparatory school set on a hill on the north side of Macclesfield and surrounded by trees and rhododendron bushes. The headmaster was Mr J.D.M. Hunt and the only other master's name I recall was a Mr Worthington, probably because he married Mr Hunt's daughter Penelope. The school's playing field had one notable inconvenience: if the cricket ball was hit too hard, or the football passed too wide, the spherical object in question had to be retrieved by running down an adjacent steep hill and then scrambling back up. In most games, I seemed to have had more exercise off the field than on it. I remember there being four "houses" in the school: Oak, Ash, Elm and Yew which were given the colours of red, yellow, green and blue respectively. I was in Yew and perhaps all this was a subliminal indication of my future interest in trees as well as coming political predilections.

After a while, my brother and I became weekly boarders (goodness knows why when home was less than three miles away) and I became homesick. I longed for the weekends, which only started at midday on Saturday, and even then there were interminable waits while father finished his week's business in the bar of the Macclesfield Arms Hotel before picking us up in his Daimler. I can still remember its registration number and his other love: a Leica camera which recorded all family toings and froings in the last half of the 1930s.

We moved schools in 1945. The Leas, Hoylake had been requisitioned as a RAF Convalescent Home during the war and the school had decamped to the Glenridding Hotel at the south end of Ullswater in the Lake District. We thus became term-boarders and had to count weeks instead of days away from home. Quite why we were moved was uncertain. It might have been dissatisfaction with Beech Hall or parental problems, or a bit of both, but we were happy in our new environment and it was certainly a huge benefit for me to be in the ambiance of an elder brother who was big for his age and popular. The main embarrassment I suffered was a propensity to wet my bed but I was never castigated for this; and the only thing I disliked was the early morning cold bath (one of the few rituals I detested about boarding schools).

We were ensconced in the Lake District for only two terms before the school reclaimed its home in the Wirral, but not before our sister Christine was born, all but eight days short of my tenth birthday and two months after VJ Day and the General Election immediately preceding it. I remember my parents being elated and relieved at the ending of hostilities but mystified and hurt that Winston Churchill had been summarily rejected by the electorate.

The school was situated on Meols Drive, between Hoylake and West Kirby, and had been founded in 1898. The house, subsequently greatly enlarged at the rear, was an imposing edifice on the flat landscape of the Wirral opposite Hilbre Island. Between the school grounds and the mudflats of the Dee estuary was the Royal Liverpool Golf Course and I recall the excitement when it hosted the 1947 British Open championship.

The Leas School had joint headmasters: Mr A. F. Fetherstonhaugh, a scholarly Irish gentleman of a somewhat frail and languid disposition, and Mr H. F. C. Silcock, with a more ruddy appearance and irascible temperament, doubtless acquired from his frequent visits to the Royal Liverpool clubhouse. One senior master who stood out was a portly man, K.H.M.Sutton, whose obesity was as a result of being gassed in the First World War. He had first been appointed a master just before it and was a gruff but kindly man of some means who lived with his sister in Eastbourne during school holidays. Fetherstonhaugh seemed to run the academic side while Silcock masterminded the sports curriculum and Sutton, a keen photographer, was the self-appointed school archivist. My termly reports suggest I was an average scholar but my forte was neat handwriting. My final report said I was "a keen and painstaking games player... a fearless tackler and strong kicker who stood up to hard knocks." I was a good shot with the rifle in the indoor range but by no means best in the school. While I love music, I was not at all accomplished on the pianoforte and it took me one whole term to master the hymn *Oh God Our Help In Ages Past* on three fingers. There was also a monthly Parliamentary Society when three conscripted pupils had to speak before their masters and peers about different aspects of current affairs. We were allowed access to a national newspaper and we read out our observations. My subject was Foreign and Sporting Affairs on the two occasions I was selected and I went about my task with determined enthusiasm, easily winning the contest both times. The school magazine reported that I "gave a very amusing speech" on my second appearance but I'm sure that I didn't intend to be humorous.

Other extra-mural activities were encouraged and the school had its own pack of scouts and cubs. The patrols were named after birds such as owls, swallows, seagulls and curlews and the pinnacle of my outdoor career was to be made patrol leader of the cuckoos, which I realised at the time could be misconstrued and used in evidence against me in later life.

Among my contemporaries was the 8th Marquis of Waterford and his younger brother, Lord Patrick Beresford; and Robert Sangster, whose father had founded the Vernon Football Pools firm. Robert was a big lad in his youth and after one round with him in the boxing ring I came to hate this sport. Later in life, he was to become a well known racehorse owner. By this time I was aware that it was mother who came alone to collect me at half-term or visited on special occasions. School holidays were spent at home but we occasionally made long car journeys to the north-east to visit grandparents, crossing the Pennines and traveling via Ilkley, Otley and Harrogate to join the A1. Later I got to know my maternal grandfather quite well. He introduced me to billiards in his working men's club in Chester-le-Street and a particular treat one year was being taken to Roker Park to watch the local football Derby when Sunderland beat Newcastle with Len Shackleton scoring a hatrick.

In due course, brother Michael went to Rugby School and I was to join him a year-and-a half later in the summer term of 1949.

2

RUGBY & RED BRICK

My brother Michael, shortly to be known as Chapman Major, was the sports star of his peers at Rugby School. He was six feet tall when he arrived at the age of thirteen and wore size twelve shoes. He excelled at games and was selected for the House rugby and cricket teams in his first year but he was a modest person who never flaunted his physical prowess.

By his third year he played in the school rugby XV and the cricket and hockey XIs (no soccer was permitted as this was regarded as the undeveloped form of football) and he finished up captaining the school and Public Schools XV. He played hard, ran fast (the one hundred yards in just over ten seconds) and threw the cricket ball (then a feature of Schools' Sports Days) a record distance.

The school's proudest sporting event was the annual cricket match against Marlborough at Lords. Michael did not score many runs or take many wickets in the public gaze there but *The Times* reported that he "hit a six which was a fair assault on the clock tower." Rugby's opening batsman on this occasion was Tom King, later to become a Cabinet Minister. Michael's physique did not make him a natural long distance runner but he came second in the annual Crick Run, the first ever cross country race (dating from 1837). His reports included the comment: "he may not shine academically but he has far more valuable gifts" while headmaster Sir Arthur fforde observed: "seven league boots are what he needs" and his final valediction was "he has a heart of refined gold and is a much respected and welcome person."

Rugby School was founded in 1567 and became a great institution under the 19th century headmaster Thomas Arnold (the father of the poet Matthew Arnold), immortalised in Thomas Hughes "Tom Brown's Schooldays." A statue of Hughes stands in front of the School Library (Temple Reading Room) and opposite, in the School Close, a stone plaque "commemorates the exploit of William Webb Ellis who with a fine disregard for the rules of football as played in his time, first took the ball in his arms and ran with it, thus originating the distinctive feature of the Rugby game in 1823."

When I joined my brother in Michell, one of ten boarding Houses, great things were expected of Chapman Minor (fully five foot 3 inches tall and weighing under seven stone) but hopes were quickly dashed. This sibling was no Olympian colossus striding the playing fields. I was selected for only my House third teams but my one saving grace was that brother was a stranger to the groves of academe while I was somewhat different or, as I put it at the time, my brother was brilliant at games and no good at work while I was no good at games and no good at work. The success of our academic endeavours was to reach only the Fifth Form, separated from the Sixth by the Upper and Lower Twenties.

Rugby was strong on religion (the School motto is 'By Praying, by Working') and two of its Old Boys had been Archbishops of Canterbury: Frederick Temple and his son William. We had to attend a daily morning service with matins and evensong on Sundays. The School Chapel was large and tall, dominating the town, and had been designed in 1872 by William Butterfield, the eminent Victorian architect, in polychrome brickwork or, as I preferred to call it, "a greasy bacon Keble College style." On the walls inside memorial tablets record the lives of eminent Rugbeians and several of them were poets and writers. I was deeply impressed by Rupert Brooke's

"If I should die, think only this of me:
That there's some corner of a foreign field
That is for ever England..."

He was born next door to Michell House. I remember also a triptych of memorial tablets to O.R. poets, with short extracts from their works: Walter Savage Landor's "Finis"

> "I strove with none; for none was worth my strife;
> Nature I loved, and, next to Nature, Art;
> I warmed both hands before the fire of life;
> It sinks, and I am ready to depart."

Matthew Arnold's "Thyrsis"

> "Why faintest thou? I wander'd till I died,
> Roam on! The light we sought is shining still,
> Dost thou ask proof? Our Tree yet crowns the hill,
> Our Scholar travels yet the loved hill-side."

And Arthur Hugh Clough's:

> "Young children gather as their own
> The harvest that the dead had sown."

Among other memorial tablets is one to the Revd Charles Lutwidge Dodgson, better known as Lewis Carroll.

Whatever my limitations in the classroom and on the playing field, I enjoyed life at Rugby and was reasonably well-mannered. I was found guilty of misbehaving only twice: the first was setting off a stink bomb in a Prefect's study. This resulted in my only caning and I was to meet again the offended sixth-former later in life. The second was being overheard whispering an aside when a master was talking about DDT. I innocently inquired: "Is it the same as DTs? This resulted in a detention and having to write two hundred words on DDT. To this day I recall that it stands for dichloro-diphenyl-trichloroethane and I became the school expert on the insecticide. My secret indulgence was to forge, by carving into the wood of the cupboard door in my study, the signatures of a number of the masters, keeping my effort from the public gaze. I often wonder when my work of art was discovered and what happened to it.

While a pupil at Rugby, I made my first visit to London. In the summer of 1951 we travelled by train at a very early hour from Macclesfield to Euston and then on to the South Bank to visit the Festival of Britain. To a fifteen year old's eyes it was a most impressive spectacle and the pointed 'Skylon' and 'Dome of Discovery' looked like landmarks of a future century, while the Festival Hall heralded the architecture of the second half of its century. Later in the day we joined a boat trip to Battersea Park 'Pleasure Gardens' to enjoy the fun fair and arrived back home very late and tired. Until then, Rugby was the most southern place I had been to, having holidayed in northern England, north Wales and, in the summer of 1947, Ireland when we travelled over night from Liverpool to Dublin and then by car to Galway. It was on this trip that sister Christine walked for the first time at the ripe old age of twenty-two months and I had my first beer: it tasted like soap.

Michael left Rugby in 1951 for two years' national service in the Royal Artillery. He played rugby for the Army, Birkenhead Park and Cheshire and thereafter joined Andrew Yule & Co., emigrating to Calcutta. He continued with his sporting interests in India, adding motor racing, and I have no doubt that if he had stayed in the mother country, he would have played for the England Rugby XV. Chapman Minor's public school life was to be a relatively short experience. The family fortunes deteriorated as father's business declined, principally due to ill health brought about by a propensity for pink gins and bloody mindedness against authority, although friends and professional colleagues said he was a kind and generous man.

In 1943, better known as W. Dobson Chapman, he became President of the Town Planning Institute at the age of thirty-four. He remains today the youngest ever leader of that prestigious Royal Institute. His firm had published master plans for such places as Cheshire, Aberdeen and Dundee at a time when his profession was at the dawn of a new era. He also produced a report in 1944 entitled *Towards a new Macclesfield* after voluntarily undertaking two years of spare time research. His plan was centred upon the need to increase the town's population from 35,000 to 50,000 with increased employment opportunities as the once dominant silk industry was dying. Macclesfield's population had remained static for over half-a-century and the explanation for this, he once confided in me, was that each time a new-born babe arrived a young man hurriedly left town. He had the foresight to realise that the town would not be able to rely on its silk reputation for much longer and, in any case, fervently believed that diversification of industry was essential. And so it was that Macclesfield was spared the fate of Lancashire's 'Cottonopolis' in the 1950s and today Maxonians can claim to live in a relatively affluent town.

When hostilities ceased, much of urban Britain needed redeveloping and the new Labour government introduced the great but controversial 1947 Town & Country Planning Act, which effectively nationalised planning, giving government at national and local level sweeping powers, not least in the compulsory acquisition of land with virtually no compensation. This concept and direction did not appeal to father and he followed his heart instead of his professional head, refusing to apply to be one of the new County Planning Officers (or some other similar post). It was all very well remaining in the private sector on principle but there was no longer much need for principals in private practice; and few major commissions now came his way in architecture. His firm in Macclesfield struggled on but became a shadow of its former self.

My parents eventually divorced and mother was almost penniless, going back to College for two years (she had left Durham without a degree) before qualifying and becoming a teacher at Prestbury Primary School in her forties and, a few years later, headmistress of Mottram St. Andrews' School in the next village. She was particularly upset (and rightly so) when drummed out of the Mothers' Union because of her divorce, even though she was the innocent party and had three children with Christine then aged four.

My parents' precarious partnership had had an emotional effect on me at The Leas School but was to have a practical consequence at Rugby. There was no money to pay the fees and I remained there for only three-and-a-half years instead of the customary five. Even then I was only able to do this due to a one-off bursary available for students in such a plight. We had to leave our spacious home and rent a small flat on the top floor in Butley Hall but I don't think Michael or myself suffered psychologically in ever overlooking but not now being able to enjoy the facilities of our erstwhile home and garden.

It was in this situation that I had to leave without any 'A' levels. I had not played for the School in any sport but I had enjoyed myself. The headmaster tried hard to pay me a compliment by observing "a very interesting person" and my first housemaster George Keay did praise me, writing that I was "just like Michael all over again" (he must have been commenting upon my academic progress not gamesmanship). But I did not regard myself as a failure in any way. Perhaps it was that streak of hope and optimism redolent of youth which now sustained me and I looked to the future with a certain confidence.

*   *   *

I left Rugby in December 1952 having decided to try and follow in my father's professional footsteps. When I told him, I detected a scintilla of concern and he offered me a piece of advice: "as an Englishman, Anglican and Architect, beware the three 'RCs' – Russian Communism, Roman Catholicism and Reinforced Concrete." The head of the School of Architecture at the Victoria University of Manchester was Professor Cordingley who just happened to be one of my godparents. My seven 'O' levels were sufficient to gain me entry but one of the conditions of getting a degree in architecture (at least then) was to have the equivalent of an 'A' level in a foreign language. I could not quite understand why being able to wrap one's tongue around the *cedilla* under a French 'c' or the *acento* over a Spanish 'o' helped me to become a better Christopher Wren, but mine not to wonder why...

After leaving school early I had nine months to prepare myself for University. Enter Colonel Percy Wright, an elderly architect who ran a two-roomed practice opposite my father's in Macclesfield. The colonel, who had been injured in the war, had difficulty in moving his jaw and had to have a strap attached to it. He agreed to take me on for the princely sum of ten shillings a week. After a month satisfying himself that I could answer the telephone civilly and make a cup of tea passably, he doubled my salary to £1.

It is difficult to imagine today that this was an adequate amount to live on but it was – not least because I was living rent-free at home. On the five-and-a-half days I worked, the return bus fare totalled only 3/0d (15p) and lunch 2/0d a day. This left enough for a weekly visit to the local cinema and the occasional half-pint in a pub.

The old family home had been sold to a Mr Denis Thornley, a lecturer in Professor Cordingley's department – perhaps another fortuitous circumstance assisting my entry therein. We had no television in our modest flat but Thornley's mother who lived below us did and, come The Queen's Coronation in June 1953, she invited me to watch the black and white spectacle. I was glued to the small box for most of the day. Sixteen months before, our housemaster at Rugby had announced the death of King George VI to his incredulous teenage charges.

The weeks went by and eventually I started on my architectural odyssey. Five years is a long time for any university course and, with the eighteen months requirement of professional experience, it was going to be the next decade before I could call myself an architect. The long haul began as an exciting adventure with lots of fellow students from all sorts of backgrounds; in my year alone there were overseas students from Malaya, Nigeria and Jamaica. We all had greater freedom than at school to study – or not work – and plenty of time to criticise our elders and tell them how to put the world in better shape. In the meantime I had a problem which soon became evident: I had no natural flair for design, nor much ability to understand the science of building. I was, so to speak, a rather humdrum bricks and mortar man in the coming age of pre-stressed cantilevered concrete and floating glass. Furthermore, I could not appreciate the *oeuvre* of some of the revered modern architects of the day. To me, Corbusier's *Unite d'Habitation* with use of bare concrete was ugly and his famous dictum "a house is a machine for living in" left me distinctly unimpressed. I tried hard to convert myself to the architectural fashion of the time but had to conclude that Andrea Palladio was my historical hero and I quickly concluded that the Georgian house represented the golden age of domestic architecture. However, I tried hard to be less conservative and more innovative, recognising that Wren's design for St. Paul's Cathedral was fiercely opposed by the medieval clergy.

Our lecturers seemed to divide themselves into two groups: the academically clever who disinterestedly delivered their papers on a 'take-it-or-leave-it' basis; and the others who were better communicators but had less knowledge to impart. Doubtless the reality was that they all had a bit of both and there was a particular respect for the doyen of them all, Professor Cordingley, who made a weekly visitation to tell us all about the Italian Renaissance period. It was a struggle to keep up with him as he rattled out the long names of churches, palazzas and piazzas but the old master knew his stuff for he was the editor of the then current edition of the architects' bible, Banister Fletcher's *History of Architecture on the Comparative Method.* He was a challenge to his mediocre student who laboriously typed out notes from his lectures upon returning home.

Two impressions were being firmly implanted in my mind. First, if ever I were to become a lecturer, it should be incumbent upon me to create enthusiasm and get the interest of my students. Secondly, it was essential to witness at first hand how projects were built on the ground. We were never taken to a building site to actually see how a damp proof course was inserted, a rafter placed on a wall plate or a sewer laid. It was all theory delivered in words or slides in the lecture room and it was up to us to see how it all came together by arranging our own visits during the university recesses. Clearly architects were to be trained off-site, the opposite of the traditional master mason.

One 'site visit' I looked forward to was a fortnight in York at the Institute of Advanced Architectural Studies at the end of our third year. Unfortunately, I went down with a severe dose of glandular fever and had to stay at home in bed with a large excess of white corpuscles. I spent some of the time reading through the *Oxford Book of Quotations*, which introduced me to many profound and witty observations, and listening to radio broadcasts of the Proms, which heightened my appreciation of classical music. I went to York the following year and fell in love with the city. The excuse for going was to undertake research for a required written thesis on some aspect of architecture. There was little further to write about Georgian York so I plumped for nineteenth century shop fronts. This was at least original and covered some charming Regency facades before concentrating on cast iron Victorian examples. With a borrowed box camera which took square black and white photographs, I recorded about twenty-five shop fronts and more than forty years later returned to search out these buildings and re-photograph them. It was a pleasant surprise to find that twenty of them had survived.

We also had the occasional lecture and studied all that was pleasing architecturally in the city from the Shambles to the great Minster. Pausing in front of one superb Georgian edifice, one of our more popular and friendly lecturers, Frank Jenkins, said: "Chapman, what do you think is the date of this building?" I stood on the pavement affecting studied interest and after a long pause said: "Well, sir, if the building was in London I would put its date at about 1770 but as this is York I would say between 1775 and 1780, perhaps 1777?" He was both surprised and impressed. I had got it exactly right but didn't have the nerve to tell my slightly short-sighted interlocutor that I had spotted the date recorded on a gutter head at the top of the building.

In my year, there were some star students who were to shine in later life. They included Mike McKinnell, with an intense nervous energy which he concealed with a quick laugh and cynical observation. He got a first and went on to win an international competition for a new Boston (Massachusetts) Civic Centre, saw it to a conclusion and then ran a successful practice in the States. There was Robert Martin who had a natural flair and feel for design, shared my scepticism of Corbusier and is a brilliant sketcher and water colourist. After working for Wates (the builders) and Westminster City Council, he became Head of Kensington & Chelsea's Architecture and Planning Department and eventually ran a sucessful practice. He was one of those rare breeds: an excellent designer, an articulate thinker, an accomplished DIY man and very good company. Another contemporary, albeit in the year behind me, was a quiet and more introvert student, Norman (now Lord) Foster. Today he is one of Britain's best known and most successful architects, having designed some stunning buildings in London and abroad. Rightly he is acclaimed among the world's best.

In my last full year at Manchester brother Michael returned on leave from Calcutta. Just before he went to India I had introduced him to an attractive girl, Sheila Fearnley, who lived on the other side of the village and they had corresponded while he was away. On returning, they quickly fell in love and I was best man at their wedding in Prestbury Church. They returned to Calcutta and their first child Clare was born there in 1959. Sheila's father was a car dealer in Manchester and he persuaded them both to return to England, promising Michael a job in his business. They returned at the beginning of 1960 and three more children followed: Mark, Victoria and Helen.

My quinquennial sojourn at Manchester eventually ended. I had survived by scraping through each year's course. My principal contribution had been to encourage the social side of the department and bring staff and students together in occasional beery suppers. It was all superficial, light-hearted stuff but I was agreeably surprised at the number of lecturers who quietly told me how much they appreciated such events. On the final occasion, in front of the Professor whose kindly nature had clearly overlooked my academic limitations, I announced that there would be a team photograph on the following day for all those who had so generously given of their time to help me with my recently completed design thesis – a new town hall for Macclesfield. Luckily for me the resulting eclectic design survived the examiners' scrutiny and even more fortunately for the good burghers of my local town, the project never got beyond the drawing board.

In my first three years at Manchester I had travelled each day by train from home, walking the mile or so from Piccadilly Station to the university campus. In the last two years I went into 'digs' and developed a taste for extramural activities in the evenings. "Social intercourse" is the phrase which springs readily to mind (one of the printed objectives of the Students' Union) and I like to think that I made up for the lack of contact with the opposite sex when I was at Rugby – then a boys only school.

My studies were not completed after the five years as I had decided to take the three-year part-time course in town and country planning. Usually this was accomplished in one full year by students who had read architecture but I could not afford to be unpaid for another year. I began working in my father's firm at £600 pa (by now inflation was taking root) and returned to Manchester two or three evenings a week. By this time I had become academically weary and did the minimum necessary. I passed the first year and repeated the formula in the second but failed in two of the subjects. Enough was enough. In the third year I re-took the second year subjects, passed the third year grades and wrote a thesis on the History of Prestbury to complete the course – all in nine months while in a full-time job.

Tired of university life, I left Manchester in 1961 with no degree but two diplomas and went forth into an uncertain world with my ears picking up the sound of distant political thunder.

3

A YOUNG CONSERVATIVE
& CANDIDATE

I joined the village branch of the Young Conservatives when I left Rugby. It seemed the natural thing to do, particularly if you lived in the prosperous area of Prestbury and found yourself in a financially parlous state with only a few pennies a week to sustain spare time activities. The branch was a mechanism on which to hang social activities but the village YCs did their bit when the political calendar beckoned.

Within two years I became chairman and launched a campaign to attract new members, twisting the arms of anyone under thirty. I organised social events and the odd political discussion and my chairmanship coincided with the 1955 general election. By this time the branch membership had increased from 50 to 130 and we embarked on canvassing encounters in Macclesfield. Returning home after one rain-sodden evening, I moaned to my mother that only 5 per cent of the electors seemed interested in politics. Her reply was to state that it was comforting to know that 95 per cent of people were normal.

My first public speech was when the sitting MP came to a meeting in the village hall during the campaign and I was asked to give the vote of thanks. Our candidate was Air Commodore Arthur Vere Harvey whose name I regarded as rather a mouthful so I advised the villagers that the best way to remember him was by replacing the 'Arthur Vere' with 'half-a-beer.' The audience affected amusement and the candidate wearily smiled. I thought that Arthur Vere Harvey had made a rather pedestrian speech but as we walked home mother said that he had her support because he could be trusted. This was one of my first political lessons: gaining respect and support was rarely achieved by making amusing and witty little speeches.

Sir Arthur (as he later became) had been selected as the Conservative candidate for the 1945 election after the previous choice, Guy Gibson VC of the Dambusters, was subsequently killed on a later bombing raid. Harvey remained in the Commons until the beginning of the 1970 Parliament and was chairman of the 1922 Committee of Conservative MPs at my first meeting. He became Lord Harvey of Prestbury.

While enjoying my YC days I took a sporting initiative: founding a croquet team. We played on pub bowling greens (there were quite a number of them in those days). The full name of the enterprise was 'The All Prestbury Croquet Club for professional gentlemen and their current lady friends.' We had two rules: 'Gentlemen are requested not to spit on the lawns or disport themselves in any other manner likely to arouse the indignation of other sundry bodies.' The other was crisper: 'Gentlemen are not allowed to play with weighted balls.' Programme cards were printed and I designed a membership tie, consisting of crossed mallet sticks under a tankard rampant. We toured the hostelries of East Cheshire but were rarely invited back.

I enjoyed myself immensely in my student and YC days, mostly in the environment of my home town and village rather than Manchester. Macclesfield had five cinemas with such names as Majestic, Rex, Regal and Picturedrome. Michael and I had a number of friends, one of whom was the Vicar's son with the appropriate surname of Hope. I enjoyed going to church, but with my eyes concentrating more on the opposite sex than the Prayer Book. The facilities and shops in the village were plentiful with a butcher and baker if not a candlestick maker. One shop, "Ye Olde Chocolate Box", was run by a good friend Stafford Beech who was not best pleased when I kept referring to his establishment as "The Old Brown Jock Strap." There were two pubs: the "Admiral Rodney" dating from 1780 while the other one had two names: one side of the hanging sign proclaiming "The Legh Arms" while the other side announced "The Black Boy." In my younger days I had known most of the shops by their owners' names, thus the butcher was 'Mr Samway's,' the baker 'Miss Harcourt's,' the grocer 'Mrs Peel's', the odds and ends shop 'Miss Ford's' and the garage 'Hollingdrake's.'

The River Bollin, a tributary of the Mersey, runs through the middle of the village, separating the old parishes of Butley and Prestbury. The village had a smithy and I remember horses being shod but my most abiding memory was of a corrugated hut precariously perched by the river which I knew as a cycle shop. I frequently visited this ever temporary establishment when my main mode of travel needed attention. It was run by a kindly old man called Harry Dawson and later by his son Walter who had a ruddy, cherubic face and a great sense of humour. He employed a man called Henry Cooper, a very pale imitator of his then unknown pugilistic namesake, who had been severely injured in the War by a shell through his shoulder necessitating treatment in hospital every day. I didn't know this at the time and when told admired his uncomplaining fortitude. I was a keen cyclist and occasionally rode the forty-five mile round trip to train spot at Crewe Station, leaving the bike unattended and unlocked outside. A particular feat I achieved was to pedal furiously from home up to 'The Cat and Fiddle,' the second highest pub in England ten miles away, in one hour and race back in half the time. When I was ten, I had fallen from my bike causing my nose to meet a gravelled drive and ever since it has remained slightly askew.

Recently, I visited Prestbury to attend a reunion dinner with some Old Boys of Beech Hall School more than sixty years before. I'm glad to report that the village centre is still very attractive in spite of the increased traffic through it but inevitably the shops have changed. The Post Office survives but remains under threat. The Old Reading Room is now home to an Estate Agent (with two more within fifty yards), while the butcher's premises has been turned into a clothes shop called "The Spirit of the Andes." Sadly, "Ye Olde Chocolate Box" and Dawson's hardware shop are no more. The up-market flavour of this haven in the stockbroker and football star belt of south Manchester is complete with no fewer than seven expensive restaurants in the 250 yard length of the village street.

Half way through my student days I reached my twenty-first birthday, which was marked by my mother opening a bank account for me with a cheque for £25. The Queen also celebrated the day by opening Calder Hall in Cumbria, the World's first commercial nuclear power station. A year later the space age dawned with the launching of the USSR's unmanned bleeping satellite Sputnik, followed by Sputnik II with Leika the dog. These circumventions of our globe were tracked by Manchester University's Jodrell Bank, ten miles from home. The space race was joined by the US early in 1958 and eventually "won" by the Americans landing on the moon at the end of the 1960s. It was around this time that I met a dazzling Swedish blonde who arrived in the village as an au pair to a well-heeled family. I was completely bowled over and invited her out for a drink (all I could afford if my £25 was to remain in the bank). All went well until I steered the conversation to foreign languages. Impressed with her near perfect English, I asked her how many languages she spoke. After a short contemplation, she said "four-and-a-half." I queried this and asked her what they were. "English, of course, German, French and Spanish, and because I can speak Spanish I am able to understand and speak a little Italian." I was deeply impressed and said: "well, you speak Swedish so that's another and presumably Norwegian and Danish?" "Oh, those aren't languages", she dismissively replied and then asked me how many I spoke. "Only three" I replied and quickly changed the conversation but she persisted in asking me which three I could speak. I weakly replied: "English, of course, and American and Australian". She was not amused and although our friendship continued, it veered somewhat from the direction I hoped it might take. I tried to console myself in concluding that Swedes did not have a sense of humour.

In 1957 I was elected chairman of the Macclesfield constituency YCs which had eight branches and again I managed to get many new members to join. The problem was keeping up the numbers as many of the young recruits soon left the district for university or national service. I served for three years becoming chairman of the East Cheshire group of constituencies and organising the YC input into the 1959 General Election. I had become hooked on politics and flung myself into the campaign during every spare moment. We challenged the Labour candidate to an old fashioned hustings in the market square. Rightly he ignored our invitation but we did get the headlines in a local paper.

The genius of the Conservative approach lay not just in welcoming young people into the Party but making the YCs an integral part of its organisation. Thus when chairman of Prestbury and Macclesfield I was automatically a vice-chairman of the senior association. This meant that in 1957 I was able to attend my first Party Conference. It was in Brighton and was memorable for Lord Hailsham's rip-roaring speech ending in ringing the chairman's bell with a reminder to Labour (then riding high in the polls) to beware of John Donne's words:

"never send to know for whom the bell tolls;
it tolls for thee."

If the YC movement had gained a reputation as a marriage bureau, I was the exception who proved the rule, but what a way to attract new members. Neil Kinnock once told me that he had joined his local YCs in

South Wales as, he delicately put it, "my best chance to pull the birds."

My time in the Young Conservatives taught me a second political lesson: you don't attract members by having a political argument with them; you do so by being friendly and giving them the opportunity to meet people and enjoy themselves. The icing on the cake was the 5 per cent who became deeply interested in politics and then played an active part in the Party. Labour never seemed to realise this, probably due to the basic philosophical difference between the Left and Right. The Left always wanted to change society fundamentally while the Right (so we would say) wanted to conserve what was best in it. And so the young Left were always battling with the old Left while the young Right happily co-operated with their elders (at least in my younger days). I had little interest in the activities of the Students' Union at Manchester but concentrated all my spare time with the YCs.

My first visit to the House of Commons was in the mid 1950s. Arthur Vere Harvey had arranged for me to have a ticket to the Gallery and I attended the Third Reading of the controversial Bill introducing Independent Television. Today, it seems incredible that the Opposition objected to a commercial channel and I sat enthralled at the spectacle below me, remaining to the very end. The bonus was to see Churchill and Attlee sitting in the Chamber (the first and last time I saw them both in the flesh).

At the beginning of the 1960s I was due to be called up for National Service, deferred while at University. I was quite relaxed about this impending two year break in my civvy street career even though I would have been in the very last intake before the abolition of conscription. Not aware of any impediment to my joining the army, I presented myself for a medical inspection only to discover that my annual bout of hay fever was enough to bar me from serving my country. They were taking only the very fittest and so it was straight back to the drawing board and the YCs and I was elected to their national advisory committee as Peter (now Lord) Walker was relinquishing the chairmanship. He was soon to be elected an MP as many of his predecessors had, including Anthony Nutting (the first chairman), John Hay, Bill van Straubenzee, Geoffrey Finsberg and Fergus Montgomery. Peter was followed by Andrew Bowden and I eventually followed Nicholas Scott in 1964 after being chairman of the North West Region and a national vice-chairman. The movement had reached its peak in the 1950s when it had over 250,000 members. Thereafter, changing social trends led to numbers declining to around 100,000 by the early 1960s and falling further in the 1970s. The movement was eventually wound up but not before further YC national chairmen went on to become MPs such as Alan Haselhurst (now Deputy Speaker), John Watson, David Atkinson, Michael Jack, Robert Hughes and Eric Pickles. Other ex-chairmen included Chris Gent, Managing Director of Vodafone in its growth years and now Chairman of GlaxoSmithKline, and Nick Robinson, presently the articulate BBC Political Correspondent.

One of the advantages of being involved with the YCs at the national level was access to the leaders of the Party. And so I met such people as Anthony Eden, Harold Macmillan, Alec Home and Ted Heath frequently. When I was national chairman, Alec Home was Prime Minister and he invited the officers of the National YCs to Downing Street. In those days the public could freely come to the front door and when our visit finished, he escorted me to the entrance to bid me farewell. About a hundred sightseers were outside and clearly thrilled to see unexpectedly the Prime Minister. They burst out in spontaneous cheering and it was all I could do to prevent myself from turning to him and saying: "Don't worry, sir, they're cheering you as well!" As I walked down the street, a couple of YCs from Cheshire came up to say that they just happened to be in London and decided, on the spur of the moment, to go to see the PM's official residence.

With Sir Anthony Eden (Lord Avon)
& Nicholas Scott, my predecessor
as National Chairman of the YCs
in 1963

With Harold Macmillian &
Iain Macleod in 1964

Escorting Sir Alec Douglas-Home
at the 1965 YC conference

With Edward Heath at the
1966 YC Conference

They couldn't believe their eyes when suddenly the door opened and I appeared with Sir Alec. I quickly learnt that timing was all important in politics.

One memorable event as National Chairman was to give a dinner for Anthony Eden (by now Lord Avon) our patron. This was in a dining room in the House of Commons and he appreciated the invitation, not least because he had had to resign as Prime Minister more than ten years before and, unknown to me, had wanted to re-visit the Palace (he had played little part in the House of Lords after being ennobled). He and his wife Clarissa had clearly enjoyed themselves and it was a momentous occasion for the YCs present. A few weeks later it was my thirtieth birthday and I returned home after the 1965 Party Conference to be with my mother. Awaiting me was an unexpected parcel which had arrived earlier in the week. I opened it to find a thank you note from Eden with a signed copy of one of the three volumes of his autobiography. It is one of my most unexpected and treasured presents.

I achieved a dubious record when national chairman: the first during whose term of office we lost two general elections. Those who had been chairmen for two years received the MBE. I was the first not to; Harold Wilson observing that the Beatles had done more for Britain's exports than the YC chairmen. I was persuaded not to put "MBE (failed)" after my name. It was now time to see what further tribulation I could wreak upon my Party.

*   *   *

It was when I became the North West YC chairman (Cheshire, Lancashire & Westmorland) that I finally made up my mind to become an MP. The immediate task was to persuade the Party that I was a fit and proper person. In those days there was no rigorous course of assessment by testing psychological suitability, speaking ability, people skills or business acumen. It all depended upon a general consensus by the few on the candidates' committee chaired by a vice-chairman of the Party. Their decision was doubtless based upon the cut of your coat as well as experience.

I passed muster and suspected this was primarily due to my recent election to the Party's National Advisory Committee, as well as my YC record. Thereafter, the vice-chairman in charge of the candidates' committee Sir Paul Bryan, a decent and much liked MP from Yorkshire, encouraged younger Conservatives to apply by assuring them that if Sydney Chapman could do it, so could they. Anyway, I was now on the official candidates list and could apply for any seat that came up. A twenty-seven year old without any experience of fighting a parliamentary seat (or a local council election) was not likely to be chosen for a Conservative held constituency so I looked for Labour seats where a Tory had yet to be adopted.

It was not long before Stalybridge & Hyde invited applications. This seat was the geographical "tail" of the old county of Cheshire (before Greater Manchester was created) and extended up to the Yorkshire moors. A number of us presented ourselves for the first round of interviews and I was selected from a short list of three at my second appearance. I was fortunate because it was a Labour marginal with a majority under 1,500 and it was a seat which the Tories should have won in the 1955 and 1959 elections but had bucked the trend due to the decline of the cotton industry. The Tories had refused to raise import duties to keep out cheap Asian imports and had paid a political price. Thus Labour had survived in 1951, 1955 and 1959 with majorities of 298, 155 and 1,423.

Although selected, I had to be approved by a meeting of the Association to which all paid-up members are invited. This is usually a formality and indeed it was so with me. I delivered a speech full of hype, hope and glory promising to work with them all and not sparing myself in the effort. After being endorsed, I small-talked my way around the room, finally approaching an elderly farmer at the back who had remained silent and unmoved throughout the proceedings. He studied me for sometime and then in a heavy northern brogue told me that the constituency divided itself into four distinct parts: Stalybridge which was marginally Conservative but "with a whippersnapper like thee it might go Labour"; Dukinfield which had been Labour for fifty years and would remain so; and Hyde which was Labour "but might go queer" (apparently he was referring to the Liberals). He then concluded: "thee wants to know where thy support is? See them 'ills up there, that's thine – 24 electors and 60,000 sheep." I roared with laughter and his eyes twinkled. There were actually more than two dozen electors in the area outside the three towns and they lived in exotic named villages such as Broadbottom, Hattersley (growing into an overspill town) and Tintwhistle.

Being adopted for S & H was fortunate in another way. The seat was only ten miles from home and I was able to visit two or three nights a week and most weekends. I attended all sorts of meetings and money-raising events and regularly visited the four Conservative Clubs. At one AGM, it was reported that the Club had made a net profit of £1,964 (I remember the exact figure as it was the same as the year) and the Treasurer proposed that "as our young candidate is with us and the election will soon happen, I would like to propose that this year instead of contributing our usual £10 to the Party we should donate £15." There was actually a discussion before this was agreed.

By this time I had left my father's firm and was working in Manchester at first for another small firm of architects, Vincent Booker, in an office near Waterhouse's magnificent Town Hall. The main staple of my father's and Vincent Booker's firm were consultancies to pub owning brewers, responsible for renovating old inns as well as designing a few new ones. A small pub in Poynton and a larger one in Wilmslow (on the road to Manchester Airport) stand testimony to my dubious design abilities but even these had been conceived in all but detail by others and my job was merely to draw them up. I also visited many older pubs to measure them up before renovation and it was on such occasions that I realised the importance of field research.

In truth neither my heart nor my mind was on the drawing board and I looked for other opportunities. One came quickly and unexpectedly: the post of Liaison Officer at the newly created Manchester Building Centre on Portland Street. John Griffiths, a fellow professional with a good grasp of architectural history and conservation, had been appointed the Director of this new venture which was to be a place where the public could see what new building processes, methods and materials were about, financed by companies who paraded their wares. I felt more at home in such a situation with more contact with the public. I also liked my title when I discovered that the word 'liaison' had a definition, confirmed in the OED, as "an illicit intimacy between a man and a woman." I was happy in this post which was essentially being the sidekick of the Director and it fitted in well with my political aspirations.

The 1959 Parliament was to run its full course. At the end of its fourth year, Prime Minister Harold Macmillan fell ill and announced his resignation. The magic circle did its work and the 14th Earl of Home succeeded him, with only a maximum of one year to claw back some popularity for a Party now in its thirteenth year of government and at a time when the Opposition, led by Harold Wilson, was reflecting better the new mood of Britain in the "swinging sixties".

The Conservatives were thought likely to lose the election and, more assuredly, I was not expected to win S & H and had now been at the Building Centre for three years. In such a situation it would be safe for me to seek another job if a suitable opportunity came along. It did. There was a family background on my mother's side of teaching: her two brothers and two sisters were all head teachers and she was now one. The post of lecturer in architecture at Wigan & District Mining and Technical

College came up and I applied. I was appointed perhaps surprisingly after I volunteered my political ambitions and the possibility of having to take leave of absence imminently for three weeks to fight S & H. I had managed to save £90 and put it in Premium Bonds as an insurance against loss of pay during the three week campaign, which came in the autumn six months after I had started at Wigan and six months after I became National Chairman of the Young Conservatives.

The campaign consumed all my energy. I canvassed furiously, usually alone and was generally politely received. The sitting MP was Fred Blackburn, an elderly backbencher, former teacher and councillor, who was popular and respected. I challenged him to a public debate but he did not even deign to reply to the invitation. Why should he when he was already well known and I was the new noisy interloper desperate to be seen and heard? Alec Home made a lightning visit to support me en route to a mass rally in Belle Vue, Manchester at which I had to propose a vote of thanks. This I did, ending with a somewhat cheeky invitation to him to have tea with me on the House of Commons terrace after the election.

Polling Day came. Labour won and I lost. The surprise to me was that Wilson only just won in the country. In S & H, Labour's majority increased and although the swing was a modest 2.5 per cent, this didn't prevent one wag in Central Office re-christening the seat Stalybridge & Hiding. Fred Blackburn went back to Westminster and I went back to Wigan.

4

FROM WIGAN TO WESTMINSTER

The last pit in the Wigan area had closed before I was appointed a lecturer at the College, over forty miles distant from my home in Cheshire.

Six years before, my mother had put all her savings together and taken out a mortgage to buy a house on a new estate being built by Wimpey to the north of Prestbury Station. The four bedroom property in Legh Road cost £3,400. Three years later I had bought my first car (on the HP), a Ford Anglia (the one with the rear window sloping inwards) so I was now independently mobile and the recent completion of the M6 motorway through Cheshire made it possible for me to travel by car in an hour to my new job. I even acquired a personalised number plate, SC 34, by paying £10 to the Edinburgh registration authority and in 1964 a gallon of petrol was only 4/6d (5p a litre).

My job at Wigan was in the Building Department which was housed in the original College on Library Street, a formidable structure in terra cotta. The head of the department was Eric Marsden, a jolly, approachable man who ran a loose ship and loved caravanning. His deputy was Frank McCann, competent, caring and polite. Both were extremely affable and the staff room had a happy atmosphere. Desks were squashed together and, as the most recent addition to the office, mine was on an improvised gallery approached by a wooden staircase. I felt as if I was sitting on a scaffold with not enough rope to swing a noose.

I enjoyed the work, the more so because of the wide range of my curriculum. If at a university I would probably have had to lecture in a specialised field but at Wigan there was no school of architecture and I had to cover a broader spectrum of subjects. My charges had a wide age range and so my duties involved lecturing young students on English Architecture for the GCE 'A' level Art Paper to mature building inspectors on Town Planning law. Later I was asked to take over the recommended one-hour a week Liberal Studies slot and I immediately changed its name to General Studies. The previous lecturer had spent a large part of the course showing the students, most of whom were in their late teens, films of plants growing and petals opening – or slides of anything he had laid his hands on. I wanted to broaden their focus and interest them in the wider world. My choice of subjects ranged from how Parliament worked to the role and structure of local authorities and from the demography of Britain to the geography of the world. The challenge was to engage their interest and, for example, when Budget Day approached I explained what it was all about with basic information on revenue and expenditure. We then made forecasts of what the Chancellor would do. After the event, we examined the Budget Statement to see how accurate we had been. All in all, I felt that I had generally fulfilled my ambition to get students interested and responsive.

The College catered for part-time evening as well as full-time day students and the arrangement was that lecturers undertaking evening classes could have a half-day off *in lieu*. My responsibilities required lecturing on two evenings but the understanding was that the two half-days off could not be on the same day. It was typical of the understanding of Eric Marsden, given the distance of my home from Wigan and my political interests, that he allowed me to have one full day off and made it a Friday. Thus I worked long and hard for four days and then had a long weekend to indulge in politics.

I carried out my YC national chairman duties arduously, visiting all parts of the realm. This included a weekend in Northern Ireland when John D. Taylor was the Young Unionist chairman. He seemed to spend much of the time putting down plots against him, clearly with some success. He went on to become an Ulster Unionist MP, was lucky to survive being shot in the head and after a successful political career is now in the Upper House as Lord Kilclooney.

In the two years, I travelled over sixty thousand miles and the Party paid a modest mileage allowance which covered the cost of petrol. Typically, one weekend I drove to Birmingham for an early evening YC function in the city, then on to Coventry for another one, finally arriving late for a South Gloucestershire constituency dinner-dance, staying there for the night. Up early to London for a lunch given by the *Sunday Telegraph* and hosted by Peregrine Worsthorne for some young European politicians. Little wonder that in giving a short speech thanking our hosts, my eulogy referred mistakenly to the *Sunday Express*. After some nervous laughter from the YCs present, I apologised profusely and learnt another lesson: in such a situation, stop digging and pretend the slip of tongue was intentional. On this occasion, sheer tiredness had overcome quickness of mind.

I was very touched when Edward Heath, after becoming leader of the Party, wrote to me asking if I needed any help with the cost of coming to London for the various national committees I was on as YC chairman. My tenure was extended by a few weeks when the 1966 election was called but I had backed down from Stalybridge & Hyde. The election could have come at any time and I felt obliged not to seek leave of absence again. However, I did get one crack in at the new Labour leadership. For Blair read Wilson and for Gordon Brown read George. The relationship between them seemed to be the same. I said that the state of the Labour Government seemed to be reflected in a local brewery advert which proclaimed: "Wilson's Bitter and Brown Ales." In the event Wilson hung in for seventeen months before calling the election and Labour won this time with a very comfortable majority. With my retirement from the YCs, my political life slowed down but I was soon elected the senior vice-chairman of the North West Area and continued on the Party's NAC.

At this time, I was interviewed on TV for the first time. I had been one of the scribblers of a YC publication on local government reform. With one of the other authors, Elizabeth Steel (a very attractive Solicitor from Liverpool), we presented ourselves at the BBC studios in Manchester and were duly grilled by Colin Welland, the actor and then presenter of the early evening regional programme, his eyes alighting on her more than me. Coincidentally, my sister Christine had been part of the audience of a new TV programme called *Top of the Pops* and the camera had shown her for about three seconds strutting her stuff on the dance floor. All her friends had seen her but nobody had seen me, nor heard my pearls of wisdom. Little wonder: over 10 million had watched her programme and probably only a few hundred thousand mine.

In mid 1965 my father died. After the divorce he had married again but his health was declining. I saw him from time to time but at his death I was on a tour of the north-east and Scotland. In those days the BBC used to broadcast an S.O.S. (just before the news on radio) when a person was critically ill and the next of kin could not be found but on this occasion, I was told, it was the first time after the person had died. I had missed the radio message but had telephoned my mother and, just in time, returned to Macclesfield for his funeral. Life goes on and in 1967 Christine got married. The bridegroom was Peter Bateson and it turned out that he was one of three sons of Rowland who was a much respected Conservative Party Agent, then looking after Geoffrey Rippon's seat at Hexham in Northumberland.

When I was spending less time on politics in the late sixties and had the bonus of a two month break in July and August from Wigan College, I had a passing fit of enthusiasm for walking in the hills above Macclesfield. Particularly in the summer, I would drive up to a pub on or off the main road to Buxton, usually the Stanley Arms but occasionally the Hanging Gate or Cat and Fiddle, and walk for miles along country roads, aiming to return via a different route. Limbs aching, I would drive round the route to check the mileage and the typical walk would be twelve miles over a three hour period. In the winter, on a free Saturday or Sunday, I would go for a shorter walk usually with two brothers, Godfrey and George Bermingham, who lived on the Buxton Road (not far from where I was born). They were both larger than life characters but as different as could be. George had at one time served with the Northern Rhodesia Police and eventually moved to New Zealand. Godfrey had a doctorate in chemistry and later married a beautiful girl I had introduced him to in Prestbury and they now live in Anglesey and I'm proud to be godfather of the elder of their two children, Katie, who subsequently joined the Army and served in Iraq.

In the summer of 1969 I decided to use a month of the summer break to take the car (and tent) and drive through France and Spain to the Algrave, planning to take a week getting there. In the innocence of the age I freely gave people lifts and wound my way from Calais to Rouen, on to Chartres and Le Mans, then down the N10, around Bordeaux to Spain. I then took the shortest route to Portugal meeting the Atlantic at Nazare. My first swim nearly ended in catastrophy, being sucked back by the ebb of the powerful waves. After dropping someone in Estoril, I crossed the new and impressive Salazar Bridge across the Tegus from Lisbon and finally arrived in Lagos, not far from Cape St. Vincent. My good deeds in giving lifts to all and sundry along the way paid a pleasurable dividend when two Swedish sisters put their collective thumbs up at me and I had company for the

rest of the journey and, indeed, for the first three days
in Lagos. After the fortnight of encampment, I returned
via La Baule and Brittany to meet a friend. It was an
enjoyable experience and incredibly well spent: the total
cost including petrol was not a penny more than fifty
pounds.

It was now time to renew my quest for a seat in
the Commons. The aim was to get nominated for a
constituency being vacated by a retiring Tory MP or one
with a small Labour majority within reasonable distance
of home or Wigan. I watched and waited. The first safe
seat to come up in the north-west had been Altrincham
& Sale (Con. maj. 10,000) on the retirement of Freddie
Errol shortly after the 1964 election. I was interviewed
but was never in with a chance as Tony Barber, shortly
to be made Party chairman, was chosen (he had just lost
Doncaster). After the 1966 election, I was interviewed
for such safe Conservative seats as Clitheroe, Ormskirk
and South Fylde but without success. Late in 1969
two vacancies emerged: at Stretford (just outside
Manchester) which Labour had won in 1966 by 3,300
and Handsworth, where Sir Edward Boyle had just
announced his retirement. I put in for both and reached
the final shortlist for both.

Handsworth had always been a Conservative citadel
but it was fast changing in character and population.
Once an expensive residential area with a proliferation of
large Victorian houses, an influx of new Commonwealth
immigrants had set up home in many of them which had
been converted into flats. Originally in Staffordshire,
Handsworth was now part of that Mecca of municipal
magnificence, Birmingham. Sir Edward first won it in a
by-election in 1950 and throughout that decade held it
with comfortable majorities of around 10,000. However,
his majority rapidly declined to under 5,000 in 1964 and
just over 1,000 in 1966.

Sir Edward was a warm and brilliant man. Educated
at Eton and Christ Church Oxford, he was President of
the Union, became an MP at twenty-six and had had a

very successful twenty years in the House of Commons. He had been Economic Secretary to the Treasury (but resigned over Suez in 1956), then Financial Secretary and a Minister of Education before becoming Education Secretary in 1964. It was thought that it was because his good friend Edward Heath had told him that he would not be appointed Chancellor if the Tories won the election that he decided to make a mid-career change (he was only forty-six) and became the Vice-Chancellor of Leeds University. He was very much in the liberal tradition of the Conservative Party and had been criticised for his perceived views on immigration, law and order and, in particular, comprehensive secondary education – not least when he was Secretary of State.

More than two hundred hopefuls put in for the seat and the committee vetting the applications asked an official to abbreviate all their CVs. Thus I was billed as "Chapman, Mr S, Architect from Cheshire, aged thirty-four." Little chance of that description leading to an interview but chance can play a big part in politics. I learnt that the YC chairman had inquired: "Isn't that the Sydney Chapman who was our national chairman?" The fuller cv. was consulted and her query confirmed. She insisted that I was interviewed and so I was. One thing led to another and eventually I found myself on a short list of three and finally selected. The favourite had been a home grown Brummie, Alderman Anthony Beaumont-Dark, a stockbroker who had been initially judged to be the best prospect for holding the seat, not least because he had fought next door Aston on two previous occasions. He became a good friend and eventually a colleague when he was elected for Selly Oak in 1979.

My formal adoption was no pushover. Indeed there was a rumour that I would be rejected when the local press quoted me saying that I did not agree with what Enoch Powell (who represented a nearby seat in Wolverhampton) had said in his recent "rivers of blood" speech, warning about the effects of the large scale immigration taking place, largely from the Caribbean and the Indian sub-continent. He had advocated a much stricter limitation on future people coming into Britain and I most certainly agreed with that but disliked the calculated and inflammatory language he had used and the unnecessary fear caused to the new immigrants, many of whom had come to fill much needed jobs. Enoch had also made his speech without telling his fellow shadow cabinet colleagues. Edward Heath had no alternative (in my view) but to sack him but this only added to the explosion of deep resentment which was released, both for and against him – not least from many dockers and other left-wing trade unionists who vigorously supported him. Apologists for him averred that his richness of language with classical illusions was what was necessary to jolt the political class into realising the extent of public unease about the issue. In the event, he was proved right in his predictions about the numbers of foreign born Britons there would be by the end of the century. Luckily for me Enoch's local supporters did not come out to my adoption meeting on the night – or if they did, they kept their peace – and it was probably a warm letter of support from Sir Edward which ensured that I was confirmed as the prospective Conservative candidate.

The Labour Government had become very unpopular soon after the 1966 election. The economy had taken a decisive turn for the worse; the pound was devalued and Labour was slaughtered in local elections. However, the opinion polls improved for them in early 1970 and Wilson decided to call a snap election in mid-June. I had been a candidate for only five months and, in one sense, this was a blessing given the cost and frequency of travelling from Wigan or Cheshire to the Midlands. Nevertheless I had visited Handsworth on more than twenty separate occasions covering sixty days and Edward had made his constituency flat available to me for as long as needed.

At the outset of the campaign a number of people were furious that the election had been called in mid-summer, then effectively denying those on holiday a vote. They felt Wilson had cheated and I know of some voters who curtailed their plans or came back specially to vote on the day. The Government had also used its majority to reject the boundary changes proposed by the independent commission. This blatant gerrymandering disadvantaged the Conservatives but exceptionally helped me. In Birmingham there was the ridiculous situation where the electorates of the thirteen constituencies ranged from over 96,000 in Northfield to under 19,000 in Ladywood. The campaign did not go well for the Tories, though it's sometimes difficult to judge the national mood when canvassing locally for long hours. The opinion polls made bleak reading, consistently showing a Labour lead throughout the campaign. Four days before polling, one opinion poll gave Labour a 12 point lead and Birmingham's *Sunday Mercury* forecast that only four Conservative MPs might retain their seats in the West Midlands. One half of me exuded self confidence that I would hold the seat; the other half told me to prepare for Armageddon and worse.

June 18th arrived and I wondered whose Waterloo Day it would turn out to be. When the Polls close candidates repair to the count with a restricted number of supporters who can oversee the checking of ballot papers and votes. There was a straight fight in Handsworth and my opponent was Mrs Sheila Wright, a Birmingham City Councillor since 1956, who had fought Sir Edward on the two previous occasions and was hoping it would be third time lucky. Unfortunately for her it wasn't and fortunately for me the massive (then post war record) national net swing of nearly 5 per cent to the Conservatives just exceeded the demographic swing against me. I had managed to raise Sir Edward's majority by a few hundred.

I humbly thanked those present and expressed the hope that my majority of 1812 would be an overture to many years of service. We won two seats that night in the City: Jo Kinsey, a florist and councillor, succeeded in next door Perry Barr while Derek Coombs, director of a family company operating stores, won Yardley. We now had six of the thirteen seats in the city; the other three being held by Jill Knight (Edgbaston) a former Councillor from Northampton, Reggie Eyre (Hall Green) a solicitor and Harold Gurden (Selly Oak) formerly a company director in the food industry. The Brummie Conservatives in Parliament were nothing if not an eclectic bunch. However, we were more than matched by the city's seven Labour MPs: Roy Jenkins (Stetchford) former Home Secretary and now former Chancellor; Roy Hattersley (Sparkbrook) a junior Minister; Denis Howell (Small Heath) a Minister of State; Julius Silverman (Aston) and Brian Walden (All Saints). They were joined for the first time by Doris Fisher (Ladywood) and Ray Carter (Northfield). As for the *Sunday Mercury*'s gloomy forecast for the Tories in the West Midlands, we actually secured 29 of the 54 seats in the five counties.

After ten years of dreaming and nearly six years since my first parliamentary contest, I was at long last on my way to Westminster.

5

EARLY DAYS IN THE
CORRIDORS OF POWER

The Palace of Westminster is a huge building, covering eight acres with over one thousand rooms and three miles of corridors. The Commons is at the north (Big Ben) end with the Lords and massive Victoria Tower to the south. In the middle is Central Lobby, a large octagonal space where the public can come, giving access to both Houses and the Committee rooms on the first floor. The old Palace, consisting of chapels and houses, had been destroyed by fire in 1834, save for the dominant old Westminster Hall. The new Palace, in the ever continuing tradition of great British buildings, had been estimated at £700,000 but finished up costing £2.4 million.

After I was elected nothing happened. I waited eagerly for a Royal Warrant or whatever to summon me but nothing came. After making enquiries and consulting the public prints, I eventually discovered when to arrive and on the appointed day presented myself at the public entrance. Policemen converged on me from all directions and politely inquired after my business. What impressed me was that never again was I asked who I was. The staff were trained to recognise all of us.

In a setting unequalled in historical associations, it didn't need an architect to admire the sheer genius of the Victorian building with Charles Barry's classical plan clothed in the neo-Gothic design which was becoming the rage of the age. When Barry won the international competition, he employed a young architect in his twenties, Augustus Pugin, to design the interior and

Pugin's Gothic fervour led him to design every detail and decoration from the stonework, timber panelling and wallpaper to the chandeliers, desks, tables and chairs, letter racks, penholders, ink wells and even the screws in the doors. Pugin, I had learnt in my student days, was a workaholic who died in his early forties after fifteen years of an incredible output of mainly churches. He was a genius.

But if the design and atmosphere of the Palace was superb, its facilities were not. The role of an MP had changed dramatically in the one hundred and twenty years between the building's completion and my arrival on site. I was first allocated a locker, so designed that a briefcase didn't fit into it. Sometime later a desk and filing cabinet were provided. Unfortunately, the locker was two hundred feet from the Chamber in one direction and the desk and filing cabinet two hundred yards away and across a road in the other.

It is not unknown for a new MP to get lost in the labyrinth of this Royal Palace but I was fortunate in that I had studied the building when a student and could readily navigate myself between the Chamber, Library, Committee Rooms and, off New Palace Yard and near Big Ben, the Members' Entrance. This was a dark, long space with a peg and coat hanger for every Member, placed in alphabetical order. On each hanger was a piece of pink ribbon. After a few weeks, curiosity got the better of me and I asked a senior Member what the ribbon was for. "To hang your sword on" was the abrupt reply – and he wasn't joking. The Chamber can be recognised by most people even though relatively few have visited it. Those who have been there generally make two comments: it is smaller than expected (only 68 x 46ft); and the atmosphere is quite informal.

At the beginning of each Parliament, MPs meet first to elect The Speaker, who then becomes completely independent of any Party. Mr Horace King was re-elected (the first former Labour incumbent) and during the next few days members are sworn in before the State Opening takes place, when The Queen processes to the House of Lords and "desires the attendance of the Commons" (the only time the three parts of Parliament physically meet). Her "Gracious Speech" outlines the Bills to be presented.

It was into this unique environment that I arrived. As I looked around at my colleagues and across the Chamber at Opposition members, it was hard to believe that I was one of their peers and, at least in theory, the equal of any one of them in Mr Speaker's eyes. Nevertheless, I decided that prudency was better than pugnacity and bided my time, listening to the early debates before committing myself to the ears of my equals and the print of Hansard. Sitting on the Opposition benches with Harold Wilson were the likes of Richard Crossman, Michael Foot and Tony Benn, but the most remarkable result was the re-election of S.O.Davies who had been Merthyr Tydfil's MP since 1934 but failed to get renominated by his Association, probably because they felt he was too old at eighty-three. He stood as an Independent against the new official Labour candidate and was returned with a whopping majority.

On the Government front bench with Edward Heath were Reggie Maudling, Alec Douglas-Home, Willie Whitelaw, Keith Joseph, Anthony Barber and Margaret Thatcher. Iain Macleod had become Chancellor but tragically died a month later and I never saw Quintin Hogg in the Chamber as he was appointed Lord Chancellor and went immediately to the Lords. Other colleagues included Robert Carr, Duncan Sandys, Ernest Marples, Maurice Macmillan (son of Harold), Christopher Chataway, Peter Walker and the indefatigable Dame Irene Ward (aged seventy-five). There were also some heroes from World War II such as Sir Fitzroy Maclean and Airey Neave, who famously escaped from Colditz Castle. I had just missed George Brown (beaten) and Manny Shinwell, Bessie Braddock and S & H's Fred Blackburn who had retired. The father of the House was Sir Robin Turton who had been Thirsk & Malton's MP since 1929.

If the House had to wait for me, I had time to assess who I was representing. Handsworth is in north-west Birmingham two miles from the city centre. 200 years ago it was the home of some of our leading industrialists such as Matthew Boulton, James Watt and William Murdoch. Boulton established the Soho Manufactory (Foundries) in 1802-03 and had been the founder of the Lunar Society in the 1770s, whose select members met every full moon to discuss philosophy and science. Watt was the inventor of the steam engine and Murdoch had invented the gas mantle. By the end of the 19th century the Parish had become densely developed with mainly terraced housing. Handsworth was added to Birmingham in 1911 and eventually became an indistinguishable area from Ladywood and Lozells to the south, while newer lower density housing in Handsworth Wood merged with contemporary development in Perry Barr to the north. To the east was Aston with West Bromwich to the west. For football fans, the constituency extended roughly from Villa Park to the Hawthorns but didn't include either ground.

In the second half of the 20th century the influx of commonwealth immigrants was supplemented by some Ugandan Asians just after I was elected and it was estimated that nearly 15 per cent of voters in Handsworth were West Indian; over 10 per cent Asian and 8 per cent Irish. Of all the then Conservative held seats, it had the second highest proportion of electors born outside the UK – the highest (perhaps surprisingly) was Hampstead.

While I had no previous connection with England's second city (such is democracy), I had always been intrigued as to why it had become so. It was not on a major river, dominant on the crest of a hill, nor otherwise strategically placed - other towns in the Midlands had access to water power and were nearer to coal fields - yet there had been a massive and rapid growth which had led to it becoming the city of 'a thousand trades' and 'the Workshop of the World.' James Brindley created a network of canals (more than in Venice) which gave

Birmingham access to navigable rivers and the sea. The citizens of Birmingham also had a super sense of civic pride which at times transcended party politics. Joseph Chamberlain created the finest municipal services (water, gas and electricity) and established the Birmingham Municipal Bank. One of his sons, Austin, became Foreign Secretary while the other, Neville, followed Baldwin as Prime Minister in 1937 after being Lord Mayor earlier in his career. When the Liberals had a landslide victory in the 1906 General Election, the Liberal Unionists and Conservatives still held all seven seats in the city.

City pride remains, as instanced by the President of my Association, Alderman Fred Hall, a shrewd businessman who manufactured nails. When he was Lord Mayor, it was reported to me that he had attended a municipal conference and met another civic head who bluntly told him that Manchester was the second city in the country. Unphased, Fred looked down at him and dryly observed: "Funny, I always thought it was London." I have to admit that I've told that one in Birmingham and the other way round in Manchester.

All this was the backdrop to the seat I was elected to represent but a young MP's thoughts soon turn to the future. Fellow newcomers to the Commons in 1970 included Ken Clarke, Norman Fowler, John Gummer and Norman Tebbit (all to become Cabinet Ministers); Neil Kinnock and John Smith (both to become Leaders of the Opposition) and John Prescott (to become Deputy Prime Minister). Also elected was Winston Churchill (the grandson), who had been selected for Stretford – he told me he was glad that I had won the Handsworth nomination. We were all relatively young but an interesting fact about the 80 Conservatives MPs elected for the first time was that a dozen were over fifty, as were a further ten who had won back their seats or been adopted for new constituencies after being defeated in previous elections.

The State Opening was only a few weeks before the long summer recess. I held my peace and it was well after the return of Parliament that I made my maiden speech at the beginning of November. Bowing to convention, I paid a tribute to my immediate predecessor, said something about my constituency and made a short and uncontroversial contribution. I began by saying of Sir Edward that Handsworth was a better known place for his having been its MP and that as long as courage, compassion and conscience were the hallmarks of the House, his name would be remembered. Of Handsworth, I opined that it was part of a great city with problems to match, observing that parts were declining physically and were "a blot on the conscience of any nation that called itself civilised." In a ten minute speech delivered in a debate on the re-organisation of government, I welcomed the introduction of the Department of Environment but regretted that its responsibilities did not include air transport which I considered to be "the arch polluter of our age."

After rumbling on about the importance of the environment (a relatively new word in those days) and the need for it to be more prominent on the political agenda, I made two suggestions: that a new Environment Act should consolidate all relevant legislation including the Housing and Town & Country Planning Acts; and that "Urban Parks" should be designated (along the lines of National Parks) with the aim of tackling and eradicating the worst scars in our conurbations. I finally pontificated on pollution in all its ugly forms and portentously concluded that if we did not safeguard our environment "one thing is certain: we shall become the curse of future generations." I had followed Willie Whitelaw who opened the debate and Tony Crosland for the Opposition. Jo Grimond followed me and was particularly complimentary about my endeavours. I was pleased and lucky to be called so early in the debate and was relieved I had got through my parliamentary baptism of fire unscathed. Re-reading Hansard over thirty-five years later, I cringe slightly at the odd turn of phrase and some ill-fitting grandiloquent words, but I immodestly reckon that my first contribution still has a certain relevance today.

The first debate on which we had a free vote was about British Summer Time. In the previous Parliament approval was given for a two year experiment to keep it all year round. This seemed to suit those living in the South East and possibly the Midlands but was more inconvenient and controversial the further North and West you lived. I decided to vote for what I thought was best for the U.K. as a whole and plumped for returning to the status quo. I was surprised to find that a very large majority of MPs held the same view. In the debate, Joe Grimond (Orkney & Shetlands' MP) said that he didn't mind which option was chosen as they were both irrelevant to his constituents.

I threw myself into a frenzy of activity and began early. On most days I would come in and collect my mail by 8am and proceed to the Library to open it and deal with as much as I could before repairing to the Members' Tea Room for a coffee and round of toast. Other early birds I saw regularly included my new colleague David Mudd who didn't employ a secretary but replied to every constituency letter in his own hand, Tam Dalyell and George Thomas who had been Secretary of State for Wales in the defeated Labour administration and was to become a future Speaker. Invariably in the Tea Room was a clutch of elderly Knights from the shires such as Anthony Fell, John Langford Holt, David Renton and Harmer Nicholls.

I took an instant interest in Question Time, always the first hour's business on Mondays to Thursdays, and immersed myself in the detail of a select number of topical issues. I submitted oral or written questions, the former being subject to a ballot and, if selected and dependent upon the time available, permitting supplementaries. It was even more difficult to be called for a supplementary on someone else's question. One of the memorable replies at Question Time was by the new Transport Minister, Michael Heseltine. A colleague and friend Eric Cockeram was exercised about the delay in building a much needed by-pass around his town. When told that it would be two years before the project would be considered, he asked the Minister with a mixture of frustration and sarcasm whether he was aware that the delay was longer than the gestation period of an elephant. "Ah" said Michael "I often wondered why they were called trunk roads." I was sitting next to Eric at the time and he swore that the Minister's reply was off the cuff and had not been pre-arranged.

I campaigned on such diverse issues as lorries in residential areas, sex magazines displayed in shops and for women to be able to travel alone on joint passports. Some issues seem just as relevant today: graffiti, obscene unsolicited mail and NHS waiting lists. When I asked Health Secretary Sir Keith Joseph how many people were awaiting treatment and he replied "half-a-million" I said this was a scandal. He politely disagreed with my choice of word, preferring to call the situation "disgraceful."

I was soon to blot my copybook when I was the only Conservative MP to vote against the second reading of the National Museums and Art Galleries Bill. This measure introduced charges for entry and I was against denying the traditional free access to such establishments. I make no apologies for doing so but soon learnt a political lesson. If you disagree with any measure, it is far better to draw attention to the fact by sitting and remaining in the Chamber when all about you are walking into the Division Lobbies. Thus the very few Tories who abstained got their fifteen minutes of parliamentary fame while yours truly got only the contemptuous disdain of the Conservative Whips. The Chief Whip was Francis Pym and I didn't help myself by referring to his colleagues as Pym's Nos. 1, 2, 3, and 4. In rebelling I was probably looking for an early opportunity to show that I was no lobby fodder.

In my first Parliament, too much of my time was spent in Committee examining Government Bills. This was not the most profitable way to use one's time or energy, so it was usually new Members who had to undertake this necessary chore. My first Committee was on a Bill to 'denationalise' a few pubs around Carlisle which had been bought by the state in the First World War in an attempt to limit the drinking time of workers in armaments' factories. Shortly after this I was put on the Housing Finance Bill Committee, a highly controversial but long overdue attempt to bring some sense to the rental market. I remember a senior Whip drawing me aside to say how much the Minister needed my expertise on the measure and how I must go on it. The Bill had absolutely nothing to do with design but I didn't have the heart nor inclination to decline. This proved costly. We sat for over 200 hours before the Government got a guillotine motion after which there was at least some structure to the debates on the various provisions in it. We finally came out of committee after 257 hours – then a record. From that time onwards I became a firm believer in the time-tabling of all Bills but it was to be more than a quarter of a century before this became a reality (and then it was carried out in the wrong way).

There was a very small overall Conservative majority on the Committee of about thirty MPs and after debating a motion on the sitting hours we examined remorselessly each clause "line by line and word by word" with any member being able to submit an amendment, though the chairman had the right to select those to be debated. When the last amendment to each clause had been debated, there was then another debate on "Clause Stand Part." As Opposition MPs were strongly opposed to the measure, they took all these opportunities to filibuster and delay its progress. This could be remedied only by a guillotine motion on the floor of the House which spelt out a timetable for the remaining stages. The flaw in this system was that, if the filibuster route was taken, hours could be spent on the first few clauses of a Bill followed by an inadequate time on all the rest. And so it was.

The leading Minister for the Government was Julian Amery, son-in-law of Churchill and a larger than life character with a manner of speaking which I described as 'oratorical rotundity.' He attended the proceedings only sporadically leaving most of the legwork and detail to Paul Channon, a first class junior Minister with a complete mastery of his brief; courteous and never showing an iota of irritability (we often sat until the early hours of the morning). On one occasion Julian Amery and Tony Crosland (leading for Labour) returned unexpectedly to the committee late one night showing every sign of having had a long and agreeable dinner together. A Labour MP was moving an amendment excluding terraced housing from a clause in the Bill. When he was done, Julian rose to reply immediately. In a most conciliatory manner, which was surprising, he profusely thanked the MP for his amendment and expressed complete sympathy with it, immediately recognising the difficulties of people living in terraced housing. He said that the Government at first had not been minded to accept the amendment but, after hearing the Member, he would like to reflect on the matter again and not least because he himself lived in a terraced house. The look on Tony Crosland's face was a sight never to be forgotten as he, and most of the Tories present, knew that Amery's home was in that exclusive and terraced part of SW1 known as Eaton Square. The Labour MP was delighted, the rest of the opposition were baffled and the Committee moved on immediately to the next amendment. Such was the way to make progress in the face of a sustained filibuster.

Also suffering with me on the Committee was another new Conservative, Andrew Bowden (MP for Kemptown). The other member for Brighton was none other than Julian Amery (MP for Pavilion) and after Amery's terraced housing intervention, Andrew told me about one of his earliest Advice Bureaux shortly after winning back his seat. Many people had come to see him on the particular day and after an exhausting session there was finally an elderly couple who had waited patiently for well over an hour. They introduced themselves immediately as two of Mr Amery's constituents but told Andrew that they had written to their MP on a rather urgent matter some weeks before but had not received any reply and they had come to him in some desperation. Andrew was seized of the situation immediately and told them that if they would like to give him the details, he would contact Julian immediately, helpfully observing that the boundary between the two seats ran somewhat arbitrarily through the middle of town. Because of this he had an agreement with Mr Amery, who as they would know, was a senior Minister and therefore a very busy person. "At such times" Andrew declared "we have resolved that I will look after the people of Brighton while Mr Amery looks after the rest of the world."

There were other characters in Parliament, most of whom were no strangers to self-publicity. High on this list was the moustachioed Sir Gerald Nabarro whose affectations may have been enormous but whose company was never boring. He took up 'issues' and became extremely knowledgeable about them. He had a style of speaking which was unique, though some were glad that it was. I encountered him one afternoon in the tea room and he said to me: "My boy, I've just been speaking to a large gathering of distinguished people at lunch and of the many who came up to congratulate me afterwards was a person who introduced himself as an architect. I asked him if he knew that there was now an architect in the Commons and if he knew you. He said he knew there was now an architect among us but hadn't met you. I said to him that he ought to appoint you as a consultant to his distinguished firm and gave him your name." I almost groaned aloud at the personal embarrassment this might have caused my unknown professional colleague and the professional embarrassment it could cause me (RIBA rules specifically forbid touting for business). Nonetheless I thanked him and tried to forget the matter. A week later, Hector MacDonald, the senior partner of the architectural firm MacDonald, Hamilton & Montefiore, contacted me and asked if we could meet. I went to his practice in Jermyn

Street (not on the sunny side) and with him were Tom Hamilton and Derek Montefiore. They said they would like me to join them but I had not practiced for some years and could not give them much time. They persisted and so I visited them occasionally and offered advice on mainly planning matters.

Sir Gerald not only gave the nation regularly the benefit of his views orally but also wrote a memoir ("not an autobiography, dear boy") in 1973 entitled *Exploits of a Politician.* Replete with photos of the good and the great in his company were many cartoons and, of course, his view of what was right and wrong in the world. Only he could devote over seven thousand words and the first chapter entirely to an escapade when he was charged with reckless driving, found guilty, secured a retrial and was finally found not guilty with costs. Naturally, his car had the registration number NAB 1.

It was into such situations and surrounded by such people that I had come.

6

IN & OUT OF PARLIAMENT

At the beginning of each parliamentary session a ballot is held so that twenty MPs can introduce Private Bills. In my very first session I drew tenth place. Success usually depends upon the measure being uncontroversial as it only requires a handful of opponents to talk out the Bill (time is limited) and scupper its chances. I appreciated this and would have been wise to have consulted Ministers, possibly accepting an "off-the-peg" measure which any Government of the day wanted but had not yet had the opportunity nor time to introduce. Instead, I had my own grand design to introduce an "Urban & Rural Environment Bill."

Like Gaul my Bill was divided into three parts and like a vicar's first sermon it tried to cover too much. Proud of being labelled an environmentalist I was determined to close some loopholes in the protection of listed buildings and I wanted also to give people greater notification of significant planning applications in their neighbourhoods. The third part was designed to give greater protection to more trees not already subject to preservation orders. When my Friday came up, I was second on and the non-contentious Bill before mine got its second reading, leaving a couple of hours for my offering. This was insufficient and my measure was talked out but unexpectedly got its Second Reading the following week 'on the nod'. Nevertheless, there was no further time available and it was doomed, leading to *The Guardian* headline: "Chop for Trees Bill."

I was less active in the main debates on the floor of the House, not least because of the time involved in sitting and hoping to be called. There was one occasion when

I was desperate to make a contribution and I dutifully wrote to the Speaker telling him why and hoping I would be able to "catch his eye." This was a debate on the Roskill Report which recommended Cublington in Buckinghamshire as the site of London's Third Airport. I disagreed profoundly with this conclusion and wanted to have my chance to tell the nation why.

I was in the Chamber well before the debate began at 3.30pm and never left it. When there was no sign of my being called at 8pm, I approached the Chair, occupied at that time by the Deputy Speaker, Sir Robert Grant-Ferris. In the most oleaginous manner I could muster, I asked him what chance there was, adding that I was the only architect and planner in the House. He cut me short with "yes, yes, but have you designed any airports?" My exchange with him proved fruitful in that I was called at 9pm before the front bench wind-up speeches concluded at 10pm. The reason I was well down the list for being called was understandable – priority is given to members with a constituency interest and it could hardly be argued that the good people of Handsworth were affected either way. The Report's recommendation was eventually rejected.

When VAT was introduced to replace Purchase Tax I was exercised about the effect this would have on inflation, which should have been neutral. There was evidence that most retailers and service providers took the opportunity to increase their prices when substituting the tax. I was in favour of the new tax and had a public exchange of views with the local Football Club chairman in the public prints (never a wise course of action). Aston Villa's Doug Ellis railed against having to impose the tax on his club's fans, asserting that there would be a severe drop in attendances. I suggested that Aston Villa supporters would be willing to pay 55p instead of 50p (then the standard entrance charge) and that their loyalty to the Club would overcome such a modest increase in the price of admittance. Answer came there none but

Doug survived much longer than I did in Handsworth. He remained chairman for a further thirty-five years.

The most important decision in my first Parliament was the vote to join the EEC. This was taken in October 1971 and Conservatives were given a free vote but Labour imposed a three-line whip against joining. At the end of the long debate 69 Labour MPs voted with the Government while about twenty Tories voted against entry. I was decidedly in favour and the motion to join was carried by over a hundred votes. The UK formally joined on 1st January 1973 but not before Edward Heath had to change his suit after a pot of paint had found its target before the signing ceremony. Another particularly contentious piece of legislation was the Industrial Relations Bill which occupied a sizeable amount of time on the floor of the House. The power of the Opposition to delay and disrupt business (now heavily circumscribed) was all too evident when, one evening, the Government successfully moved a closure motion after a lengthy debate on a group of amendments. This meant that progress to the next set of amendments could be made but not before voting on the group, the subject of the closure. Normally there would be one vote but there was nothing in the rules to prevent voting on all 57 amendments separately. Labour seized this opportunity and there were continuous Divisions all through the night and into the following day (each vote taking about fifteen minutes as we trooped through the lobbies). It was estimated that we must have walked thirteen miles around in circles over a period of fifteen hours. In one Division I arrived early in the Lobby to find Edward Heath already there. It was at a time when the media were criticising him for taking time off to sail his beloved yacht "Morning Cloud" one weekend. Any doubt I might have had about the Prime Minister lacking a sense of humour was dispelled when he dryly commented that apparently it was acceptable to sit on an island watching the boats go by (a reference to Harold Wilson taking his annual holidays on the Scilly Isles) but quite wrong to be sailing one of the boats.

A particularly unpopular decision taken by the Government around this time was to increase MPs pay by nearly 40 per cent from £3,250 to £4,500. We all received apoplectic letters from a few constituents, irrespective of having had no increase since 1964 during which time the salaries of others had risen by two-thirds. Coincidentally Edward Boyle (now Lord Boyle of Handsworth) was chairman of the Review Body which recommended the increase. I could never understand why MPs could not be treated like most other people and have regular reviews until I realised two things: many of our constituents would still complain and only MPs could approve the recommendation and therefore we were deemed to have our snouts in the trough.

Speaking of which, I was to go on parliamentary visits abroad on two occasions. The first was to Sweden when I was part of a small British delegation attending a Council of Europe seminar on house building standards. It was a defining experience for me. Arriving in Stockholm for the three day event, I was fired up with enthusiasm and attended every session with due diligence, listening very keenly to all that was said. The object of the conference was to encourage adequate building standards through-out our continent and it soon became clear that most present thought it would be a good thing if the same regulations were applied to every country. I remained silent until the final day when the draft resolutions were being framed and consensus was in overdrive. When one resolution was about to be approved which began: "Housing in all member states should have double-glazed windows" I innocently observed that while I could see the point of having double-glazing, even triple-glazing, for housing in the Arctic Circle, I doubted this would be necessary in sunny Sicily. This did not go down at all well and I was considered a naïve MP at best and a downright troublemaker at worst. This was, in truth, my first encounter with a different political culture. Whereas we would want to be precise about every word and its meaning before agreeing to a resolution and then rigorously adhering to it, some of our continental neighbours would readily agree to what sounded good but, if minded, ignore it later.

My second overseas outing was to undertake a fortnight visit to East Pakistan (Bangladesh), India and Pakistan in 1973, shortly after being appointed to the Select Committee on Race Relations & Immigration. We were led by Bill (W.F) Deedes, a Cabinet Minister in the Macmillan and Douglas Home administrations who left Parliament in 1974 to become editor of the *Daily Telegraph*. On the delegation was Norman Fowler and we got to know each other well during the visit. When in East Pakistan, we visited the 'world's largest village' Sylhet with a population of over a million and were given an insight into the thriving cottage industry of forging passports. We liked to think we worked hard as well as travelled widely and on our only day off, a Sunday in New Delhi, some of us accepted an invitation to visit the Taj Mahal about one hundred miles to the south. This involved a dawn start and a hair-raising car journey but it was well worth it. It may have been the wrong time of day to see the building (early afternoon instead of sunset) but this did not matter to me as it is one of the most beautiful buildings I have seen. Whether the fortnight visit was a success or not is for others to judge but I did note that after meeting the leaders of all three countries they all had untimely ends: two assassinated and one hanged.

After the setback to my Private Members' Bill I wanted to pursue one part of it in a constructive way and started campaigning for a national tree year to encourage planting on a massive scale. Completing the groundwork, I put down an oral question to Environment Secretary Peter Walker, fully expecting his answer to be along the lines that I had a good idea but it wouldn't be the most appropriate time when local government was being reformed. It subsequently turned out that this was precisely what he was going to say but on the spur of the dispatch box moment he designated 1973 as National Tree Year (to the surprise and consternation of his civil servants). I went into the Tea Room after and was greeted with shouts of "doggies delight" (I was also Hon. Secretary of the All Party Animal Welfare Group).

The event became known as "Plant-a-Tree in '73" and the initiative succeeded in raising public awareness about the need for trees in our towns and the countryside, where Dutch Elm Disease had reeked havoc in many parts of England. The civil servant put in charge of the initiative was Alastair Gordon, the Prefect who was the recipient of my stink bomb at Rugby. Many planting ceremonies took place and I attended a number of them during the year, deriving great satisfaction when the Post Office issued a special stamp depicting an English Oak. As for my doomed Bill, most of its provisions were resurrected by Sir John Rodgers in the next Parliament and eventually enacted.

There was one chance meeting I had at Westminster which taught me to help others whenever possible. I wanted my mother to visit Parliament and eventually a day was arranged and she had strict instructions to take a taxi to Westminster on arrival at Euston. A proud son arrived early at the Public Entrance on a lovely summer's day to greet her. While waiting, I heard two elderly Americans asking where the entrance to Westminster Hall was. I turned and saw the couple with two children standing just behind me. Trying to be helpful, I told them the entrance was fifty yards down the road but, if they wished they could come with me via the 'back entrance.' They readily agreed and saw the Great Hall from the top of the ceremonial steps (the best initial view). They were immensely grateful and I pointed out some of the features and a little of the long history of the Hall (including the nine hundred year old walls and the six hundred year old double-hammer beamed roof). On the spur of the moment I asked if they would like to come on a short tour of the Palace, telling them that I was about to show my mother around on her first visit. They were delighted and we arranged to meet half-an-hour later. I asked them where they came from and they said Boston. "Ah," I said "that's the land of the bean and the cod, where the Cabots talk only to the Lodges and the Lodges only to God." They roared with laughter and I gave them my name and asked them theirs. "Mr and Mrs Large" he replied "and these are our two grandchildren."

Mother arrived in Central Lobby where I had also arranged to meet a girlfriend of my sister Christine who was over from Canada. The Larges then reappeared and the girl immediately recognised Mr Large and almost swooned. I introduced my mother to the visitors and he politely said: "no, my name is Lodge, not Large." The penny dropped. He was Henry Cabot Lodge who had been Nixon's Vice-Presidential candidate when Kennedy had won by a whisker in 1960. The family was in London for a few days before Henry was to take up an appointment in Rome. A chance meeting, indeed.

My most unnerving event in the Chamber was when someone threw a gas canister from the public gallery. The instinctive reaction was that it was a bomb and the war-serving generation of MPs knew exactly what to do - lie flat on the floor - but the younger MPs seemed transfixed and only when the choking fumes of the missile quickly reached us did we hastily depart the scene. A more pleasant happening was when I was called for a supplementary at Prime Minister' Questions after the previous interlocutor had asked him how he intended to celebrate the first anniversary of our joining the EEC. I seized the moment to tell him that the best way he could do so was by announcing immediately that the Government would give the go-ahead for the National Exhibition Centre to be built near Birmingham. The House laughed and appreciated the local plug for my city. Heath gave a non-committal reply but as soon as Questions ended his PPS, Tim Kitson, rushed over to me to tell me that he was to make the announcement that very evening. I had no idea about this and regarded my contribution as the most nicely timed intervention of my career.

A more personal memory in this Parliament was towards the end of it when I was appointed a PPS, an unpaid post which mainly involves being the eyes, ears and bag carrier of a Minister. I was seconded to two of them, Paul Dean and Michael Alison at the then DHSS. Always one to emphasise any personal achievement, I remember claiming the longest title in Parliament as Parliamentary Private Secretary to the Joint Parliamentary Under-Secretaries of State at the Department of Health and Social Security. I was also to have the post for the shortest time ever as the general election was to come soon after.

Before it did, and it came suddenly in the sense that the Parliament lasted less than forty-four months in spite of the Government's reasonable working majority, near neighbour Dennis Howell asked me if I had seen a recent edition of *Socialist Worker*, a way-out leftie weekly which wasn't likely to be the bedtime reading of any up and thrusting Tory MP. I told him as much but he said that I ought to as I was mentioned in it rather unflatteringly. I repaired to the Library and held my breath as I read an article about Dennis Howell's business activities with a Birmingham building firm alleging all sorts of dubious goings on and worse by the former Labour Minister. I was confident that Dennis was a man of impeccable propriety and though doubtless he had some connection with the firm (why shouldn't he, now that he was no longer in the Government) I could not believe the allegations to be true. However, that was a matter for him but suddenly my jaw hit the floor when the article went on to state that another Brummie MP was involved with the firm. It stated that I had shares in the company, giving a precise number. This upset and baffled me. It upset me because there were strict professional rules governing an architect's association with building firms (we acted for clients and were not permitted to have any conflict of interest). An architect could not be a director of a building group and although I was not then a practising architect, I paid my annual subscriptions to the RIBA and the Architects' Registration Council not least as I may have needed to find gainful employment after the Election. But what baffled me was the confidence of the reporter in asserting that I had a particular number of shares when I had none. Suddenly I realised that the writer had confused me with Donald Chapman, the Labour MP for Birmingham Northfield from 1950 to 1970. It was he who had shares in the company and not his namesake from the capitalist Party. I contacted our leader of the Conservative Group on Birmingham Council, Neville Bosworth who was a well known solicitor in the city, and he acted for my reputation. I dreamt of a huge amount of damages being awarded and the attendant publicity helping to secure my re-election but all I got was Neville's costs and equal prominence to the article in a subsequent edition of the paper apologising for the error. In short, no nationally known household name had been libelled, only an obscure backbench MP.

My Party's 1922 Committee (all our backbenchers) met weekly and this was the occasion to raise matters of concern confidentially (or so it was hoped). One of the burning issues in the early 1970s was whether MPs should declare their outside interests. I took a somewhat ambivalent view on the issue but some of my older colleagues were resolutely opposed to such a radical departure from the long held convention that we were all "honourable members" and behaved accordingly. In the short debate we had, Sir Derek Walker-Smith and Enoch Powell spoke eloquently against declaration and were clearly in the majority, while one or two younger members were more relaxed about the issue. Something impelled me to catch the chairman's eye and Sir Edward du Cann called me. Most of the assembled, I calculated, expected me to side with the minority but my short invention was:

"Mr Chairman, I have thought long and hard about this issue but have concluded that, on balance, I remain firmly opposed to any declaration of interests."

I detected a feeling of surprise followed by semblance of warmth towards me and continued:

> "My conclusion is that if we had to reveal our interests, I would be in the embarrassing situation of being probably the only one among us who had nothing to declare."

Luckily there was laughter all round and as we left the room, Julian Critchley smiled and assured me that my words would be mentioned in his diaries when he published them. They were not.

The 1970 Parliament was not a happy time for the country. Edward Heath's administration was beset with problems: violence in Northern Ireland, war in the Middle East, the quadrupling of oil prices and increasing unemployment with industrial unrest. In 1972 the miners and dockers went on strike; in 1973 the trade figures worsened, interest rates rose, the miners rejected the wage restraint policy and a state of emergency was declared. When over 80 per cent of members of the NUM voted to strike at the beginning of February 1974, the Prime Minister called an election for the end of the month.

During the campaign things got worse for the Conservatives. The visible monthly trade gap was the worst in history, the director-general of the CBI called for the repeal of the Industrial Relations Act and Enoch Powell, who had refused to stand as he put it "in an essentially flawed election," advised people opposed to the EEC to vote Labour. In Handsworth, I scurried around but soon realised that the danger to my survival was not so much in the traditionally marginal areas of the constituency (there was evidence that some Labour voters might be with me on the issue of who ran the country) but in my stronger area of Handsworth Wood where most of the electors were more concerned about the recently imposed three day working week to save energy; and this time my electorate had the opportunity to vote Liberal.

Come polling day and the British electorate gave a somewhat indistinct reply with no party having an overall majority. Labour got four more seats than the Tories but 300,000 fewer votes. The permutations were almost endless and Heath hung in, trying to cobble together a coalition with the Liberals who had won only 14 seats but nearly trebled their vote to six million. In the event they refused to join in any arrangement except a grand coalition so Heath went to the Palace to resign and Harold Wilson returned to Downing Street. He was probably more surprised than anyone else.

With the disadvantage of boundary changes and the intervention of a Liberal candidate securing 5,000 votes not least by raising the immigration issue, I was out by 1,600 votes and desperately looking for a job in pastures new.

7

"FAREWELL, HANDSWORTH"

To be kicked out of the Commons is a chastening experience and the more so after only one Parliament. There is nothing more "ex" than an ex-MP. One day you strut the corridors of power and are recognised not for any talent you may possess but simply because you are deemed to have some influence (though far less than yesteryear). After being rejected, you're a nobody.

To be defeated clearly brings an immediate practical problem: no job. An MP is paid until polling day and the prudent or pessimistic candidate will have saved for a rainy day. It positively chucked it down after I was defeated but my immediate cash flow problem was softened by three months severance pay.

Then there is the question of where to live. It is necessary to be in London when Parliament is sitting, usually thirty-four weeks in the year. I had rented a room in the house next to Robert (the architect) and Trudie Martin in Barnes. Their elderly neighbour, Mrs Lester, welcomed the extra income and it gave me the opportunity to keep in touch with the Martin family. My loss of seat also meant Mrs Lester's loss of rent and I had decisions to make. The best chance for finding gainful employment was in London but there could be another election at any time. I decided to take a two week break in Marbella, where I had been on holiday before, to lick my wounds, take stock and spend some time with Ian Granger, a larger than life character who lived in Spain and had acquired a new wife, Ena. Ian, a former army officer, was a big and ebullient man who had a fund of true but seemingly incredible stories about his latest escapades. Disaster was no stranger to every initiative he took but this only increased his appetite for adventure.

On returning home I decided I must sell up in Handsworth and buy a property in London. And so it was with a heavy heart that I moved from Birmingham and went to the metropolis to seek financial survival if not political resurrection. The local Conservatives chose Bob Tyler, a master butcher, to replace me. He was a local councillor and when the General Election came in October he made a respectable showing, given the national swing against us. I had put in for the few Conservative seats which became available, including Chelsea, Chichester and Petersfield, but without success.

I sold my house in 1975 for exactly twice the amount I had paid for it four years before. This was my introduction to being on the right end of rising house prices and was perhaps reassuring to those worried about falling values in immigrant areas. It was time to write to my mortgagor. I stated my position openly: I had £5,000 (after repaying the mortgage) and had spotted a two bedroom flat in a newly renovated early Victorian block near Paddington Station on the market for £18,000. I needed a £12,000 mortgage. The Building Society manager wrote back emphasising the downside: an application to triple the mortgage; no job or salary and not even the income of a wife to help. Nevertheless, he would take a risk on me; after all, the value of the property was unlikely to decline immediately by a third if I was to default on the monthly repayment. It didn't and I didn't.

And then there was the job problem. I didn't want to go back to the drawing board, not least as I hadn't practised architecture for thirteen years, except for the odd housing extensions for friends. Fortuitously, I had been writing a weekly column for *Building* since September 1973 and the House Builders Federation asked me to advise their members with planning problems. I was not paid a retainer but could charge the member directly if he sought my advice. A few did and with the addition of a modest retainer from the architectural firm in Jermyn Street I was able to keep the wolf from the door.

The RIBA had contacted me when I became an MP and asked me to keep in regular touch with them. I was happy to do so but insisted that this was on the condition that I was not remunerated; and they accepted this. Half way through the Parliament I decided that it would also benefit me if I got to know more about my professional institute, so I stood for the RIBA Council and was elected on their national list – being an MP clearly helped me. At the quarterly Council meetings politics occasionally reared its head but I resisted attempts to fuel the fire of such discussions. Alex Gordon was then the President and he was followed in 1975 by Fred Pooley, Buckinghamshire's County Architect, who asked me to be one of his vice-presidents with responsibility for Public Affairs and Membership. The President, then elected by the 70 member Council, had the right to choose his 'cabinet' and I was delighted to accept this honorary post. I stayed on the Council until 1977, leaving over the issue of architects advertising their services. This was a controversial issue and after much navel gazing we resolved to allow discreet self-advertisement but were immediately criticised by one of the architectural journals. Three months later the Council reversed its decision and it was the U-turn rather than the issue which filled me with despair. I resigned.

On a happier note, I went on a ten day visit to the USSR with a group of architects from Wessex in the Spring of 1975, visiting Moscow and Leningrad. The Kremlin, the hub of Moscow, encircled by 15th century brick walls enclosing cathedrals and palaces, was magnificent and there was an undeniable grandeur about the city with its monumental buildings, vast parks, impressive squares and the wide sweep of its streets. What depressed me was the drabness and mediocrity of the modern buildings. Variety and individuality had been stifled by a dull conformity and the vast edifices, all too readily recognised as the Russian wedding-cake style, were oppressive instead of impressive. Moscow then contained over seven million people and in spite of one-third of the city being covered by boulevards, parks and gardens, the density of population exceeded 20,000 per sq. mile simply because there were no semis or straddling suburbias: virtually everyone was housed in multi-storey tenement blocks. On the plus side, the communists practised conservation with a commendable determination. Old buildings had been preserved and restored and even yellow paint on stuccoed brick had invested unexceptional classical buildings with a certain charm.

After four days we travelled to Leningrad. It took eight hours by train on wooden seats with no refreshments available as we traversed a massively drab landscape of flat plains and pine trees. However, the journey was worth it. Leningrad must rank as one of the truly beautiful cities of the world. Founded at the beginning of the 18th century by Peter the Great and built on millions of oak piles driven into marshland at the mouth of the River Neva, its splendid classical buildings were designed by Italian, French and Dutch architects brought in by the Romanovs. The first imperial decree of Peter limited the height of all buildings, except cathedrals and churches, and so spires and towers still dominate the townscape. The Winter Palace (Hermitage) housed a handsome collection of European art and, with the Summer Palace outside the city, was worth every penny of the visit.

Around the time of my Russian sojourn, the new Government introduced the Community Land Bill and the National Farmers Union, Country Landowners Association and British Property Federation agreed to have a combined campaign against the measure and asked me to spearhead it. The CLB was designed, in the Government's words:

> "to enable the community to control the development of land ... and to restore to the community the increase in the value of land arising from its efforts."

The Bill, according to the Chapman interpretation, frustrated the main purpose of land planning – to ensure the right land was developed in the right way at the right time for the benefit of the community – and would give excessive powers to local authorities to control what development could take place and who should develop the land. I published a fifteen hundred word pamphlet detailing the harm the Bill would have on housing and industrial schemes, farming, occupational pension funds and even charities. I railed at the costs of implementing the proposals and the opportunities for malpractice. The pamphlet was distributed widely and I organised a series of meetings throughout the country. The result of all this? The Bill received Royal Assent more or less unscathed but the Government did back down on some of its original proposals (though not, I suspect, because of my efforts).

When Labour came back to power, Denis Howell was re-appointed Minister for Sport in the Environment Department to which was added Drought, Rain or any other problem which emerged. He had specific responsibility also for matters arboricultural and one of his first decisions was to set up the Tree Council to carry on the impetus of National Tree Year. The first chairman was the doyenne of the landscape world, Dame Sylvia Crowe, and the Council resolved to have an annual National Tree Week to highlight its efforts. I was overjoyed to accept their invitation to organise the first one in March 1975. A civil servant from the DoE, Ken Davis, was seconded to act as Secretary and we were given a modest room from which to operate.

Denis got the Prime Minister to officially open the first Week by planting a tree at Chequers and this was to be my second visit there (Edward Heath had invited me four years before). Harold Wilson, with pipe and Paddy the dog in tow, ensured a good photo opportunity and response from the media. He told me that, of all the PMs, Neville Chamberlain was the keenest tree-planter and Sir Ralph Verney, one of the Chequers' trustees, added that

With Margaret Thatcher, Leader of the Opposition,
tree planting in Marylebone. 1975

it was a tradition for every PM to plant a tree. Churchill had planted an oak (which had since died); Attlee a hornbeam; Eden a plane and Baldwin a flourishing oak. Wilson planted a sapling holm oak (which should grow to ninety feet high in one hundred and fifty years). To ensure political evenness, I got Margaret Thatcher, who had just become Leader of the Opposition, to plant a thirty feet high lime on a new housing estate in Lissom Grove, Marylebone. The following year I organised a multi tree-planting event in Hyde Park with a dozen well known personalities representing all walks of life. Denis Howell and Sylvia Crowe were joined by, among others, Sir Ralph Richardson, Lord Lichfield, Charles Forte and the comedian Graham Chapman. I left the Tree Council after the 1976 Week but was honoured to be appointed one of its vice-presidents and remain so to this day.

Shortly after, I was asked by Sir Eugene Melville, Director-General of the British Property Federation, to be their part-time Director of Information. Sir Eugene had retired after a distinguished career in the Diplomatic Service and I had met him on a number of occasions during the CLB campaign. I accepted with alacrity and though I was expected to work only three days a week, I usually turned up every weekday. Membership included most of the larger property and development companies and the Small Landlords Association. The BPF operated from a pleasant building in the corner of Catherine Place near Buckingham Palace. I enjoyed the work immensely, monitoring Parliamentary Bills, attending meetings and writing in their quarterly *Property Journal* introducing a chatty column which I dubbed "Pedlar's Place." At the time I also wrote a pamphlet for the Conservative Political Centre entitled *Town and Countryside – Future Planning Policies for Britain.* As well as providing background and briefing material on a variety of political topics, the CPC published a series of books and pamphlets to stimulate new ideas for future policies. The theme of my contribution was that while 'Planning' was anathema to most Tories, 'Town & Country Planning' was vital for Britain, with (then) 56 million people living on a small, densely populated island. I set out proposals for unclogging and improving the development control system. My little tome was published after Environment Secretary Anthony Crosland had rejected all the proposals of Mr George Dobry QC who had been asked to review the whole system by the previous Conservative minister, Geoffrey Rippon.

Just before joining the BPF I was introduced to an attractive and elegant twenty-something year old girl called Claire, who had been married to Colin McNab, coincidentally vice-chairman of the Scottish YCs when I had been chairman in England & Wales. Claire had worked for a time in Conservative Central Office and had seen me there. Her marriage had been dissolved but it did produce a son, David, who was born twelve days before I was elected to Parliament in 1970. After first meeting Claire, I invited her and David to London Zoo. We started seeing each other regularly and she came to various events including the tree-planting event in Hyde Park and my 40th birthday party. At this party, my brother Michael met Rosemary, who had been married to Terry Wray, a former YC national chairman (I am a godfather to one of their three children, Amanda). Michael subsequently married Rosemary, while Terry married a former friend of mine, Jenny Riley. Meanwhile Claire and I married in April 1976, a day before her 30th birthday. Having been a bachelor for too long, I suddenly found myself with three mouths to feed.

The marriage had a beneficial effect on my parliamentary ambitions. I had continued to put in for seats but was having only a 50 per cent strike rate in obtaining an interview, let alone getting any further. My bachelor status was not proving helpful in the immediate post-Heath Premiership period. However, as soon as my marital status was written into my cv, I was interviewed for virtually every seat which came up. Yet I was still failing to become the candidate. Frequently I got to the very last round but no further. A by-election came up in the Cities of London and Westminster and I was in the last three but pipped at the post; and from Morecambe & Lonsdale to Sevenoaks it was the same story. At Wycombe I actually reached the last two and appeared before hundreds in the Town Hall. Normally when the candidate is chosen, he would be asked to come out of the waiting room and be told the good news alone, while the rest of us were thanked and discharged via the back door. At Wycombe, Claire and I worked out that the reverse would happen so that the unsuccessful candidate could be told quietly and slip away. And so it was, but we insisted on returning to the hall to thank them for seeing us, congratulate the successful Ray Whitney and promise to come canvassing on the first day of the by-election campaign. This surprised the audience but did us no harm.

I was to have another but quite different encounter. When I first arrived in the Commons, there was a very successful firm of architects called Chapman Taylor and Partners and a number of colleagues enquired if I was the Chapman. I told them that I wished I were and wondered who my namesake was. He was Bob Chapman and he wanted to know who I was. A mutual friend arranged for us to meet and Bob asked me to have lunch with him at his offices in Kensington Church Street. The small talk flowed and I mentioned a coincidence: his partner John Taylor had the same name as my father's last partner and successor in Macclesfield. Then for some inexplicable reason I told him about a greater coincidence: on my first day in the Commons I had gone to the Library, opened *The Times* and saw the obituary of my namesake, Sydney Chapman, a distinguished mathematician who had been president of the International Geophysical Year in 1957, with a crater on the far side of the moon named after him. Bob Chapman replied: "I'll tell you of a greater coincidence: that Sydney Chapman was my father." He had died on the very day I had been elected in 1970. Incidentally, at the Chequers Tree-planting ceremony Harold Wilson had asked me if I was related to him as he was one of the PM's tutors at Oxford.

In the autumn of 1976 plans were being laid for the celebration of The Queen's Silver Jubilee in the following year. It was decided to have a series of themes and events in London and various informal committees were set up to organise them, chaired by some of the good and the great – and me. Thus, Lew Grade ran the show business side and Jimmy Hill the sporting contribution. I was asked to chair tree-planting schemes and I had the advice and expertise of a number of London Boroughs, the City and the Royal Parks. At the initial meeting of all the committees, we waxed lyrical about the importance of our specific areas and I was moved to observe that whereas all their efforts would be ephemeral bread and circus events, my committee's endeavours would be longer lasting. We did organise various planting events and there was one very special one. On the exact day of the 25th anniversary of her accession, 6th February, The Queen planted a tree in the park to the south of the Palace of Westminster (near the statues of Emile Pankhurst and the Burghers of Calais). This was carried out in the morning and was her only official event on that day.

In the late autumn of 1977 our daughter Laura (named after my mother) was born and on my mother's sixty-sixth birthday a month later they were introduced to each other. Sadly this was the first and last time they met, as my mother died six months later. The first signs of early dementia (subsequently to be known as Altzheimer's) had appeared six years before and the last years of her life were spent in a mental hospital, albeit tenderly cared for. Thank God that sufferers today are not condemned to such an end.

By the beginning of 1979, I was getting more and more dismayed about my lack of political success and it cannot have been easy for Claire – time and time again playing the dutiful and supportive wife to the has-been politician and would-be statesman. At Wycombe, shortly after giving birth to Laura, she was asked, with a heavy touch of meaningfulness, if having a baby would inhibit her from supporting me if I became their MP. She gave a splendid retort: "No, anymore than it stopped Diana MacKay from helping her husband Andrew to win Stechford in the recent by-election."

My self-confidence was taking a bashing and I felt it was time to move on and get a full-time job. I would forget any further foray into politics if I had not secured a seat by the next election, which was widely expected in the autumn of 1978 when the Liberals ended their pact with the Government. Having dropped hints to the electorate and with his party workers and trade unionists fired up for action, James Callaghan finally declared (to the astonishment of many) that he would not be going to the country. Nevertheless, an election would have to come by the autumn of 1979 and in the meantime I applied to become a Planning Inspector, took a written exam and after being interviewed by the Chief Planning Inspector, Mr Eric Midwinter, was selected and agreed to start work in the summer.

8

CHIPPING BARNET & REGGIE

Much happened in the Spring of 1979 after the winter of discontent. A succession of strikes and disruptions caused chaos and public anger. Mountains of rubbish accumulated in the streets, pickets appeared outside hospitals and fire stations and there were empty shelves in the supermarkets.

At Westminster, the Labour Government staggered on. At first they had a slim overall majority of four but this soon evaporated and survival depended upon the "Lib-Lab" pact. When this ended after eighteen months in the autumn of 1978, James Callaghan turned to the Nationalists but they made their support conditional upon the Prime Minister driving through Devolution. Callaghan knew he could not deliver with a score of Labour rebels who had supported the Opposition getting a proviso put in the Scottish Devolution Bill requiring 40 per cent of all Scottish voters to support the establishment of an Assembly. In the Referendum on March 1st the Scots backed the Assembly but not in the required strength. Mrs Thatcher now had her chance. She put down a motion of "no confidence" and on this occasion the Liberals, Nationalists and Ulster Unionists joined the Tories and the Government fell by one vote.

Six weeks before, Reggie Maudling, the former Chancellor and Home Secretary, died and this heralded a by-election in Chipping Barnet in north London. After the funeral of Reggie, the local Conservatives moved quickly, not least because the Tories wanted to be at full strength in the Commons. Over 260 would-be MPs applied and a committee of twenty was appointed to sift through the individual candidates' details. The committee decided to interview forty of them, after which the number was reduced to seven. It had then been the intention to reduce the number to three and put them before the Executive Council. However, when the Government fell, the committee had to take a decision quickly to ensure there was a candidate before the start of the election campaign. They met on Sunday April 1st resolving to submit only one name to the Executive.

The chairman of the association, Don Goodman, was asked to ring me immediately to accept the invitation to be the candidate. Unfortunately, blissfully ignorant of all this, Claire and I were having lunch with Jeremy and Verna Hanley in Northwood. It turned out that he was also one of the seven still in the running and it wasn't until the early evening that we returned home and finally got the telephone call. Inevitably, there were a number of disappointed people and I had to tread very carefully, not least because the president of the association, Bob Brum, had high hopes of being selected and the Executive Council members might feel they had been bounced into accepting someone they were required to take on trust. It was, after all, thirty-three years since they had last chosen a candidate. Thursday came and I survived, being taken immediately to the Conservative Club in the High Street by Don Goodman who winked as he told me that they would review their decision before the end of the next Parliament. The president of the Club, Eric James, who was waiting to greet me with a badly needed pint, expressed the hope that I would visit the Club at least once a year. I told him to expect me many more times than that.

"Plucked from limbo at the last moment" a headline in the *Daily Telegraph* proclaimed when my selection was announced. The reporter was at pains to stress that I "had been a member of a 'travelling circus' over the past five years and had appeared before thirty or more selection committees across the country." This was an exaggeration. I had been to only twenty-eight. Other newspapers referred to the "added warmth in his smile as he canvassed his new-found constituents" and my "breathing a sigh of relief at getting a seat at the eleventh hour." On my first day of canvassing, my very experienced Agent, Arthur Fawcett, suggested I visit the old people's homes to introduce myself and to remind them about applying for postal votes. As I toured the various establishments and was politely received by the matrons and other staff, I could see the unspoken comment in their eyes: "he comes here when he wants our votes, but we won't see him again until the next election." I made a promise to myself that I would visit each home at least once a year. And I did. The campaign was one of intense activity. We had a few public meetings because that was the tradition, but I crammed six days a week with canvassing as many homes as I could, leaping dwarf walls, sprinting across driveways and running up and down steps. Don Goodman was worried that I was overexerting myself but my strategy was simple: forget the political issues (they were being fought out in the media); just meet as many voters as possible and introduce myself as an active, reasonable, interested person, anxious to help. I called at about 7,000 homes during the campaign but these were less than 20 per cent of the total and even then nearly half the households had no one at home. Candidates soon learn to endure stoically the all too frequent doorstep remark: "Why haven't you come until now?" or "We've never seen you before," no matter how active and ubiquitous we are.

My opponents were Peter Dawe, a thirty-year-old Labour candidate who was a schoolteacher and Methodist lay preacher and David Ive, a twenty-nine-year-old solicitor representing the Liberals. I liked them both. There was also a fourth candidate, Ronald Colc, a fifty-years-old design engineer who was fighting the seat a second time for the National Front. He was the most local candidate, living round the corner from the school he had first attended. Reggie Maudling had had a majority of just under eight thousand over Labour with just less than half of the total vote and I was hoping to achieve the rounded figures of over 50 per cent and a five-figure majority. By polling day, Don Goodman was confident of a 12,000 majority. I joked and said I wanted more than that and he promised me a case of wine for every 1,000 above the figure.

The London Borough of Barnet had four constituencies, the others being Finchley, Hendon North and Hendon South. All the counts were held in different parts of Hendon Town Hall. Chipping Barnet was consigned to a large room at the back and the plan was to concentrate resources so that the Finchley result could be declared as soon as possible and Margaret Thatcher could return to Central Office and hopefully the next day via Buckingham Palace to 10 Downing Street. It turned out that Chipping Barnet was the last to declare, at 3.15am. We trotted over to the Council Chamber for the result to be declared but the media circus attending Margaret had long departed with only three local reporters staying on while TV crews dismantled lights and rolled up cables. My consolation was to receive over 25,000 votes with a 14,000 majority and 57 per cent of the poll in a turn out of over 75 per cent. Labour secured just over 11,000 votes, the Liberal less than 7,000 and the National Front less than 1,000. It was, on any criterion, a very satisfactory result for me with a 6.4 per cent swing from Labour. I was on my way to Westminster again, this time with two cases of wine.

*   *   *

Back in the House, I now had time to reflect on my new constituency and the people who had decisively put their trust in me. 'Barnet' is Anglo-Saxon for 'a place cleared by burning' and its most famous historical event was the eponymous Wars of the Roses battle in 1471 when Edward IV beat the Earl of Warwick around Hadley to the north, just outside the town. The word 'Chipping' means 'market' and King John had granted a charter in 1199. East Barnet was the earliest settlement in the area with the oldest (originally Norman) church. A new Chipping Barnet church was built in 1420 and this was restored and enlarged in 1875 by Rugby School Chapel's architect William Butterfield (not, thank God, in his 'greasy bacon' style). It is said that the keyhole in the south door was positioned in line with the top of the cross on St. Paul's Cathedral. In 1573 Queen Elizabeth Grammar School was founded on a site opposite the church and its Tudor Hall still stands today. The famous Barnet (Horse and Cattle) Fair dates from 1588, thus the cockney slang 'barnet' meaning hair. Samuel Pepys "took the waters" at Barnet in the 1660s (the covered Physic Well still survives).

When the coach and horse became the fashionable mode of travel, Barnet was the first staging post on the Great North road from Charing Cross to York, bringing prosperity to the area. One hundred and fifty coaches would stop in the High Street in a day. The town was also the highest point on the journey, fully four hundred feet above mean sea level, leading to my inevitable boast: "after Barnet, its down hill all the way". On a literary note, Barnet was where Oliver Twist first met the Artful Dodger and Dickens observed: "every other house in Barnet was a tavern, large or small." When the railway replaced the coach and horse, a station at New Barnet was built on the Kings Cross to Hitchin line and a branch line was constructed from Finsbury Park to High Barnet in 1872 (part of this has been a spur of London Transport's Northern Line since 1940).

To some of my new colleagues in the House, Chipping Barnet sounded as if it was in the Cotswolds. The seat used to be called Barnet but the creation of the new London Borough in 1965, with a population exceeding 300,000, made it necessary to change the constituency name, if only to avoid confusion. Thus Chipping Barnet, named after a Parish covering part of the market town, became the official name. The reason that one of the largest Boroughs in London was called Barnet was a political compromise. The place with the largest population in the new area was Hendon and the second largest Finchley. The representatives from Finchley refused to accept the name of Hendon and the people of Hendon would never agree to the name of Finchley. And so Barnet became the choice.

Chipping Barnet is where the metropolis meets the countryside. It is a pleasant, mainly residential area (with only a few small industrial estates) consisting of 1930s suburbs interwoven around and attached to much earlier villages such as New Barnet, East Barnet and Whetstone with three further villages, Totteridge, Arkley and Monken Hadley remaining almost separate. Half the total land area of the constituency was Metropolitan Green Belt or Open Space, which doubled pressure for housing on the other half. The Green Belt has prevented Barnet from exploding into the countryside, not only to the north but also westwards and even southwards into the Totteridge valley, only ten miles (as the crow flies) from Hyde Park Corner. However, the price for this has been a great amount of infilling development with blocks of flats replacing large Victorian family homes and their gardens covered with tar macadam for off-street parking.

Most descriptions of places in England are too neat and simple to be absolutely true but it would not be an over exaggeration to claim that my new constituency was an agreeable and convenient place in which to live, with relatively easy access to the heart of the metropolis to the south when the trains on the Northern and Piccadilly Lines are behaving. Chipping Barnet is situated very conveniently in the "box" formed by the M25 to the north, the North Circular road to the south, the A1 to the West and the A111 to the East. As for Barnetonians, I soon came to realise that they were pleasant, generally successful people who were conservatives with a small 'c' and interested in politics with a small 'p'. They wanted peace and quiet at home and a sensible and sensitive approach to matters beyond their front doors. Many of them give much of their spare time to voluntarily work for local charities and play a distinctive part in the community.

For the second time, I was following a brilliant man as MP. Reggie Maudling had been chosen as the new Conservative candidate shortly after the Labour landslide victory of 1945 when Barnet, a newly created constituency (previously it had been the southern half of St. Albans Division) had returned a Labour MP by less than 700 votes. Reggie nursed the seat assiduously for four years and (after a favourable boundary change) received a 10,000 majority in the 1950 election. Twenty months later, the Tories returned to power and the following year Churchill appointed Reggie to his first ministerial post, aged thirty-four. Soon after, he became Economic Secretary to the Treasury and in 1955 Eden made him Minister of Supply and a Privy Councillor at the age of thirty-eight. Macmillan appointed him Paymaster-General and after the 1959 Election he was promoted to the Cabinet as President of the Board of Trade. In the summer of 1962 he became Chancellor of the Exchequer at the age of forty-five.

When Alec Douglas-Home resigned as leader of the Opposition in 1965, Maudling stood for the post and was the favourite at the outset among Conservative MPs and the national press. He was well regarded and had few enemies but his campaign was almost non-existent and his supporters went about promoting him in an amateurish way. Ted Heath, his main rival, was a colder person but a consummate politician, backed up by a younger but more professional team of parliamentarians who organised his campaign with ruthless efficiency. The other challenger was Enoch Powell who was felt to be almost a token candidate - the standard bearer of free market economics. He was not expected to get more than a score of votes. Under a new system of voting among Conservative MPs, the result of the first round was Heath 150, Maudling 133 and Powell 15. Although there was provision for a second ballot on such a narrow result, Reggie had felt there was little point in "asking people to say the same thing over again" and conceded victory. Heath made him Shadow Foreign Secretary and Deputy Leader and when Heath became Prime Minister, Reggie was appointed Home Secretary (which then included Northern Ireland) and number two in the Cabinet (but not deputy PM). However, in 1972 he resigned over the "Poulson Affair" and was never to become a Minister again.

I got to know Reggie quite well, first when chairman of the YCs and later as an MP. Unfortunately, losing my seat in 1974, I did not see him in the last five years of his life. I remember him as a man with a brilliant mind coupled with a laid-back approach. This was typically evident when delivering speeches. He extemporised on a few scribbled notes. He could grasp the essential points in any paper quickly and he had the ability to speed-read any document. When the Tories lost office in 1974, he had been a Minister for more than 12 years and his salary as Chancellor was a mere £5,000 pa. This was now reduced to an MP's salary of £1,750. An immediate priority must have been to improve his family's finances and this led to his association with Poulson and others. Reggie was involved in promoting building projects abroad for Poulson and was in no way concerned with the architect's business at home, which was securing contracts in the public sector by corrupt means.

Lewis Baston, in his definitive biography "Reggie" (published in 2004) states:

> "the general consensus among parliamentarians about Maudling's business involvements was that he displayed bad judgement in being taken in by crooks like Poulson. If pushed, his colleagues would admit that he was greedy for cash and was less than diligent about checking up where it came from."

Reggie was a popular man, immensely liked on both sides of the House and respected by many leading politicians abroad. He was a big man who seemingly never bore a grudge. However, his failure to get the leadership of his Party in 1965 did affect him badly and he was uncharacteristically bitter and critical of Margaret Thatcher after she sacked him as Shadow Foreign Secretary in 1976, uttering the comment "hired by Churchill and fired by Thatcher." He didn't live long enough to realise the irony of this remark.

A Select Committee looking into Maudling's (and two other MPs) involvement with Poulson reported in 1977 that it did find "matters of concern" including not making a declaration of interest in a speech ten years before. The main criticism was his resignation letter as Home Secretary in July 1972 (read by Ted Heath to the House) which was "lacking in frankness." Maudling strongly challenged this and had considerable sympathy from a number of MPs. When the House debated the findings, a Tory MP moved an amendment inviting the House to "take note of" instead of "agreeing with" the Report. This was carried and that was the end of the matter. Nonetheless, Reggie's front bench career was firmly ended and he was bored and frustrated. His drinking became heavier and his condition suddenly worsened in January 1979. He was taken into hospital and suffered a painful end to his life, dying of cirrhosis on 14th February, aged sixty-one. There was genuine sorrow beyond his own Party at the death of a popular politician who had just failed to make it to the top of the greasy pole.

9

THE EARLY
THATCHER YEARS

The first woman Prime Minister heading a new
Government following an election caused by a motion
of no confidence carried by one vote was an unique
time in British politics; and I was glad to be back at
Westminster. It had all been so sudden. Within five weeks
I had been transformed from an ageing bridesmaid at
selection meetings into an MP with a five-figure majority
and every prospect of a long tenure.

The Palace of Westminster had hardly changed. The
two most notable exceptions were the Committee rooms,
which had been enlivened with re-printed Augustus
Pugin wallpapers; and a new underground car park
beneath New Palace Yard turning the area in front of Big
Ben from a car pound into a lawn with pleached trees
and a fountain celebrating The Queen's Silver Jubilee.

Among the new MPs in this Parliament was Sheila
Wright from Handsworth who had failed to win the seat
from me at her third attempt in the 1970 Election. John
Lee, who beat me in 1974, announced that he would not
stand again half way through the Parliament because of
ill health and the likelihood of an election at any time,
only to make a full recovery after his successor had been
selected.

Within the first week back, a Whip asked if I had
seen Cecil Parkinson, the MP for next-door South
Hertfordshire. He had just been appointed Trade
Minister but had immediately left on a ten-day official
visit to South America. By the time he returned, I had
put two-and-two together and realised he wanted me to

be his PPS. Unfortunately fate intervened when Margaret Thatcher decreed that the Trade & Industry Department should not have more than two PPS's. Trade Secretary John Nott had already appointed one as had the other - Minister for Consumer Affairs Sally Oppenheim - and so Cecil had to share Sally's choice, Michael Spicer. On his return, he approached me in the Division Lobby covered in confusion and explained the situation. I said that I perfectly understood and in any case my father had warned me, as a good professional man, never to go into trade. The relief on his face was palpable.

It was time to make my re-entry speech and I was anxious to get this out of the way before the summer recess. The best opportunity came when the Opposition put down a motion deploring the proposed cuts in public services. Again, I was fortunate to be called first from the government backbenches and I tried to put the issue as factually and bluntly as I could. Public expenditure had risen from £28 billion to nearly £70 billion in the five years of Labour but inflation had more than doubled and therefore the real increase had been minimal. I went on:

> "The truth is that our taxpayers and ratepayers have been asked over the past quinquennium to pay more and more ... for less and less; and this in a period when there has been record inflation, record unemployment, record debt and record disillusionment."

The new Conservative Government proposed to cut back the planned increase in public spending by 3 per cent, so that it would rise by 17 per cent instead of 20 per cent. I asserted that such a modest cutback could be undertaken without affecting the quality of the vital public services and that the voters were fed up with profligacy and wanted prudency.

Re-reading the speech over a quarter of a century later, some passages in it seem eerily familiar today and, back in my new constituency, some of the problems facing Barnetonians were even more so: the erection of aerial masts, graffiti, the closing of a post office, commuter services, the local taxation system and the NHS.

The last three became perennial problems for my constituents and the bane of their MP's life. Two London Underground lines serve Chipping Barnet: the Piccadilly Line to the east and the Northern Line coming up the middle of the constituency to High Barnet. The latter became known as the Misery Line, with antiquated rolling stock, outdated signalling and old track. There was ever a shortage of drivers who disliked working in the longest tunnel in the world (from East Finchley to Morden) while service frequency was limited by the number of trains that could pass through its pinch point at Camden Town, where its other spur came in from Edgware. All the long suffering commuters wanted was a clean, safe, reliable and affordable service but investment had been inadequate for many years on the false assumption that the ever increasing ownership of cars would mean a reduction in use of public transport. Until the end of the 1970s there had been a steady fall in numbers using the Underground system but there was to be a massive increase in passengers thereafter.

Local taxation – then the Rating system – was unfair, illogical and out-of-date. It was unfair and illogical because people did not pay according to their means or the services they used; and out-of-date because central government had to meet nearly two-thirds of local authority expenditure. The problem was to find a fairer alternative and few people today would suggest that the best solution has been found.

The third continuing problem was the crumbling state of Barnet General Hospital which consisted mainly of early 19th century buildings, including a former Workhouse on which Charles Dickens had based "Oliver Twist." Prefabricated huts built in the 1930s with an intended life span of ten years had survived for over four decades by the time I arrived. One-third of the beds in the hospital were in these huts and patients had to be taken to and from operating theatres on trolleys in the open air. Under successive governments promises to rebuild the hospital had been reneged upon and I took all this up with equal doses of energy and frustration.

When the House returned from the summer recess, Norman Fowler needed a new PPS and I was delighted to accept his invitation. His ministerial office was small with only one junior, Ken Clarke, and I was encouraged to participate in a number of issues. One was a new vehicle registration system - the old one using three letters and three numbers was running out - and it was eventually decided to use an additional but separate letter indicating the year of issue of the vehicle. My suggestion was to add an extra number, introducing an additional 9,000 numbers (from 1000 to 9999) for every variant of the three letters giving an additional 150 million registration numbers, but this was not accepted.

In the 1970 Parliament I had unsuccessfully campaigned to replace the road tax (Vehicle Excise Duty) with a surcharge on petrol tax. If this had been done then it would have involved only an additional 4.5p on a gallon (1p per litre). When I told Norman about this, he warmed to the idea and put it forward, but it was fought bitterly by the Treasury on the simple basis that they wanted to keep every avenue of revenue open (unless for mega-political reasons). Norman told me later that he won the argument in the Cabinet sub-committee but the Chancellor insisted on bringing the matter to the full Cabinet and Geoffrey Howe won when he said that a charge would still have to be made by the DVLA for running the registration system. Support for the idea melted away as ministers realised that even a minimal initial charge would be increased yearly and we would soon be back to 'square one.'

At the end of 1980 my Agent, Arthur Fawcett, retired. He had read classics at London University before joining Conservative Central Office. He was to become Churchill's agent in Epping at the 1935 election and after serving in North Africa and Italy during the war resumed his career, being appointed to Barnet in 1949. He had seen Reggie through his nine successful elections as well as my first one and with twelve campaigns under his belt and, approaching his sixty-ninth birthday, he felt it was time to call it a day. At his farewell meeting, I tried to find a suitable description in my eulogy to him but felt that "from Churchill to Chapman" was the wrong way round and did not do him justice.

It was a few months before Arthur Fawcett's successor was selected. The Association chose Geoffrey Ellis who had been the Agent at nearby Hampstead for five years. Happily he and his wife Shelagh already lived in Barnet and she happened to be Cecil Parkinson's Agent. I had known them for some years with our common Y.C. backgrounds. During the 'interregnum' Andrew Pares voluntarily stepped in as acting agent. He was a modest man who had everything to be immodest about, not least as a former Mayor of Barnet and Leader of the Council who had been awarded both a military MBE in WWII and civilian OBE for public services.

When interviewed by selection committees, I was invariably asked if I would live in the area. I always replied with an enthusiastic 'yes' believing in the obvious: that it would benefit electors (and me) to be locally accessible. And so it was with Chipping Barnet but now I was married the only problem was how quickly I could move as this involved David's education. In mid-1981 he was eleven and was ready to move to his next school. This gave us the opportunity to sell our home in Putney and we bought a relatively more spacious late Victorian house in Ravenscroft Park, not far from the High Street in Barnet. Our new home had last been modernised in the 1930s (newspapers under the linoleum flooring in the bedrooms confirmed this) and the house needed drastic surgery, with re-wiring, central heating and a new kitchen. The property cost £57,000 but a further £35,000 was needed for the improvements, with a hefty mortgage to match, though our home in Putney was sold for £61,000 (well over triple the price I had paid three years before).

Meanwhile a happy event had intervened. In May 1981 our third child Michael was born, the day after our annual visit to the Whitsun Bank Holiday Carnival at Barnet Rugby Club. At one stage Claire wondered if she was about to give birth at the Club but it was a false alarm and he was delivered at Queen Mary's, Roehampton. Michael was christened in the Crypt Chapel of the Palace of Westminster eight weeks later and with the kind permission of Speaker George Thomas (he had been elected in the previous Parliament) the Reception was held in his State Rooms. The christening was conducted by our new Chipping Barnet Rector, the Revd Adrian Esdaile, and at the exact moment a loud clap of thunder penetrated the ceremony and the heavens opened. The Speaker joined us during the reception and was photographed holding the infant Michael in his arms.

In the first major Cabinet reshuffle, the Prime Minister appointed Norman Fowler Secretary of State for Health and Social Services and I moved with him from Transport. This vast Department was housed at the Elephant & Castle in a ghastly, impersonal 1960s concrete jungle difficult to reach from Westminster and, like the Home Office, reputedly the graveyard of ambitious ministers. Ken Clarke went with him, as Minister of Health, and the total ministerial team numbered eight. Health, pensions and the benefits system are high profile and politically controversial areas and I used to say to Norman that if he had dropped only one of the many political eggs he had to juggle with come Saturday, he had had a very good week. He not only survived his ordeal; he proved himself a competent team leader with a safe pair of hands.

Another change in the reshuffle involved Cecil Parkinson who was appointed to the chairmanship of the Party. This meant that the Prime Minister occupied the seat to the immediate south of mine and now the Party Chairman was to the immediate north. I felt I was

I once described the job of an MP as "part Vicar, part Doctor and part Personnel Manager of a large works!" A House of Commons policeman presented me with this cartoon.

Drawn by a friend and fellow architectural student, Robert Martin in 1979 on my appointment as PPS to the Minister for Transport.

being watched or, as Claire put it after the re-shuffle (and many subsequent ones): "I see you're being overlooked again."

A short time later I was deeply saddened at the early death of Edward Boyle. I knew he was not well when, late one evening leaving the House, I heard his unmistakeable voice greeting me and I could hardly believe my eyes when I saw a slim and gaunt looking man, literally a shadow of his former self. He had succumbed to bone cancer and died a few weeks later. When I succeeded him in Handsworth, he immediately invited me down to his home in Sussex and royally entertained me for a weekend after the arduous campaign. It was only then that I saw another dimension to his interests: a deep love and knowledge of music (we went to the opera at Glyndbourne nearby) and an expertise on roses. He died at the age of fifty-eight, a most accomplished man who was successful in the two worlds of politics and academia.

Towards the end of the summer recess in the following year, I made my first visit to the United States. President Reagan had come to London in the preceding June and had been the first US President to address both Houses of Parliament. This historic occasion witnessed his use of the transparent autocue, which made him much more fluent and much less forgetful than he probably was. I now felt it my duty to return the compliment and visit his country and went with six other MPs, including John (now Lord) Cope and Malcolm Thornton. Our Parliamentary Group first went to Washington for a few days after which we each repaired to the district of a Congressman seeking re-election (which they have to do every two years) and then to New York. The Federal Capital is, of course, laid out on the grand scale with the main axis from the Houses of Congress on Capitol Hill to the Lincoln Memorial. It is city planning at its most deliberate, with buildings and monuments befitting the capital of a great nation and we did our share of sightseeing, including the Oval Office in the White House. However, I was surprised to find that I began to tire of the architecture and began taking a liking to the smaller scale, evolved growth of the nearby suburb Georgetown. As for New York, I experienced the reverse emotion. I was half dreading the noisy, crowded, towering scale of this city of disorder and it seemed certainly that when we arrived at Grand Central Station. Nonetheless, after a few days, I began to enjoy the hustle and bustle of the place, in spite of the then practice of painting the outlines of people on the pavements where they had been killed. The city had a vibrancy and excitement about it and I discovered something else. With skyscrapers galore, I expected Manhattan to be a series of dark canyons with little light reaching ground level. But not so: because the city had a grid plan, light flooded in horizontally.

In between Washington and the Big Apple, I was allocated to Chicago and met Congressman John Porter of the 16th District of Illinois, spending the weekend in his constituency in the northern suburbs of the 'windy city.' One of his aides met me at O'Hare airport and drove me immediately to a non-political dinner. I arrived after the meal had started but American hospitality took over and after a couple of short speeches which included a personal welcome to me, I assumed that I was expected to reply. I went to the rostrum and expressed delight at this my first visit to their country and, with a touch of theatricality, brandished a letter from the Prime Minister thanking the American people for their support and understanding during the Falklands campaign. It brought the diners to their feet. I had asked Margaret for a short letter and she had willingly obliged, writing it in such a way as to make it relevant for almost any occasion. The following day John Porter had me glad-handing at a Supermarket with Miss Illinois, with strict instructions for me to speak in my English accent. In the afternoon he dragged me around a tea party for well-to-do Republicans and I met a certain Cyrus, with a story to tell.

Cyrus began with a monologue containing two distinct strands. The first was a glowing tribute to "your wonderful Prime Minister and your Falk-lands war" and how she had a wonderful sense of fair play "in giving the Argentine invaders a month to get out which, Sydney, is how I understand you play your game of cricket." The second strand was all about his friend Elmer, who unfortunately couldn't be present but had scored the greatest commercial success that year in the whole of the US of A. I thought it best not to explain the logistics of getting an armada half way across the world but I couldn't quite understand what Elmer had to do with the Falklands, until it all came together when he said: "Elmer's into sweat shirts, Sydney, but I guess you call them T-shirts in England. When you regained your little colony, Elmer brought out the best-selling sweat shirt ever. Nothing multi-coloured, just plain white but written across the chest was 'Don't cry for me Argentina' and underneath 'The Empire strikes back.'"

I warmed to Elmer and when I returned to London and met Margaret at her room in the Commons, told her about the shirt. She was clearly delighted and suddenly said to her PPS Ian Gow: "Come on, let's go and have dinner." We adjourned to the Members' Dining Room and I ordered a bottle of Chablis. "How did you know it is Margaret's favourite wine?" purred Ian in a quiet aside. I felt things were going very well until the PM suddenly looked at me and said: "Sydney, why did you go into politics?" The question was well intentioned and was said not in a sense of 'why on earth did you come to Westminster' but more with the purpose of eliciting some profound answer along the lines of realising that as every day passed I shared absolutely Conservative principles and values and wanted to do my bit in advancing them and helping to create a prosperous and happy society for all our people. Unfortunately, I failed to fully comprehend the opportunity to impress and as my mouth opened the awful realisation came to me that I was digging a deep hole for myself and incapable of changing tack. I responded: "Well, many years ago I had a dream, which I subsequently realised was a vision. The purple clouds parted and a voice from above intoned 'Chatham, Chamberlain, Churchill, Chapman.' But don't worry, Prime Minister, I'm in no hurry." There was a distinct stifling of breath and an eerie silence was quickly followed by a stilted change of conversation. Less than half-an-hour later, the bells sounded for a division and waiting for me on the message board was a note from the PM enclosing money reflecting her exact share of the cost of the Chablis. She always insisted on paying her way.

Another occasion when a group of Conservative backbenchers met Margaret at no.10 was early in 1983. She sat fifteen of us down with a drink and methodically went round the room asking each in turn when we thought she should go to the country. About half those assembled told her that whatever she decided would be all right by them, while the other half said she should go soon (after four years, instead of waiting the full five). I happened to be the last to be asked and said a precise date in September. There was complete silence and so I explained that it seemed a waste to go early when we were going to win; she should get the House down in July for the summer recess and then come on television on the first Monday in September (which I still regard as the first day of a new year) to announce the event. I added that the nation, knowing that an election would have to come within a few months, would be grateful to get it out of the way as soon as possible. There was a grudging recognition that my view had the hallmark of originality, but the assembled seemed unimpressed. Above all, the Prime Minister failed to act upon my advice and we had a mid-summer election.

10

THE MOMENTUM OF
THE MID-EIGHTIES

The Conservatives were riding high in the opinion polls when the Election was called, in contrast to most of the previous four years. There had been full scale riots in Brixton, Toxteth and Moss Side in 1981, unemployment had reached over three million in 1982 and there was the Maze Prison Hunger Strike in Northern Ireland. However public expenditure and borrowing were eventually curbed, inflation cut and taxation reduced. Margaret Thatcher had also won a £2.4 billion rebate from the EC Budget and the council tenants' Right-to-Buy scheme was proving popular. Less so, at least initially, was the privatisation programme. The National Freight Corporation, Amersham International, British Aerospace and Cable & Wireless had been de-nationalised and BA, BT, British Gas and British Shipbuilders were planned to follow. A piece-by-piece reform of Trade Union legislation was also under way. When this and the restructuring of the economy faced difficulties, the resolve of the 'iron lady' remained steadfast ("the lady's not for turning"). If ever the electorate doubted this, her response to the invasion of the Falklands dispelled such thoughts and the recapture of the islands turned public opinion. On the day the islands were attacked, Defence Secretary John Nott was having lunch with me when he received a note and suddenly left. When he didn't return, I was soon to learn that it was because of the invasion and not something I had said.

Before all this, there had been a fundamental split in the Labour Party. When Mr Callaghan resigned, the left-winger Michael Foot beat Denis Healey by ten votes for the leadership. Immediately the 'gang of four' and ten other Labour MPs renounced the Party Whip. A new Party, the SDP, came into being and initially commanded more than 50 per cent in the opinion polls. In March 1982, they vied with Labour on 33 per cent to the Tories 31 per cent (probably the first time a governing party was in third place). After the recapture of the Falklands, the Tories jumped to 46 per cent with Labour on 27 per cent and the Alliance (Liberals and SDP) 24 per cent. This poll almost reflected the share of votes in the General Election nearly a year later.

The 1983 Election was a triumph for the Tories and Thatcherism, a disaster for Socialism and a mixture of success and bitter disappointment for the Alliance. The Conservatives won 397 seats with an overall majority of 144. Labour secured only 209 constituencies while the Alliance doubled its number of MPs (from 11 to 23) and nearly doubled its vote (to almost 8 million). The Tories' vote was actually down by 700,000 on 1979, while Labour lost 3 million supporters. The Alliance disappointment was due to the difference between the votes cast for them and the seats they won. They were only half-a-million votes behind Labour but secured just over one-tenth of their seats and the Conservatives did particularly well because support for the two main opposition parties was almost evenly split.

I felt a scintilla of disappointment in Chipping Barnet. My vote was slightly down and so was my majority even though the reduced vote was explained by a slightly lower turnout and the reduced majority by the Alliance candidate overtaking and comfortably beating Labour. Also it had been a five horse race. The Alliance candidate was Christopher Perkin, a thirty year old photographer, while Labour's was Nigel Smith, a 35 year old teacher, whose wife Angela was subsequently to become the MP for Harlow and a Minister. There was also an Ecology Party candidate and an Independent.

Every candidate has his own story to tell about a campaign and there were some surprising remarks made to me on the doorstep. The first was the number of electors who said "I'd never vote for you or that woman but I agree with her abolishing the GLC." The other frequent observation made was "I was thinking of voting for you on this occasion but I don't want your Party to get a massive majority" and this became my major worry. I took a day off during the campaign to go to Richmond and help Jeremy Hanley in a seat which was threatened by the Alliance. After canvassing in the morning, Jeremy asked me to accompany him to a lunchtime meeting at a school where the candidates were to face questions. One girl enquired as to what they would do first if they won the election. Jeremy gave an adequate reply; followed by Alan Watson (Alliance) who gave an unnecessarily pompous answer saying he would win and had already agreed to be interviewed by Robin Day on television. The Labour candidate was twenty-six-year-old Keith Vaz, born in Aden, who replied: "If I won, I would go into the nearest Christian Church and thank God for a miracle." The pupils enjoyed that and although he came a bad third in the contest – Jeremy winning by 74 votes – I was able to greet Keith when he was elected for Leicester East in 1987 by reminding him of his reply.

The achievement of Mrs. Thatcher's first term was that she had created a sense of reality, hope and purpose among the British people and I was fascinated by her. As her next door constituency neighbour I felt a double obligation to be loyal and I admired her sense of purpose, indefatigable determination and boundless energy. Yes, she had a down side: deep prejudices and an over-readiness to divide her adherents too easily into "one of us" or "a wet." I felt instinctively that she did not regard me in the former category but that did not stop me from supporting her when I had some reservations about policy and her arbitrary manner in declaring them. One such one was the decision to abolish the GLC which came out-of-the-blue to Tory backbenchers from the metropolis, who had no inkling of this last minute decision. We were not consulted before the decision was taken but, had we been, I suspect we would have been deeply split on the issue and that, in all likelihood, may have been the reason for keeping it from us until the publication of the manifesto. I was in favour of the decision and, as I witnessed during the campaign, there was some enthusiastic support for abolition even though public opinion in the capital turned against us during the long legislative process to make it a reality.

I had resolved to do something different in each Parliament and so, by mutual agreement, resigned as Norman Fowler's PPS. I had been his House of Commons "eyes and ears" for nearly four years and immensely enjoyed the experience, but there was one drawback: I couldn't speak out publicly on any matter relating to health and social security matters although I could lobby privately and directly to ministers. I had become particularly interested in the new Select Committee system which had been set up in 1981 by the then Leader of the House Norman St. John Stevas. Virtually every Department had a Select Committee shadowing its work and it had the right to call for people and papers and inquire into any aspect the Department's responsibilities. I applied to join the Environment Committee and was selected. There were eleven members and the places, as with Standing Committees, were allotted proportionally to the number of MPs in each Party. In the new Parliament, the Conservative had seven nominations and Labour four (or three with another Party getting the other place). It was done with mathematical precision, as were the chairmanships, with the minor parties represented on some but not all committees. At our first meeting we elected Sir Hugh Rossi chairman and it was a wise choice. He had been a minister in the Environment, Northern Ireland and Social Security Departments, so he clearly knew his way around government. We took two initial decisions: not to inquire into highly contentious party political issues; and to seek, wherever possible, all-party consensus on the reports we published. Apart from some necessary annual inquiries into the Department's estimates and spending, we covered in depth over the next four years such diverse matters as water pollution, metropolitan green belt policy, acid rain, nuclear waste and historic buildings.

While Select Committee work usually occupied about two hours once or twice a week (excluding time involved in reading up written evidence and other material), there were still the Standing Committees (examining Bills) to be manned. I found myself appointed to one or two each session and the time involved usually depended upon the degree of controversy in them. I agreed to be on most Housing and Planning Bills and in addition attended the Committee meetings of Private Members' Bills I had supported. All these activities were scheduled for mornings so did not cut across the daily Question Time on the floor of the House. As appropriate, I used these occasions to advance various campaigns, usually as a result of constituency cases. Car insurance coverage, misuse of air guns and disposal of asbestos were just some of the issues that I raised.

I wanted a change in the law so that drivers involved in an accident had to report the incident to their insurance companies. This was because many blameless people lost out when they applied to the other driver's insurance companies to pay for the damage. The other insurance company often denied any responsibility simply because the accident had not been reported. The appalling misuse of air guns was another local issue with cases of young people firing at dogs and cats and causing horrific injuries. Any seventeen- year-old could legally buy an air gun and then pass it on to a younger child. The publication "Cats" had been organising a national petition and the editor of this moggies' magazine asked me to present it to Parliament. I had been liaising with a veterinary surgeon, Michael Stockman, whose practice was round the corner from my home and who was on the national committee of the British Veterinary Association. All this resulted in my being elected an Honorary Associate member of this professional body and I was flattered to remain so until I retired from Parliament, when they immediately upgraded me to honorary membership.

I was also exercised about the disposal of asbestos waste, which was then double-bagged before being buried three feet under earth. The problem with this was that the asbestos remained toxic and a continuing health hazard, not least because the ground could be disturbed. A Sheffield firm had invented a process of vitrification, whereby the waste could be transformed into a harmless glass substance, making it safe for all time so that the land did not need to be sterilised.

A new draft circular on green belts caused me anxiety and after a meeting with the specific minister and a letter to *The Times* (as well as support from many colleagues) the draft was eventually withdrawn. I was less successful with other campaigns. On the fortieth anniversary of the end of the war in Europe, I wrote a joint letter with our local MEP, John Marshall, to none other than Mikhail Gorbachev, asking the USSR leader to reconsider his policy of not allowing Russian Jews to leave his country. We sent the letter when I made my first visit to Strasbourg but I have to report that there was no answer to our missive. Since my Handsworth days, I had taken a particular interest in the plight of Soviet Jews and had become the President of the Architects and Construction Industry's Committee for the Release of Soviet Jewry. I was to meet Gorbachev many years later but felt it prudent not to remind him that I was still waiting for a reply.

If I was unable to influence the Russian leader, I have to report that I caused a little embarrassment to the British leader and it was all to do with Sunday trading. The law was in a mess and the Government decided to act. After appointing a committee to look into the issues, Mr Justice Auld's team recommended a complete deregulation of trading. Mrs T decided to act. After a debate on a free vote asking the House to agree with Auld's recommendations, the Commons voted to do so. With this authority, the Government introduced the Shops Bill and put a three-line whip on the measure. They did so with complete propriety as they had the support of a majority of MPs in the free vote. However, I believe that they made a tactical error in putting on the three-line instruction to their supporters and the whips eventually backed down and made it known that the three-line whip was there to ensure attendance, not to dictate which way to vote! The problem for the Government was not of its own making. When there had been the free vote some MPs (presumably not exercised one way or the other on the issue) decided to return to their constituencies early and did not vote. When the Government brought forward its Bill, many more MPs voted at the Second Reading and the measure was defeated. I had voted against Auld's proposals and I voted against the Second Reading. I recognised that the existing law needed changing (some of the anomalies were preposterous) but I was opposed to sweeping away all legislative restrictions. The present compromise was eventually introduced and I gave this my wholehearted support.

I felt impelled also to rebel on the issue of the Third London Airport. After the Buckinghamshire site had been rejected in my first Parliament, the Government now came forward with the expansion of Stansted. Again, I felt deeply that the heart of beautiful countryside was the wrong place for a new international airport and I was sufficiently concerned to be one of 70 Tory MPs to vote against the proposal. I was not opposed to a modest expansion of the existing Essex airport – it could take up to 5 million passengers a year without fundamental expansion – and I was not opposed to a fourth terminal at Heathrow but with the second terminal at Gatwick about to come on stream, I remained implacably opposed to a third London Airport. With my double rebellion on Sunday trading and Stansted, I concluded that my ministerial ambitions were now completely shattered.

At the end of 1986 I was able to make two journeys abroad on 'official' business. The first was in the autumn when I accompanied the Duke of Gloucester, who was a qualified architect, with some other members of the Foreign Office Diplomatic Estates Advisory Panel, to Moscow. The then Foreign Office minister Baroness (Janet) Young had appointed me to the Panel and a major decision had been taken to build a new embassy in the USSR capital. The existing one was a converted house just outside the Kremlin walls and the sight of the Union flag waving at the window of Joe Stalin's bedroom had irritated the Russia dictator in his remaining years after the Second World War. The Duke and I were part of a small committee advising on the siting and design of the new buildings. We spent two days there, being driven hither and thither in the Ambassador's Rolls Royce. Although I still found much of the city (outside the Kremlin walls) depressing, I did discover that at least one Muscovite had a sense of humour. As we were passing a mean looking seven storey building, the Russian chauffeur of our man in Moscow informed me in broken English that it was known as the tallest building in the city. I thought he had mistakenly got his English words mixed up and politely pointed this out. "No, no," he insisted, "zat is zee KGB headquarters and eet is the only building in Moscva from vere you can zee Ziberia."

In December I was appointed to be leader of a Commonwealth Parliamentary Association visit to Barbados. Among the delegation of five was the distinguished and retired diplomat Lord Greenhill of Harrow. On any criteria, he should have been our leader as he had been Head of the Diplomatic Service from 1968-1973 but an MP from the Government party always had to preside. We stayed at the Rockley Resort and Beach Club which became our base for the week, during which we met Prime Minister Errol Barrow and almost everyone who was anyone in this island in the Caribbean. We had time also to visit a rum distillery, cement plant, housing project and the famous Sandy Beach Hotel (for an official lunch). When I told the Manager that I envied him his job, he told me not to go too green as he had just been told that his next assignment was a hotel at Gatwick Airport. Barbados, the most windward of the Windward Islands, was about one-quarter the size of Greater London with a population of only 250,000 and had just celebrated twenty years of independence. The weather was perfect but the leader of the delegation found it frustrating not to be able to enjoy holidaying in such a paradise.

When I returned to Barnet and Westminster, it was likely that the next general election would be held the following year. I felt confident in as much as I had worked hard and one or two political commentators were mentioning me as being one of the top ten MPs in terms of workload in the Commons. It was reported that I "was one of the most frequent oral questioners of ministers, had made twenty-nine major speeches on the floor of the House, had a 100 per cent attendance record on the Environment Committee, was serving on the Services Committee and had chaired a special committee looking into the Norfolk and Suffolk Broads Bill." I was flattered and made quite sure the local Press were informed!

Outside Parliament, my environmental interests were recognised by being elected President of the London Green Belt Council and my national tree year antics had led me to the presidency of the Arboricultural Association. The previous President had been John Parker, the Father of the House, who was first elected in 1935 and had retired at the previous election. Back in Barnet, my political base seemed secure and my happiness in my job was only occasionally disturbed by the deaths of friends, not least when my President, Bob Brum, died in April 1985 and a constituent, Major Derek Stuart-Brown who had been awarded the MBE during World War II, collapsed as he stood to put a question to me at my AGM in March 1987. Another blow for me in the mid-eighties was the collapse of my marriage and separation from Claire. We had grown apart, perhaps understandably with my commitment to politics and the long weeks in

Westminster; and we divorced in 1987. Before this, I had turned fifty and wondered what the next election and the future held for me.

11

THATCHER'S THIRD TERM

The 1983 Parliament heralded the rise of popular capitalism. The right-to-buy policy was in full flood and millions bought shares in privatised industries. There was steady economic growth, low inflation and unemployment was at last beginning to fall. The living standards of those in work were improved and Britain's international reputation was enhanced. The human cost of the reconstruction of the economy, and much of industry necessary to achieve this, was all too evident but all of us supporting Mrs Thatcher believed that this sea change was essential if Britain was to have a competitive economy at home and political influence abroad.

Labour's disaster in 1983 had resulted in Michael Foot's resignation and by October Neil Kinnock had replaced him as leader of the opposition. In the same month, Cecil Parkinson resigned in the wake of his affair with Sarah Keays. I knew Sarah quite well; she was a secretary to another MP and had an office next to the one I shared with five others in Old Palace Yard when I was first elected. She had invited me to her sister's twenty-first birthday party at her parents' home, a beautiful Georgian country house in Somerset. When her father made his displeasure known about the affair, BBC TV News led with the story showing the family home. I recognised immediately the building and had a shock, thinking something dramatic had happened to someone I knew, as of course it had but not in the way I feared - the IRA was making itself known on the mainland at the time. Indeed, a year later, the bomb at the Grand Hotel in Brighton failed to assassinate the Prime Minister but did kill a number of friends, including the Chief Whip's wife, Roberta Wakeham, and my Whip, Anthony Berry. Anthony was a popular colleague with impeccable manners. His Southgate seat was next to mine and I felt his death very keenly. Luckily for me, I had taken a sabbatical from our annual trip to the seaside: if I hadn't, almost certainly I would have been in the bar off the Hall below where the bomb exploded.

1985 began with a sterling crisis (the pound sank to US dollar 1.08) and another coal strike but this time the Government was fully prepared. By March it ended with total defeat for Arthur Scargill. But nothing stays still in politics and towards the end of the year the Anglo-Irish agreement was signed, setting up a forum for British and Irish ministers to discuss political, security and legal matters affecting Northern Ireland. The Ulster Unionist MPs vehemently objected, resigned their seats *en bloc* and fought the ensuing by-elections, winning 14 of the 15 seats.

Early in 1986 there were two senior ministerial resignations. In January, Michael Heseltine walked out of a Cabinet meeting over the Westland helicopter saga. There had been a leak of the Solicitor-General's letter to the Defence Secretary pointing to inaccuracies in a Heseltine letter and Leon Brittan (Trade & Industry Secretary) admitted he had authorised this leak and also resigned. Odds on bets in the Chapman Ministerial Chase shortened briefly but with my Sunday shopping rebellion they soon lengthened considerably. This led a colleague Roger Moate to congratulate me one morning upon my election to the Horse Guards Parade Club. I was perplexed as I had absolutely no knowledge of equines, never having sat on a sturdy steed nor plonked my posterior on a pony in my youth. I innocently asked him to explain and fell right into the trap. "Well," he said, "we had a committee meeting last night and you have been made an honorary life member as you meet the qualification for membership perfectly: always being overlooked by 10 Downing Street."

The two ministerial resignations inevitably led to some severe setbacks. We lost four by-elections and just crawled back in West Derbyshire by a paltry 100 votes when we had held the seat in 1983 by 15,000. This by-election was caused by the resignation of Matthew Parris to take over Brian Walden's Sunday lunchtime interview slot on ITV. By now it was obvious that the electorate did not take kindly to any "unnecessary" election but I was astonished that we held West Derbyshire when we lost the even safer Ryedale seat where the much respected MP, John Spence, had died. We also took a thumping in the 1986 local elections.

This was also a time of Tory rebellions: on capping rates, abolition of the GLC and top people's pay. Our huge majority encouraged some on our backbenches to provide an unofficial opposition but the other parties also had their own problems with Labour suffering from its unilateral defence policy, its promise to reverse trade union reforms and its contradictions over taxation policy. The Alliance was also split on whether to merge with the Liberals (which it eventually did) or pitch its tent with the SDP.

By the beginning of 1987 the Tories were again comfortably ahead in the opinion polls and the Prime Minister opted once more for a June election. There were hiccups during the campaign but the Government again won comfortably and Mrs T. had now triumphed in three successive General Elections, then without precedent in modern politics. The Tories had an overall majority of 101, losing 20 seats net to Labour but containing the swing to under 2 per cent.

In Chipping Barnet, the result exceeded my expectations. I increased my vote, percentage of the poll and majority, helped by Labour recovering slightly from its 1983 debacle but not sufficiently to reclaim second place. The figures looked even better for me on paper, 24,686 to the Lib/Alliance's 9,223 and Labour's 8,115. The Alliance candidate was James Skinner, fifty-four, an economist and Old Etonian who continued to blame the electoral system, while the Labour candidate was Dave Perkin, the youngest of us at thirty-four, who had studied nuclear physics in a post-graduate research course and was a member of CND and ASTMS. He attacked the Government for the reduction in acute beds and the growing waiting lists at Barnet General – echoes of the past. After the count, I praised my opponents and this was noted by the local press who billed me as the "winner of a good, clean fight" and "a refreshing change from the histrionics (in the same room) of the Finchley result earlier." It was decidedly not a 'flaming June' election and I described it later as the gumboot campaign and the last stand of the wets.

We had given mutual aid to Hornsey & Wood Green, which Hugh Rossi was defending with a 4,000 majority and a shifting population (bed-sit land was spreading into hitherto salubrious areas). We managed to ensure that the seat was widely canvassed and made a point of tackling the high-rise tower blocks. A small but significant number of electors therein were delighted that Tories had called and the whole exercise proved the point that no area was the fiefdom of any one Party. Hugh survived by nearly 2,000 votes in spite of the demographic changes and wrote a most generous letter to me asserting that but for our help he would not have been re-elected. At the start of the campaign, I had taken an afternoon off to be at son Michael's sixth birthday beano. The Sunday after the poll I attended a surprise party to celebrate Hugh Rossi's sixtieth birthday.

Winning for the third time in my constituency seemed to establish me as a fixture in the local neighbourhood and this reflected itself in a spate of invitations to open not only the annual round of fetes and fairs but also some new buildings with the unveiling of a plaque. Vanity always got the better of me and I employed the well worn remark that I was flattered to see my name on a wall in my constituency and for once not in graffiti. The event which gave me most satisfaction was the opening of the new Memorial Hall in Monken Hadley, built on the site of the old prefabricated building which had been put up forty years before as a memorial to those who had died in the War. The mastermind behind this project was Dennis Nicholson, son of the Barnet Constituency Conservatives first chairman in 1945. Helped by some local charities, the fundraising committee collected £95,000 and the new Hall is now widely used by residents and groups far beyond the parish.

Another attractive village in my patch is Arkley, to the west of Barnet. This is my north-west Frontier and after induction into the Horse Guards Parade Club I began to take an interest in equestrian matters recognising that Arkley was, as I put it, the 'horseyculture' centre of north London. Over eight hundred horses were stabled in the area and the problem was that the best riding grounds were on the other side of the dual carriageway A1, where the traffic was lethal on this last stretch of open road before the metropolis. Enter the chairman of the North London branch of the British Horse Society, the appropriately named Mr Stephen Oates. The BHS is a prestigious body which champions the welfare of horses as well as the interests of riders. A thoroughbred horse had been killed and riders had to take their lives in their reins to cross the A1. The answer was a bridge so that horses, cyclists and pedestrians could cross in safety. But this was an expensive solution as Transport Secretary Paul Channon reminded me when I questioned him on the floor of the House. I discovered that a bridge for the same purpose had been built a few miles to the north but this might not help my case if it was judged that it would be uneconomic to provide another one relatively near. There was the possibility of a compromise: providing safe gathering areas for horses to assemble at both sides of the road with a railed refuge on the central reserve. I would have settled for this but, a few months later, I was surprised and delighted to be told by the Roads Minister, Peter Bottomley, that a new bridge would be built. The equestrian world was ecstatic and the British Horse Society invited me to open the

124

structure when it was completed. Ever after I have called
it my Sydney Bridge.

At the beginning of 1988, Barnet's first MP died aged
seventy-seven. Dr Stephen Taylor had been elected in
the Labour landslide of 1945 before he lost to Reggie
Maudling in 1950. He had a distinguished career in
medicine and after his defeat in Barnet became a member
of Harlow New Town Development committee. He was
appointed to the Lords as one of the first Life peers and
Harold Wilson made him a junior Minister in 1964. Three
years later he became Vice-Chancellor of the University
of Newfoundland. He parted company with Labour in
the early-eighties when the then opposition promised to
abolish private beds in NHS hospitals and thereafter sat
on the cross-benches. His wife Dr Charity Taylor was
the first woman governor of Holloway Prison at the time
when Ruth Ellis was the last woman in Britain to be
hanged there.

Later in the year my first agent Arthur Fawcett died at
the age of seventy-five. In my tribute to him I wrote: "Apart
from the war when he reached the rank of captain, he
devoted his career to politics becoming one of the most
experienced agents in the country and a substantial
authority on election law and party organisation. His grip
and knowledge on our local political stage was such that
he forecast, with devastating accuracy, the result of my
1979 election, employing his legendary secret formula
on our canvassing returns."

Constituency problems continued to occupy me during
my third Parliament, including the crumbling Barnet
General and inadequacies on the Northern Line. Apart
from perceived cuts in the NHS, the latest plan for
hospital provision was to close Edgware General and
expand Barnet General. The thinking was that since
Barnet needed a new surgical wing, two separate
facilities did not make economic sense. With local
MPs John Gorst and John Marshall, I countered with
the somewhat tart observation that hospitals were for

the benefit of patients, not accountants, and that poor transport facilities between Edgware and Barnet made two separate units essential.

Another NHS decision which caused huge controversy was the closure of the Victoria Maternity Hospital in Barnet. "The Vic" was hugely popular, not least because many of my constituents had been born there. The problem, which triggered at first its temporary closure, was a shortage of midwives and a lack of success in recruiting other necessary staff. On purely medical grounds, the decision was understandable: an inability to guarantee that mothers and babies could be cared for in clinical safety, even though Barnet General was only a quarter of a mile away. If the Vic had been replaced by a new maternity unit at the Hospital, the political fall-out could have been contained but for the next decade babies had to be delivered at Edgware Hospital. A few years previously, my agent's wife Shelagh had given birth at the Vic and I put into practice a piece of advice given to me by Speaker George Thomas, who in such situations sent a letter not to the proud parents but to the new born. Thus my epistle declared: "Dear Master Ellis, Welcome to this wonderful world and allow me to congratulate you on the first two decisions you have made in it: your choice of parents and your place of birth in my constituency ..." The matron asked to have a copy of the letter and promptly framed and displayed it in the reception area. Perhaps another reason I did not want the Vic to close!

The Northern Line continued to provide an unsatisfactory service for its passengers and more fury was generated when it was announced that fares were to be increased by 12 per cent. LT claimed that the service had improved and it was unfair to the taxpayer not to ask the user to pay some of the cost of improving facilities. The problem was that the users could not detect any improvement in the service and felt rather deeply that any further hike in their contributions should come after new rolling stock and a more reliable service had been provided.

Another local issue (experienced by many other London suburbs) surfaced towards the end of the 1980s at the height of the housing boom (soon to end) with the threat to the scale and character of many pleasant residential areas. This came in three ways: pressure for development on green field sites not in the Green Belt; individual housing extensions; and, the most serious, demolition of large family homes to be replaced with blocks of flats. In an article in the *Barnet Press*, I described the problem as one of infilling, overfilling and flat filling. In fairness, developers were trying to meet the increased demand for homes at a time of economic growth and increasing prosperity. Furthermore, there was a dire need for smaller dwellings brought about by an ageing population and more single-parent families, as well as provision for those manning the vital public services who could not afford to buy even the cheapest home.

I led a group of MPs campaigning for stricter planning controls and advocated a second category of Conservation Areas which I suggested might be called Special Priority Areas or SPAs, wherein the local authority could refuse permission if the proposal was "out of character with the neighbourhood, either in style, scale or density." One of my colleagues, Hugh Dykes, called for planning permission to be required before a building could be demolished, whether it was listed or not. This campaign generated some publicity and not a little controversy, with the Royal Fine Arts Commission being somewhat critical. Their Secretary, the extremely urbane and accomplished Sherban Cantacuzino, diplomatically observed that "on the whole the commission tends to be against designating more specialised zones or areas because this only creates more confusion... we don't necessarily go along with tighter controls but what we do need are more discerning controls." Not unexpectedly, the Government turned down our proposals, resting their case on the view of the RFAC.

Reflecting on the first half of the 1987 Parliament, it seemed to be a hyperactive time for me. In a local newspaper, I recorded a typical weekend in Chipping Barnet as follows: "Friday evening began with a briefing by the Royal College of Nurses at Barnet General ... this was the first in a series of NHS meetings to glean up-to-date information before I lobby the Regional Health Authority and Ministers. Later in the evening I attended our High Barnet branch social. On Saturday morning I met Conservative councillors to discuss various issues with planning cases and traffic conditions high on the agenda. In the afternoon I went to our Monken Hadley branch garden party before visiting constituents in their homes in Lyonsdown and Whetstone; and then looked in at the Totteridge Horticultural Society's summer show." Sundays were not a *dies non* for me. Many Conservative branches held social events on the Christian Sabbath, probably because of the multi-faith complexion of the population in North London and it was quite typical of my diary to show twenty-four hours of time spent on constituency business in a weekend.

I continued to open annual events and visit businesses and schools. One such encounter was at Church Hill Primary School, East Barnet where I toured the classrooms with the Head Master, Mr John Savidge, before planting a tree. Arriving at the senior class, John reminded the children that my visit was part of their week's study about Parliament and asked them if they had any questions to ask me. One boy's hand shot up and invited to ask his question said: "Please sir, can a man become Prime Minister?" On reflection, I realised that he had been born after Margaret had become PM ten years before.

During this Parliament, I was asked to take on a particular type of Private Bill which involved a Second Reading on the floor of the House. There was nothing exceptional in this (nearly all measures have their initial debates in the Chamber) but this was a British Railways Bill. Whenever BR wished to carry out substantial works, it had to introduce a Private Bill and this necessitated a Second Reading on the floor of the House before going into Committee upstairs. Convention demanded that a Government backbencher introduced the measure and any Member had the right to raise any issue relating to BR when debated. Normally, BR introduced one or two Bills at the most in any Session but in this particular one it had four, including the Thameslink measure which facilitated a direct link from the north to south of London between Farringdon and Blackfriars. At the beginning of each Parliament, BR usually asked a particular MP to look after its Bills and for some time Sir Geoffrey Finsberg, after he had ceased to be a Minister, accepted the task. However, there was a limit to the number he could supervise and he asked that someone else should introduce this one. As it was preferable to have a London MP for this Bill, the list of available Government backbench members was not inexhaustible and I suspect in some desperation our railways' overlords had to turn to me. I willingly obliged.

Come the day, I rose from our backbenches to propose that the British Railways (London) Bill be given a Second Reading and began to address its various provisions. Within a minute a series of interventions from various MPs on all sides of the House asked me if I was aware of the particular problems facing their constituents as a result of actions taken or proposed by BR. For example, Alan Beith was exercised by the intention to no longer stop the night sleeper from Edinburgh to Kings Cross in his beloved Berwick, while Greg Knight was worried about inadequacies in the service from his Derby constituency to St. Pancras Station. I had to sympathise with all of them and promise to contact the chairman of BR about their grievances before gently reminding them that the measure I was proposing would be good news for all their electors if and when they were travelling through London. Eventually I was able to proceed to what the Bill intended, including what I considered to be an environmental plus: the removal of a Victorian rail bridge which blocked the view of St. Paul's Cathedral from the west. I declaimed:

> "Finally, Mr Speaker, this measure brings some good environmental news; it will replace an overhead railway line and bridge with a shallow cut tunnel and thus restore the historic prospect of Christopher Wren's masterpiece from Fleet Street."

At this point I paused and said to the House:

> "It may be helpful if I declare a possible personal interest.Sir Christopher and I have two things in common: we have been both architects and Members of Parliament. We realised that this might cause confusion so our agents have reached an agreement which has successfully stood the test of time: Sir Christopher would promise not to make any more speeches if I would promise to design no more buildings."

The Chamber had relatively few Members in it (even allowing for those with a grievance against BR) but the Gallery was full (probably because it was a wet summer's evening) and there was a roar of laughter from above me which surprised those below and suitably fed my vanity. The Bill got its Second Reading.

12

COMMITTEES, CORRESPONDENCE & CHANGE

In the late 1980s I took part in two special types of Committees. The first was a procedure for considering "hybrid" Bills - Public Bills affecting private interests. This involved an additional and separate stage: a committee to receive and consider all representations. The main participants employed barristers (some well known) to examine and cross-examine witnesses. These lawyers were paid generous fees and seemed in no hurry to expedite matters. Five MPs acted as judges and had to recommend to the House whether the provisions in the Bill satisfactorily dealt with the private interests affected or whether amendments should be made to ensure this.

In the previous Parliament I had already chaired the Norfolk and Suffolk Broads Bill setting up a new authority with increased planning powers in the relevant part of East Anglia. This involved a few weeks of deliberations, including a visit to the area, and I found this an agreeable experience. Now I was asked to chair the Dartford Crossing Bill which took longer, was more contentious and divided the committee in unexpected ways. When we convened, our first duty was to determine whether there was the *locus* to consider the private interests. There clearly was – some properties had to be compulsorily acquired to build the bridge – but this didn't prevent days of argument. When we eventually got to the provisions in the Bill, the main issue was whether the Bridge should have "wind baffles" in its structure. These were to be provided on the Second Severn Bridge, so why not on this one? The reason the new Severn Bridge was to be better shielded from gales was that the first Bridge didn't have them, thus making it less likely that both bridges would have to be closed in stormy weather. But, argued some, there would be only one bridge across the Thames and so it must have this additional wind protection. No, said others, gale force winds would be very rare and the alternative route through the Dartford Tunnel, already existed, so wind shields were unnecessary. And so it went on.

When all the arguments had been extensively examined, that was not the end of the matter for we then had to decide upon the name of the Bridge. As the existing link was the called the Dartford Tunnel, Thurrock wanted the new engineering feat to be named Thurrock Bridge and also called in aid that there was already a Dartford Bridge, providing photographic evidence of a road crossing over a stream. Dartford responded by saying that nobody knew this insignificant bridge by its name and to call the proposed one Thurrock would confuse people. I suggested a compromise: "how about calling it The Queen Elizabeth II Bridge or as there's a little jetty nearby called Botany Bay, how about naming it after the chairman of this committee and calling it Sydney Bridge?" Eventually it was decided to name it after Her Majesty but all the signposts refer to the Dartford Crossing which carries the traffic going south over the four-lane Bridge and going north in the two tunnels. Since it was opened, the Bridge has rarely been closed because of high winds. Incidentally, we were told that the toll charges for the Crossing would only apply for a limited number of years (fifteen, I think it was) but I note that we are still paying today.

The other special Committee was one of very few to consist of members from both Houses. The Ecclesiastical Committee of Parliament was established under the 1919 Church of England Assembly Act and is composed of fifteen Peers and fifteen MPs, nominated by the Lord Chancellor and The Speaker respectively. It is the only

Parliamentary Committee on which Ministers can sit as individuals (John Gummer was an example) and its only function is to consider and report on any measure passed by the General Synod. Our job was to decide if the measure before us was 'expedient' or 'not expedient' (not 'inexpedient'). The precise meaning of the word is uncertain but has generally been taken to indicate the Committee's views about the merits of the measure and particularly in relation to the constitutional rights of all people.

After cross-examining appropriate witnesses, we had to agree a draft report and send it to the Legislative Committee of the General Synod. This gives that committee the opportunity to withdraw the measure which they probably would do if we were minded to find it not expedient but there is nothing to stop them putting the issue to both Houses. The Ecclesiastical Committee cannot amend any measure, nor can either House. I was appointed to the Committee for four Parliaments and perhaps the most controversial measure we examined was the Ordination of Women Priests in 1993. In the General Synod's House of Bishops it had been passed by three-to-one and in the House of Clergy and House of Laity by about two-to-one. When the measure came to our Committee, we agreed that it was expedient by 16 to 11. I voted for the measure basically because I would need to have had good reason to find it not expedient when it had been passed convincingly by the General Synod, provided it did not adversely affect the constitutional right of any person. A good deal of our time was spent on the provisions designed to safeguard the position of those in the Church of England who were in all conscience unable to accept the ministration of women priests.

We had considered another controversial measure in the 1987 Parliament, about the ordination of Clergy and the then absolute bar to a man being ordained in the C of E if he had married a second wife while his former spouse was still living or if his wife had a former spouse still living. The sole purpose of the Clergy (Ordination) Measure was to enable an Archbishop, on the application of a diocesan Bishop, in an exceptional case to grant a dispensation from disqualification. After six meetings spread over a year, the vote in the Ecclesiastical Committee was to find it expedient by ten to nine. Though sympathetic to the measure, I voted with the large minority because we were led to believe that there would be very few applications to the archbishops when on further enquiries we were told that there would be many, so I felt the Synod should reconsider the matter. Having scraped through our committee, the House of Commons actually rejected the Measure in July 1989 but in the next Session of Parliament the House reversed its decision.

These two types of special committees did not take up too much time in any session but with a commitment to taking a fair share of Standing Committees and sitting on a number of backbench committees and private Bills, I can truly say that MPs quickly have to come to terms with committee-itis.

*   *   *

A time-consuming burden on any MP is his constituency correspondence. During my first year in Chipping Barnet, I calculated that I had received two tons of mail. A large part of this weight was represented by reports, journals and official documents but the majority of items were constituency mail and the most frequent question I'm asked is how many letters does an MP get from constituents? At first I received an average of about one hundred per week but this figure inexorably rose over the years to two hundred. In the twenty-six years that I represented Chipping Barnet, I reckon that I sent out about a quarter of a million letters. In addition to constituents, many pressure groups and local and national organisations regularly bombard your MP.

Most of my personal mail from Barnetonians related to housing and social security problems and much of this was a matter for the local council. However since people had taken the trouble to contact me, I looked into the problem before passing it on to the appropriate council official and then sent the reply to my constituent. This may or may not be the end of the matter and it is a rare occurrence to have to send only one reply. I calculated that I sent the 250,000 letters to about 40,000 constituents – but these were only a small proportion of all constituents over one-quarter of a century.

It was not untypical of me to spend the first two hours of Mondays to Fridays opening, reading and dictating replies and writing to government ministers, chiefs of nationalised industries or council officers on behalf of my electors. A very small proportion of my mail was about national or international issues, except when a campaign had been organised. If most of my mail was about housing or social security matters, in later years an increasing amount were immigration cases or health and hospital issues, while the perennial problems of planning, parking and pavements doggedly continued.

*   *   *

Life at Westminster and in Chipping Barnet was ticking along normally and it is at such times that a person should expect the unexpected; the more so in politics. My life was about to be changed by two completely unrelated events in successive months. In early November 1988 the telephone rang in my office and my ex-wife told me that my sister was trying to contact me. As she had been unable to do so, Claire felt impelled to give me the message that my brother Michael had died. Apparently he had had a heart attack while driving to work. I was absolutely devastated and the first emotion I felt was one of guilt – guilt at not having seen him for some months and guilt at having seen too little of him for some years.

To a certain degree this was inevitable: I was locked into a committed vocation that kept me in London while he lived and worked in Derbyshire. Nevertheless, whatever justification there might have been for not meeting up more often, I blamed myself for even thinking of the need to search for any justification. I remember only walking around in a daze and when a colleague asked if I was not feeling well, blurted out the news. He got in touch with the Government Whips' Office and a car was arranged to take me back home. The next day I travelled up to Matlock to see Michael's wife Rosemary and to help with arrangements for the funeral. She told me that the first she had heard about the event was when a phone call from Derby Hospital asked her to come with a friend and bring some overnight clothes with her. When she arrived she was told he was dead and that no one else had been involved in the incident. It appeared that Michael had realised his plight and managed to steer his car to the side of the road.

When I returned to Barnet, my House of Commons mail had been forwarded to me and there was a four-page handwritten letter of condolence from the Prime Minister. I was told later by Mark Lennox-Boyd (her PPS) that she had penned her sympathy late in the evening before leaving very early next morning for a European environment meeting in Oslo. After the funeral I handed the letter to Rosemary, the contents of which were extremely touching and she was deeply moved.

My brother's untimely death at the age of fifty-four caused an inevitable degree of self-introspection and I became a much less cheerful and a more morose individual, at least for a time. Matters weren't helped by feeling impelled to vote against the Government on the issue of charging for eye tests in the month before. I felt deeply about the issue and there had been no mention of it in our manifesto. Having found it necessary to wear spectacles permanently since 1970 (save for a short time when I wore soft contact lenses), my interest in matters ophthalmic had been registered on the political radar screen for some time and I was certain of two things, whatever the arguments for introducing charges. First, fewer people would have their eyes tested – or tested as regularly as before – and regular eye testing was essential to catch early signs of glaucoma and thus prevent deteriorating eyesight and blindness. My whip, Michael Neubert, an extremely civilised, courteous and likeable man whom I had known from my YC days, was somewhat put out by my action, even though I had expressed my views to him politely but unequivocally. The problem was that there had been a vote immediately before on the introduction of charges for dental examinations. On this, I had stretched my conscience as far as I could and abstained. He assumed that I would do likewise on eye testing. His understandable misjudgement may have been my fault in not being more explicit, but we had had no opportunity to see each other between the votes and I had promised to attend the debate before deciding upon my course of action.

With this and my brother's death, I was yearning for the Christmas Recess but in the last week before it there was yet another ministerial resignation. Edwina Currie, a junior Health Minister, was forced to resign over some injudicious remarks she made about salmonella, upsetting egg producers (not just the hens) far and wide. In the small reshuffle, Michael Neubert was promoted, leaving a vacancy in the Whips' Office. The telephone rang and the no-nonsense Chief Whip David Waddington wanted to see me immediately. When I arrived in his office he didn't beat about the bush. "We want you to join us in the Whips' Office." I was completely taken aback and mumbled something about needing time to consider the unexpected offer. As it was the penultimate day before the Recess, I asked him when he wanted to know, thinking that early in the new year before the House returned would be the answer. "Well, let me put it this way. In five minutes I'm going to our daily Whips' meeting and I would like you to come with me. Yes or no?" I walked in with him and so, eighteen-and-a-half years after I was first elected, I had finally got my foot on the first rung of the ministerial ladder. If I was amazed at what had happened some of my colleagues were more so, hardly countenancing that a "senior and respected backbencher" (not my words) had been appointed to the lowliest position in government. That evening I went into the crowded members' Dining Room and was greeted with a hail of friendly derision (mock cheers rather than heartfelt jeers). By tradition and in order to ensure confidential conversation, Labour MPs sit at one end of the long, high-ceilinged room and Tories at the other with a couple of tables for the other parties in the middle. I looked for somewhere to sit and a voice behind beckoned me to his table. At it were three venerable knights of the shires. They asked me to join them, profusely congratulated me and asked what I would like to drink. I said that a glass of wine beginning with the first three letters of my surname would suffice, thinking that I had covered two of my favourites; Champagne and Chablis. Without batting an eyelid, one of the knights summoned the waiter to tell him that "Mr Chapman, our new Minister, would like a bottle of Chardonnay." It was a most welcome bottle (shared with them, I hasten to add).

The next morning I began to take stock of what had happened. The good news was that I had had a most friendly reception and not least in the Press. Instead of merely giving the name of who was the last small piece in the minor reshuffle jigsaw, The *Daily Telegraph* wrote a prominent piece on its Parliament & Politics page, replete with a 5 x 3in photo headed: "Whip's job for conservation MP" stressing my 'Plant a Tree' campaign in 1973 and my special interest in conservation, inner city regeneration and arboriculture; while Robin Oakley wrote a six paragraph piece in *The Times* which began: "Mrs Thatcher yesterday gave new hope to Tory MPs who thought they had been overlooked for office." I was quite moved by all this and some extremely generous remarks from colleagues.

Members of the Whips' Office are the only Ministers not chosen by the Prime Minister. When a vacancy occurs, the Whips themselves decide and submit their choice to the PM. She has the right to refuse their request but, equally, the Whips do not have to accept any name proposed by their leader. Put another way, a mutual blackballing system operates, though it is highly unlikely that Mrs Thatcher would propose anyone as a Whip simply because she could appoint that person a departmental Minister.

A new Whip never knows how or why he has been elected by his new peers but in later years I gained a strong impression that my name had been submitted on a previous occasion but was rejected and, on this occasion, the Whips' had submitted another name with mine as an option, judging that the PM was even less inclined to favour the alternative. However, that was complete conjecture and I preferred to convince myself that it could not be true. More certainly, when she came into the Commons' Chamber the first time I was on bench duty, she greeted me with a smile and profuse congratulations. Shortly after news of my promotion reached Chipping Barnet, I attended a pre-Christmas Branch social in my Hadley Ward. When I arrived late and entered the large room of a private house, I was greeted by an ear-splitting raucous round of cheering. When the noise subsided I felt that the most apt response was to utter one of the three eternal truths: "Thank you. I'm from the Government and come to help you all."

The day after I was appointed was the last before the Christmas Recess and news came through about the Lockerbie air disaster. And so an unexpected and personally exciting week at Westminster came to a chilling end. I did not know what to expect in 1989 but prepared myself for the heat of the government kitchen.

13

WHIPPING THEM IN

The origins of the whipping system are uncertain. In earlier times there was concern about non-attendance and at first messages were only sent to 'friends' to ensure a quorum and secure a vote. The earliest were sent to King James I's parliamenentary friends in the 1620s. When this practice became generally known, MPs not of the royal persuasion objected, regarding it as unconstitutional. It was decided that MPs should be summoned by Proclamation only.

By the 18th century, the issuing of these circular letters to friends had become part of the party political system but the Whigs and Tories were not monolithic organisations and various groups within the two coalitions rallied their own supporters. Consequently, even if the government of the day had a large majority it could find itself in danger of defeat. After the 1832 Reform Act a system not dissimilar to the present day was established by the opposition parties as well as the government. The first use of the word 'whip' dates from 1828 but the word 'whipper-in' goes back to around 1770 when ministers sent messengers to bring supporters back to Westminster when there was a crisis. It was Edmund Burke who compared such messengers to the 'whippers-in' of a pack of fox-hounds.

When I was appointed, there were fourteen of us in the Government Whips' Office and the tradition was such that, apart from the Chief and his Deputy who were appointed by the Prime Minister, the remaining dozen were chosen by those left in the office when there was a vacancy. Seniority was based upon length of service and the most recently appointed had the unofficial title of 'Junior Whip.'

It was into this august post that I found myself catapulted at the tender age of fifty-three, even though I was the fourth oldest in the office. The Chief Whip was officially known as the Parliamentary Secretary to the Treasury (and unofficially as the Patronage Secretary) while the Deputy Chief Whip, then David Hunt, had the grand title of Treasurer of Her Majesty's Household. Number 3 in the office, Tristram Garel-Jones, was the Comptroller of H.M. Household and Number 4, Tony Durant, was styled the Vice Chamberlain of H.M. Household. The next five Whips in order of seniority were known as Lords Commissioners of the Treasury and the remaining were Assistant Whips.

It was often said that the Whips' Office is the sewerage system of the Government: essential, unseen and dirty. It has the crucial role of being the link between ministers and backbenchers. The Chief Whip attends every Cabinet meeting and is responsible for organising the timetabling of bills and getting the Government's business through the Commons. The pivotal role he plays in the ordinance of political power can be illustrated geographically. The Prime Minister's older and other title is First Lord of the Treasury and his official residence is, of course, 10 Downing Street. Next door is the Chancellor, the Second Lord of the Treasury, and the Chief Whips' Office is closeted in 12 Downing Street. Most of the Whips' work is necessarily done in the House of Commons and most of us went to No.12 only once a week for a two-hour meeting to discuss matters of the moment more fully and agree the draft agenda for the business in the Commons the following week (subject to approval by the Cabinet). The Government (and Official Opposition) Whips' Offices in Westminster are off the Members' Lobby with easy access to the Chamber. The Chief Whip is helped considerably by his Private Secretary, a Civil Servant, who is known as the "usual channels" in dealing with the other Parties. The ubiquitous and engaging Murdo

Maclean occupied this role from 1979 until 2000 and was only the third person to do so since World War I. Diplomatic skills are essential since the Opposition, if so minded, could disrupt Government business on the floor of the House and in Committees. It is common practice for the Government to accede to any reasonable demands from the Opposition and, in return, the Government has the right to expect its legislation to be enacted subject to a majority in the Commons. Murdo Maclean was the lynchpin in negotiations and had to be seen to be even-handed and so enjoy absolute trust by all.

A Whip is given responsibility for a Department of State and a group of colleagues. The first is a moveable feast and his responsibilities were changed each session to give a wider experience. I was first appointed the Environment Whip and became the conduit for all issues and legislation within that Department. Thus I was thrown into the turbulent waters caused by the introduction of the Community Charge ("Poll Tax"), a replacement for the domestic rating system. The new tax had been the centrepiece of legislation for the first session of the 1987 Parliament and it was first introduced in Scotland in 1989. Such had been the hostility to it from the public that plans were unveiled to reform it within the first week of its introduction in England & Wales.

The second function of a Whip was to look after some of his colleagues. They were grouped geographically and I was given my home area of Greater London North as it had been Michael Neubert's territory. There were 30 Tory MPs north of the Thames entrusted to my tender care, including three Cabinet Ministers (the PM, Peter Brooke and Michael Portillo) and three junior ministers. I also had Norman Tebbit and Dr Rhodes Boyson, both of whom had recently left the Government, and 22 other backbenchers. What I soon realised was that my age and length of service became an advantage, especially as ageing backbenchers usually did not take kindly to a younger overzealous Whip remonstrating about a missed vote. I found that when I had to enquire into such an event, it was as if I were looking into a mirror and a more sympathetic conversation ensued.

Not long after becoming a minister I was invited again to lunch at Chequers. As well as Margaret and Dennis hosting these events, there were always other guests from beyond the political spectrum. One such person I had met on a previous visit was Arthur Bryant, the distinguished historian. He was a small man with a beaming face and he was clearly delighted to be asked. He told me that the only other time he had been to the PM's country residence was over fifty years before when he happened to be cycling past the house and on the spur of the moment rang the bell to say hello to Ramsey Macdonald. Another very enjoyable Sunday lunchtime was to be invited by Michael Heseltine to his country home, Thenford Hall near Banbury. Michael is a keen tree-planter who had started an arboretum some years before and was beginning to see the fruits of his endeavours. He had long wanted me to visit and among his and Anne's other guests that day were Tony Crosland's widow Susan and the Poet Laureate Ted Hughes. Both these invitations were most agreeable interludes in my new parliamentary duties, one less pleasant consequence of which was a significant drop in income. Ministers, quite properly, can have no outside interests and since 1980 I had been a non-executive director of the property company Capital & Counties and a couple of years later had joined Lovell Construction, a subsidiary of YJ Lovell. A few hours before joining the Government, I had agreed to be a consultant to a large firm of West End Surveyors and had the embarrassment of having to telephone immediately to withdraw. The result of joining the Government meant that although my Parliamentary salary increased by £10,000 (the then ministerial element of it), my overall loss of income was £11,000 and, to put it bluntly, I was financially embarrassed for the next two years.

There are some who believe that MPs should have no paid outside interests but I would disagree. It seems to me that Parliament benefits from its legislators having continuing experience in a business, trade, profession or any other walk of life, thereby providing hands-on experience. Others will disagree, asserting that being an MP should be a full-time job. It is, but that does not mean that there is no time for other interests, be they social, sporting or business. I had also to give up some other outside but unpaid activities such as the presidencies of the Arboricultural Association and the London Green Belt Council but I was able to stay on as president of local organisations, such as Friends of Barnet Hospital and the Barnet Society.

1989 was not the most propitious year to be in the Whips' Office. The Prime Minister's ten years in office, unparalleled in the twentieth century, was overshadowed by a series of events which weakened the Government's standing. Inflation hit 8 per cent; Chancellor Nigel Lawson was at odds with Alan Walters who had been recalled as Mrs Thatcher's Economic Adviser; the Tories were trounced in the European Parliament elections in June; and Margaret had agreed at the Euro Summit in Madrid that Britain would join the Exchange Rate Mechanism "one day" - we did not know at the time that Geoffrey Howe and Nigel Lawson had threatened to resign if she hadn't said as much. In July, a Cabinet re-shuffle removed Geoffrey from the Foreign Office to Leader of the House and in came John Major. Nicholas Ridley went to Trade & Industry and Chris Patten succeeded him as Environment Secretary. David Waddington was promoted from Chief Whip to Home Secretary and Margaret appointed Tim Renton to run 12 Downing Street, our first Chief Whip without any previous experience in the Office. In October interest rates were raised to 15 per cent and the Chancellor resigned and was replaced by John Major. Douglas Hurd became the new and third Foreign Secretary in four months. In November there was a "stalking horse" challenge to Mrs Thatcher's leadership (the first time since she was elected leader of the Conservatives in 1975) by Sir Anthony Meyer -

unkindly called "the stalking donkey" - and although she won easily, sixty Tory MPs voted against her or abstained.

In the first half of 1989 my responsibilities had kept me in close touch with the Environment Secretary Nicholas Ridley, one of Margaret's most trusted lieutenants and a fully paid up member of the Market Forces Club. His principal Ministers of State were Michael Howard (Housing and Planning) and John Gummer (Local Government). Nicholas's laid back approach didn't make him too many friends but I soon came to admire his ability to soak up the pressures of his job and his support for ministerial colleagues in the DoE. With increasing frequency the Department had to make unpopular statements in the Commons and Nicholas always insisted on delivering them. On the rare occasions when there was good news to report, he would invite the appropriate Minister of State to take the limelight. But there was another side to him. The younger son of a Viscount, he was no introvert aristocrat but had interests as diverse as membership of the Institute of Civil Engineers and being a most accomplished water colourist. His landscape and garden paintings were brilliant and distinctive. One of his junior ministers was Virginia Bottomley and when I congratulated her on her appointment, wryly observing that her environment portfolio was the one I secretly coveted, she replied in a similar vein, wanting to have become our first female Whip. Her husband Peter had become an MP in 1975 and was regarded as being on the left of the Party. When she was adopted for a safe seat in a by-election in 1984 rumours reached us of her being well to the left of him. Upon her arrival at Westminster she proudly introduced herself as the red in Peter's bed.

In the autumn my Whipping responsibilities were moved from Environment to the Employment Department, at first headed by Norman Fowler and then Michael Howard; and the Education Department under John MacGregor who had just followed Kenneth Baker.

I spent relatively little time in these two ministries but I did get a sense of feeling about both of them. The top civil servants in Employment seemed positive about implementing ministerial decisions and proactive in seeking solutions but those in Education seemed to act as if they were the arbiters of what the policy should be with Ministers being mere transient visitors.

When the House returned after the Summer Recess in 1990, I was transferred to the Ministry of Defence. On my nephew Mark Chapman's thirtieth birthday I rang him to offer congratulations and told him the second eternal truth: that the cheque was in the post. I also informed him that I was the new Defence Whip and would be keeping a beady eye on him. He had become a professional soldier in the Light Infantry and at his wedding two years before told me he had been appointed the ADC to the GOC Southern Command and would soon be moving with his new wife Ruth to near where I lived. On further enquiries this turned out to be Aldershot, fully fifty-five miles away beyond the other side of London from Barnet but to a northerner it was 'down my way.' He now informed me that his boss had been made C in C of our land forces in the Gulf and he was flying out within the week as his Military Aide with the rank of Major. The C in C was, of course, Sir Peter de la Billiere – a name unknown to me at that time. Saddam Hussein had invaded Kuwait in August, since when the allies had been building up air and naval forces in the Gulf and planning an armed invasion.

In November, I was asked to head our annual Parliamentary delegation to the United Nations in New York. This involved five days visiting their HQ; meeting our Ambassador David Hannay and staff; and having talks with the President of the Assembly and heads of organisations such as UNESCO and UNICEF. I was disturbed to see that we were due to fly from Heathrow on the morning of Remembrance Sunday and commented on this to the Foreign Office official making the arrangements, expecting him to say that it was a very tight schedule and there were no alternative flights available. I was agreeably surprised when he looked at me, confirmed that I was leader of the delegation and declared that it was for me to approve or alter the programme. We flew in the late afternoon and I was able to attend the wreathe-laying and Remembrance Service in Chipping Barnet Parish Church for the twelfth year running.

It was a hectic visit almost entirely spent within the Lake Success complex but I had made sure that we would have the last afternoon and evening free before flying back at the weekend. I had arranged to visit Montclair across the Hudson River in New Jersey. This was one of the places twinned with Barnet and their Mayor Clifford Lindholm came to collect me at my hotel and show me some of the sights of Manhattan before taking me to his township, an attractive suburban area on the first bluff to the west of the Hudson River. I attended a town council meeting and read out another letter from Margaret Thatcher sending her greetings to them. In my speech, I mentioned my first contact with some of their fellow countrymen near my home before the allied invasion of Europe in 1944. I was presented with the Stars and Stripes flag and a Congressional Certificate of Merit. The Mayor also escorted me to Montclair Kimberley Academy, which was twinned with my daughter Laura's school and a reception given by the Friends of Barnet. Finally, he took me to a high point in the north-east of his town to see the historic view of Manhattan, dominated by the then Twin Towers, with the sun setting behind. It was truly a most magnificent panorama and, with the Taj Mahal, is on my list of the top ten sights in the world.

It was while we were in New York that Geoffrey Howe made his devastating resignation speech inviting a challenge to Margaret's leadership. Returning from the UN, I soon realised that this was no time for the faint-hearted and Michael Heseltine announced he would stand. Once it was known that there would be an election, the Whips had to act in a neutral way though, of course, we could vote in the secret ballot. Our main task in the short six day period of the campaign was to assess the way things were going and, in confidential talks with North London MPs and gossip in the coffee houses, two things were apparent: Margaret would win comfortably but a sizeable number of colleagues were extremely critical about some of her policies as well as the manner of her management of the Government. I had determined to vote for her but there was little doubt that after her third General Election victory she had become even more arbitrary in her decisions and more peremptory in rejecting any other viewpoint.

When the result of the vote was announced, I was somewhat surprised to realise that the Prime Minister had secured support from only four-sevenths of her colleagues. She had won by 204 to 152, but not by a sufficient margin to prevent a second challenge (the rules were complicated). In the half-hour between the declaration of the result and an emergency Whips' meeting, four of my North London colleagues sought me out to affirm they had voted for her but would not do so in the next round. Tim Renton began our meeting by going round the room asking for each Whip's assessment. It so happened that I was the last to be asked. All the other Whips had expressed reservations given by their colleagues but all were bullish about her chances in the second round. I had to mention my four colleagues' intentions and this heralded a flood of second thoughts. I had a gut feeling that one of the Whips, a diehard supporter of the PM, passed this information to her at a late night meeting in No. 10, with the inference that I was against her. This deeply hurt me. I remained stoically in support but it would have been a dereliction of any Whip's duty not to pass on all information received. Immediately after the vote, which she heard at a EU meeting in Brussels, Margaret confirmed that she would fight on but when she returned the majority view of her Cabinet colleagues, who she saw one by one, was that if she stood in the second round she would lose and

Michael Heseltine would succeed her. With little sign of prevarication, she announced that she would resign and later in the day gave a barnstorming speech in the Commons which was hailed on both sides of the House.

Her decision now gave others a chance to stand without fear of disloyalty. Nominations closed only a few hours after her announcement and, five days later, the election took place in which John Major secured 185 votes, Michael Heseltine 131 and Douglas Hurd 56. John was short of the necessary majority but Michael and Douglas quickly conceded and we had a new First Lord of the Treasury, aged forty-seven, who succeeded a great predecessor who had occupied 10 Downing Street for eleven-and-a-half years, the longest serving in the twentieth century – indeed the longest continuously serving PM since the Earl of Liverpool (1812-27). Her end was a political earthquake which would have a profound consequence on the fortunes of the Conservative Party.

14

LORD COMMISSIONER

After being elected leader, John Major reshuffled the Cabinet and appointed Richard Ryder as Chief Whip. He then visited the Whips' Office and we opened the champagne. I had known John before he first became an MP in 1979 at a time when we were both seeking constituencies, though we never found ourselves competing at interviews. Claire and I first met him and Norma at a dinner given by mutual friends and we next met as a quartet in 1980 when Margaret had invited a few colleagues with their wives to lunch at Chequers. His political career, in stark contrast to mine, was ever upwards and onwards and when he visited the Whips' Office he brought along Norma. My first words to him were: "Prime Minister, congratulations but I have to say that I have a criticism of you already." Concern spread across every face in sight so I quickly added: "I shall never forgive you for being the first Prime Minister ever who is younger than me." Luckily they and the new Chief Whip laughed.

At the beginning of 1991, the Gulf War started and six weeks later the Iraqi forces were beaten. The conflict put the new Prime Minister on the international stage and it was to be our first televised war. The effect of this was to give an added but unexpected dimension to my job as the Defence Whip. Iraqi time was three hours ahead of GMT and the Government was concerned that MPs, and indeed the public, would graphically witness the battlefield news and speculation as soon as they woke up. The top level daily MoD intelligence assessment was given to ministers early each morning and I was asked to attend a political meeting immediately after with Defence

ministers and advisers. It was clear that there was a limit
to what I could be told, knowing that what I passed on
to my fellow Whips would reach MPs and be broadcast
far and wide. And so it was that during the war there
was an additional daily Whips' meeting chaired by the
new Deputy Chief Whip, Alastair Goodlad, at which I
passed on the information given to me with due gravitas.
The tension was invariably lightened by the proverbial
mickey being ever so gently taken out of me. Typical of
this was the opening remark of Alastair: "Now, over to
the battlefront and let's hear what Chalky Chapman has
to say today."

The MoD ministerial team consisted of Tom King
(Secretary of State), Archie Hamilton (Minister of State for
the Armed Forces) and Alan Clark (Defence Procurement).
We were supplemented by Tom's special adviser Keith
Simpson and a couple of Private Secretaries. There was
a problem in this team: Alan Clark. He had a propensity
to brief the fourth estate off the record and was critical
of some of the things being done. I had to make some
considerable effort to keep the Procurement Minister 'on
message,' not an easy task when he thought Tom King an
uninspiring Secretary of State and was scheming behind
his back, sending his strategy papers to No.10. Tom
magnanimously turned a blind eye. Alan was a military
historian of some standing. His first publication *The
Donkeys* was a devastating condemnation of World War
I's High Command in which he asserted that the British
soldiers were lions led by asses. Clearly the knowledge he
had gained by researching military matters had led him
to convince himself that he was best placed to conduct
the war. However, as I told everyone around, the war was
actually won by 'the Chapmen': my nephew Mark, with
a little help from Sir Peter de la Billiere, conducting the
sand forces while I looked after operations in the MoD.
When John Major and Tom King visited the troops and
were met by Sir Peter, they asked to see Mark to pass on
regards from his uncle and he received the military MBE
in recognition of his service during the war.

By the time of the change of Prime Minister, such had been the frequency of the reshuffles caused by ministerial resignations that I had climbed a third of the way up the Whips' greasy pole and become a Lord Commissioner of the Treasury. This prestigious sounding position appealed to my vanity (my visiting cards looked particularly impressive) but the reality was absolutely no change in my status except that I had two extra duties to perform: signing Statutory Instruments and Government cheques. Statutory Instruments were issued by powers conferred in Acts of Parliament, usually to spell out the detail of orders and regulations made in them. My only role in all this was to be asked to sign the approved S.I. with the specific Minister responsible.

The signing of Government cheques was a much more exciting prospect. At any time an official from the Treasury might contact me and come armed with an impressive document full of expenditure figures. I remember one occasion well, not least because the total figure amounted to £106 billion. Two burly figures sought me out in my office and asked me to sign the cheque. I looked at the total and innocently enquired if they had checked all the amounts to see if they tallied with the total. They assured me that they had. I calculated that if I could hold the cheque in my own High Street bank account for one hour, at a conservative guess I could earn £1 million in interest on it. I asked if I could take them out to lunch but they politely declined. As I was about to sign the document, I noticed that someone else had already written on it "Elizabeth R." It was all I could do to stop my hand signing "Sydney C." I never fail to tell my bank manager, when he expresses anxiety about my overdraft, that I have signed cheques for over £100 billion.

In the last session of the 1987 Parliament I was made the Pairing Whip, perhaps the most demanding if not dreaded job in the office and little compensated for by becoming the Foreign Office Whip. These two responsibilities went hand-in-hand on the presumption that there would be no legislation to be steered through the House from that Department, thus making one element of the job lighter. Unfortunately there was a necessary piece of legislation during my watch just as there had been when I was at Defence with the quinquennial Armed Forces Bill. The Pairing Whip is responsible for the Government's majority in the House of Commons. It is he who approves or rejects colleagues' applications to be absent from the House, be it for an overseas visit, an important constituency event, or to attend a grandmother's funeral. He is smothered with approbation or opprobrium according to his decision but he has to ensure that the majority is safe. While a Tory MP can have a private pairing arrangement with a Labour MP, the Pairing Whip still has to approve since it is sometimes necessary for the Government to have a respectable number voting (in spite of the majority) and always necessary to have a sufficient number to ensure a quorum or move "that progress be made."

You would be wrong to think that a Pairing Whip's job is easier with a large majority. The 1987 Parliament began with the Govrnment having an overall majority of 100 and although this had been reduced to 88 by the time I arrived it was still a pretty healthy margin. However this happy state begat an assumption that a vote can be missed (particularly late at night) without any problem while a Pairing Whip with a small majority could count on additional loyalty on the calculation that a missed vote could spell defeat. A prudent Pairing Whip will always have a sufficient safety net – in my case I decided upon twenty-five – and be prepared to exaggerate the problem to a dissapointed colleague not being granted absence. Not that a rejected applicant necessarily stayed. More certainly, the Pairing Whip got to know his colleagues better than most other MPs.

There was one occasion when the Deputy Chief Whip took it upon himself to allow the main day's debate to finish early, instead of dragging it out until the designated vote at 10pm. Unfortunately he did not consult me and I had agreed to forty or so colleagues attending the Society of Motor Manfacturers and Traders annual dinner, provided they returned by the appointed time. Luckily, there were some, though many fewer, Labour MPs also at the function but there were shocks all round when the early vote resulted in a Government majority of only one. Next morning I was congratulated by those attending the dinner on my nerve in calculating the necessary majority and thus sparing them the need to return to the House.

I have never had to work harder or longer in my life than during this period. In the April 1991 Census, one of the questions was the estimated hours the head of the household worked a week. This set me calculating and I reckoned that when the House was sitting, I worked an average of sixteen hours a day from Mondays to Thursdays and an average of eight hours a day at the weekends: a total of eighty-eight hours a week. During the recesses, I reckoned on over sixty hours a week. Mind you, some of the work was an enjoyable relaxation and, unlike most other jobs, I had a variety of things to do and was not tied to an office desk or factory floor. I had to be in the House virtually every minute when it was sitting but there were few Whipping duties when Parliament was in recesss and so my work in Chipping Barnet was unaffected and I continued visiting schools and businesses and even more Fairs and Fetes. Ever more trees were planted and I opened everything from a revamped ticket office at Oakleigh Park station to a new steak house on the A1 Barnet By-Pass. I became an annual pilgrim to the Poor Clare monastery in Arkley where I met a dwindling number of sisters and conversed with them through a glass screen. I soon found out that they knew as much as me about the world around them in spite of their closed order. I was also invited to an increasing number of one hundreth Birthday parties and, in addition to presenting the centenarian with a House of Commons bottle of sherry and chocolates, also wrote them a letter detailing their life and age when great events took place, such as Gladstone's last administration, the Diamond Jubilee of Queen Victoria and the Great War. One lady, Miss Rose Trudie Bland, celebrated in style by speaking fluently and reminiscing for no less than forty minutes about her life in Barnet. A fortnight later I received a beautifully written letter of thanks from her, with a sad note added by the matron of the Old People's Home saying that she had asked her to post it to me before going to bed and had died peacefully in her sleep that same night.

The then largest business in my patch was the telephone giant STC, now part of Nortel, whose New Southgate site employed over a thousand people (in the war it had been 12,000). On one visit there, they told me that before long there would be such a thing as a pocket telephone, no larger than a small calculator, from which a person would be able to take or receive a call from anyone, anywhere in the world. I found this hard to believe and as a joke asked if we would also be able to see to whom we were talking. "Oh yes" came the reply, "but that technical development will take a little longer."

A secret party had been organised to celebrate the tenth anniversary of my election and the then chairman, Dorothy Wilkinson, collected me, as I thought, to take me out to dinner. She stopped the car outside the recently rebuilt Hadley Memorial Hall and I walked into a crowded room of friends and supporters. I was presented with a pair of silver early 20th century decanters. My present to my constituents was to plant ten trees of ten different species in ten open spaces in Barnet.

The need for a new hospital became more acute and by the early 1990s I was campaigning for a new surgical block with a maternity ward to replace the now closed "Old Vic" as the first phase of rebuilding. In the autumn of 1991 the go-ahead was given for a £90 million rebuild and Margaret Thatcher, John Marshall, John Gorst and myself attended a symbolic demolition of one of the old buildings on the site. This good but very overdue news was happily announced by the new Health Minister,

Brian Mawhinney, who ever so fortuitously happened to live fifty yards away from my home in Ravenscroft Park. Not so good news around this time was the emergence of illegal gipsy sites with carefully planned invasions on accessible fields which infuriated nearby constituents, not least because it took some weeks for the law to grind its course before eviction was granted. Another matter of concern was the review of local authority boundaries which led to an attempt by next door Enfield to take a slice of Cockfosters from my bailiwick. Apart from a large majority of the affected Barnetonians wanting to stay put, there was a fear that a couple of oversubscribed schools would be transferred and make it more difficult if not impossible for Barnet parents to get their children into them. This proposal was successfully resisted and there was more good news: unemployment in Chipping Barnet had been halved in three years to under one thousand, the lowest figure since constituency records were kept.

In the autumn of 1991 I was asked to represent the Government at the tenth anniversary celebrations of the Independence of Belize, which in my schooldays I saw on the globe as a little pink blob called British Honduras. Having been fully briefed by the FCO, I arrived for the five day visit and my first port of call was to meet the Governor General, Dame Minita Gordon and Prime Minister George Price, a Welshman who had emigrated to this low-lying country on the Central American mainland which was about the same size as his native land but with less than a quarter of a million people. The capital had recently been moved from Belize City to Belmopan and our High Commissioner David Mackilligin told me that the P.M. had been a fiery, left wing evangaliser in his younger days and always had a bible on his desk. After the preliminary pleasantries, I affected to be surprised at seeing the bible open on his desk and asked which part of it he had been studying. "Psalm 119" came the reply and without hesitating I nonchalantly oberved that this was the longest chapter in both the New and Old

Testaments. He picked up the book and upon seeing that the Psalm had two hundred and seventy-six verses seemed agreeably surprised at my comment. I then asked him if he knew that Psalm 117 was the shortest chapter. He turned back the page, seemed even more impressed and so I had to complete my charm offensive by telling him that I had been told that Psalm 118 was the exact centre point of the two Testaments. He confirmed this with his eyes and was clearly delighted. I was treated as the star at all the proceedings thereafter, including the actual tenth anniversary ceremony itself, held in the open with only a canopy covering the VIPs who included the US President's elder brother, Prescott Bush. The British had made only one error in granting self government to Belize. They did it in their monsoon period and the heavens opened causing alarm among those of us under the canopy and a certain merriment to those who weren't as light bulbs exploded above us. I visited their rain forest with Prescott Bush and a local businessman who I met for the first time, Michael Ashcroft.

Back in the autumn of 1989 television cameras had entered the Chamber for a six month trial period. Most Conservative MPs had voted against the proposal, including myself, fearing that our traditional debating style would be jeopardised. We were advised that the best way to appeal to the viewers was to stand still and speak straight ahead instead of turning and moving as we referred to different points made by colleagues on both sides of the Chamber. In the event, our fears were partially unfounded and we all agreed to make the experiment permanent. At the time I willingly conceded that in a democracy we had no right to deny our constituents the opportunity to see as well as hear us at work. One particular fear I had was that as Whips do not speak in the Chamber, except to move the start and end of business or 'next business,' some constituents might start complaining that they never saw me speak.

I need not have worried. When on duty a Whip sits on the Front Bench, usually half way between the Dispatch Box and Mr Speaker's Chair, and before long a flood of Barnetonians were saying they saw me regularly. It didn't matter that I was not speaking; they readily drew the conclusion that I was working hard.

At the end of the year, the Evening Standard printed London MPs' voting records for the session. As the Whip it was not surprising that I proved to be the most assiduous, voting in 95 per cent of all divisions. The simple reason for not attaining 100 per cent was that ministers do not generally vote on Ten Minute Rule Bills and other Private Members' legislation. Equally, the frequency of voting is not a perfect indicator for assessing an MP's commitment. Some Members have to be absent on Parliamentary business, such as Select Committee meetings, Council of Europe sessions and so on. Ministers also have Departmental engagements and all these considerations have to be taken into account. Nevertheless, the London MP with the worst voting record that year was Ted Heath on only 3 per cent, while Margaret Thatcher (understandably) recorded a modest 15 per cent. The third most absent London MP was a Mr Ken Livingstone (23 per cent).

The first year of John Major's Premiership did little to restore the Government's popularity. Within a week of the Gulf War ending the Tories were trounced by the Liberal Democrats in the Ribble Valley by-election, caused by David Waddington going to the Lords. The swing was nearly 25 per cent, virtually the same as two years before when William Hague was first elected in Richmond, Yorkshire, following the appointment of Leon Brittan as one of our European Commissioners. Two months later, Labour were to win Monmouth from the Conservatives with a 12.6 per cent swing. The local elections confirmed that the Conservatives were being assailed from all sides. The new Prime Minister had brought back Michael Heseltine into the Cabinet as Environment Secretary in 1990 with a mandate to abolish the 'poll tax', which was to be replaced by the Council Tax. Attention soon turned to the international stage when President Gorbachev was forced out of office for three days until Boris Yeltsin led a successful resistance against the old Communist politicians. After John Major visited Washington, Moscow and Peking, his personal standing rose and the Tories were back up with Labour in the opinion polls. The Prime Minister also gained the opt-outs on the single currency and social chapter at Maastricht which (at least temporarily) united our Party. At the end of 1991, Gorbachev resigned, the Soviet Union collapsed and was replaced by the Commonwealth of Independent States and Boris Yeltsin became leader of Russia. In the new year, by which time the Conservatives had pinned their hopes on a brighter economic environment, it was clear that the recession was still being felt and time was running out. Labour and the Conservatives were neck-and-neck in the polls and John Major decided to go to the country in early April, two months before the full five year period of the Parliament.

The campaign was one of the strangest in which I campaigned. Throwing myself into the usual marathon of door-stepping, I detected absolutely no sign of changing allegiances. I had canvassed among a cross section of the electorate during the first week and Agent Geoffrey Ellis was satisfied the canvass returns were accurate. I was baffled and began to convince myself that there was a swing against me but some electors did not want to say so. Candidates can become quite paranoid but Geoffrey was doing his sums and was quietly confident. In the country at large the campaign had not been going well for the Tories and Labour had a small lead in the opinion polls. They suggested a hung Parliament with Labour gaining a few more seats than us. This was in line with my polling day prediction but we were nearly all wrong and John Major and my agent's quiet confidence was vindicated. Although the Tories suffered a net loss of 39 seats to Labour we had an overall majority of 21. More comforting, the turnout improved by nearly 2.5 per cent and the Conservative vote was up by over 350,000 to a record of over 14 million. Labour improved its vote by over 1.5 million to 11.5 million. In Chipping Barnet my vote topped 25,000 while my majority declined slightly to just under 14,000, as did my share of the vote to 57 per cent. Labour candidate Alan Williams, who was to become leader of his Party's group on Barnet Council, came second ahead of the Liberal Democrat's David Smith, reversing the result of the previous two general elections.

The Chipping Barnet electorate had declined by over 3,500 but the turnout had increased from 70 to nearly 79 per cent, with well over 2,000 more electors voting. All-in-all, I was surprised but very happy with the result and waited impatiently to see what would happen when I returned to Westminster.

15

HER MAJESTY'S
VICE CHAMBERLAIN

Richard Ryder telephoned and asked me to stay in the Office. He was a person I had come to like and respect and truly belied the second half of Sir Robert Peel's definition of a chief whip: "a person requiring all the qualities of a gentleman, but which no gentleman would accept." I had been in office now for forty months and while I still might have hoped to become a departmental minister, I was happy to remain in the engine room. The bonus was that I was now no. 4 in the pecking order and enjoyed an even more prestigious title: Vice Chamberlain of Her Majesty's Household. Another batch of visiting cards was duly ordered.

The new Deputy Chief Whip was David Heathcoat-Amory who had returned after a spell as a departmental minister. His uncle had been Chancellor of the Exchequer in the 1950s and David cut a sauve and intellectually dashing figure with a slightly careworn face. David Lightbown who had been a Whip since 1986 and reached no.3 in 1990 remained in post. He was literally a larger than life character: tall and with an exceedingly wide girth, all of which added up to twenty-something stones. He exuded a gruff and bluff countenance but although he played up to the tough and rough image, he was a kind and generous person. Nos. 2 and 3 were as different as chalk and cheese. Nicholas Baker, Greg Knight, Irvine Patnick, Tim Wood and Tim Boswell were the Lords Commissioners, while Timothy Kirkhope, later our leader in the EU Parliament, and David Davis remained as Assistant Whips, joined by Robert Hughes,

James Arbuthnot and Andrew MacKay. We were a motley bunch but I judged that we were truly representative of our colleagues. Greg Knight followed me as Pairing Whip and as I handed over the books and bludgeon to him, I told him that he would find the task easier. How wrong I was.

The first appointment of the Vice Chamberlain was to receive his wand of office from Her Majesty. I presented myself at the Palace in morning coat (with black waistcoat and top hat) and after a short but agreeable conversation was presented with the stick in question. It resembled a billiard cue but was longer, thinner and in two pieces of simple wood which screwed together perfectly so that the inscribed words 'Vice Chamberlain' on one brass band lined up with 'of HM Household' on the other. Why Household Officers had these wands was a mystery to me but I suspect that in medieval days they had staves to surround and protect the royal person when processing in public. I was told that when their services were dispensed with, the monarch broke the stick. Perhaps the staves were refined and screwed to help Queen Victoria continue the tradition. I had three additional duties to perform: carrying messages from the House of Commons to Her Majesty (and reporting back); acting as Hostage at the State Opening of each session of Parliament; and writing to The Queen every day to report events in and about the Lower House.

The messages I had to carry were requests from the Commons which asked her to approve a particular Resolution. Most seemed to be 'Double Taxation Relief Orders' involving the UK and a foreign country and at that time many of these related to our financial arrangements with the new independent countries carved out of the old USSR. But there were others and my first was the traditional one passed by the House following the debate on the Gracious Speech at the State Opening. My second was another traditional one, asking that some signal honour be bestowed upon the recently retired Speaker,

Jack (Bernard) Wetherall. This was code language asking that he be granted a peerage.

When I went to see our sovereign, no one else could be present and I wondered what would happen and what I should say. I was assured that I should not worry about this nor when to bid farewell and bow out of the room. And so it was. I was taken by an equerry to a room in her private wing at the Palace, was announced and the door was closed behind me, I bowed, advanced with wand and asked her to receive and sign the paper. Business done, she then led the conversation and after usually ten minutes or so I knew when to thank her, walk backwards to the door, bow again and depart. Upon returning to the House, immediately after Prayers, the Speaker would call "The Vice-Chamberlain" and I would walk down the aisle bowing three times before reading out The Queen's reply. In the case of the response to the Resolution concerning the retired Speaker, Dennis Skinner, who loved to prick the bubble of pomposity on such occasions, drawled out: "I think that means that Jack is going to get the BEM." I have to observe also that I did not have a reputation for being one of the more smartly dressed MPs so the sight of my appearance at the Bar of the House attired in pin stripes and tails always engendered a certain ribaldry on the backbenches. This naturally hurt me greatly but the most tricky task I had to undertake in the Chamber, having delivered HM's response, was to walk backwards again bowing three times.

The conversations between the Sovereign and her Vice Chamberlain must remain confidential (Ministers are bound by the Official Secrets Act) but in what would be over twenty private meetings, not once did Her Majesty show any sign of partisanship and while some conversations naturally touched upon parliamentary matters of the moment, there was not even a hint of political preference. I said that our meetings were private but this wasn't strictly true. Usually a number of corgies were present and I have to confess that while I am an animal lover (and shared my home in Barnet with four cats) I'm not a paid-up member of the corgie fan club and Her Majesty's canine companions seemed distinctly unfriendly to this stranger in their midst. However, there was one occasion which I must regard as one of the more embarrassing moments of my life. Among the corgies was a dorkie, a cross between a dacshound and corgie. This dorkie had the opposite temperament and was very friendly. No sooner had I bowed to Her Majesty, the dog raced across the room and was half way up my legs, sniffing enthusiastically. I affected not to be concerned.

The requirement to attend Buckingham Palace when The Queen drove in State to open a new session dates back to the 17th century. After Parliament cut off the head of good King Charles in 1649, his son and successors were a little nervous when visiting Westminster, which in those days was regarded as the sleazy end of the city of London (has anything changed?) Monarchs demanded an important parliamentarian be kept at their official residence until safe return and over the years this hostage became the Vice-Chamberlain. Tradition was that Her Majesty could not leave Buckingham Palace until I arrived; and I could not return to Westminster until she was back home. The State Opening of the 1992/93 session was my first away day and I dutifully presented myself at the Privy Council door in good time. I was met by Col. Malcolm Ross, the Chamberlain, a tall and impressive man in court dress who allowed a scintilla of relief to spread across his face at my arrival. In his welcoming words he reminded me that I was required to stay. I was about to feign disappointment by saying that I was hoping to shop at Harrods while HM was away, but thought better of it. An equerry (always a young officer from one of the services) followed me at all times and it wasn't until much later that I realised that it was his job to ensure that I remained, if necessary with the help of his sword. I was escorted to the main entrance of the Palace to await HM's departure. After the band in the inner courtyard played the national anthem (there was another band at the front of the Palace and yet another at Westminster) the Chamberlain, equerry and myself joined the Lord Chamberlain, then the Earl of Airlee, to watch the proceedings on television. Her State procession to Westminster, the Gracious Speech and return trip only took just over an hour, after which we adjourned to one of the state rooms and had drinks before I was returned to my Palace. Fate decreed that I was to perform this duty on two further occasions. Incidentally, the Lord Chamberlain is the head of the working Household whereas the Lord Great Chamberlain is one of the seven Great Officers of State, a hereditary appointment held at present by the Marquess of Cholmondeley, who walks backwards in front of The Queen as she processes from the Robing Room through the Royal Gallery to the House of Lords.

By far my most onerous and time-filling duty was the reponsibility of writing to Her Majesty each day to keep her informed about what was going on. The Commons sat at 2.30pm and the first hour was taken up with the ritual of Parliamentary Questions to Ministers on a four week rota with the exception of the Prime Minister who answered for quarter-of-an-hour every Tuesday and Thursday at 3.15pm. Unfortunately, 2.30pm was the time of the daily Whips' meeting and so I had little more than two hours to attend the Chamber and then leave to write and check my Message (for that is what it is called) before it was sent to the Court Postmaster at 6pm.

Tradition has it that a new Vice-Chamberlain is shown one of the Messages of his predecessor and John Mark Taylor, whom I knew from my West Midlands days, duly obliged. My first report was relatively easy as I could stay in the Chamber throughout the first meeting of MPs to elect a new Speaker – the only item of business – and then write a straight account of what happened. More than half of the 320 Tory MPs preferred Peter Brooke, the former Northern Ireland Secretary who had just retired from the Government, but Labour MPs wanted the previous Deputy Speaker, Betty Boothroyd. The necessary motion was put and Betty won comfortably by 372 to 238 votes to become the first woman Speaker.

My second Message reported on the debate immediately following the State Opening. I decided that The Queen wanted to be entertained as well as informed and turns of phrase and pithy descriptions would be the way ahead. I judged also that she would prefer background detail and coffee house chatter to straight reporting, which she could always get from better writers in the public prints. I had always secretly wanted to be the parliamentary sketch writer of a national newspaper and this would be my opportunity, albeit to a smaller but singular audience. There were few rules but they included the necessity to handwrite the words, using the third person. This lengthened sentences but not to the extent of destroying the flow of thought. And so, to take an extreme example, "as I told you yesterday" became "as your Vice-Chamberlain informed Your Majesty in his last Message." It was all good, traditional practice which appealed in equal doses to my sense of occasion, boundless vanity and escalating self importance. I also determined, as my writings were confidential, that a thumb nail sketch of the parliamentarians as well as what they said might be appropriate. An innocent example of this was when Michael Portillo, the new Chief Secretary to the Treasury, opened the second day's debate on the Gracious Speech. I was able to refer to him as "unique among all Your Majesty's past and present Cabinet Ministers in that he is the first to be born after your accession to the Throne."

Re-reading my early Messages, three things seemed to dominate: the parliamentary ascension of the re-elected Prime Minister, the concomitant post-election depression of Opposition MPs and the Second Reading of the EC (Amendment) Bill giving effect to the Maastricht Treaty. However, John Major was to enjoy what was to be a only a short interlude of unassailed leadership. In July, John Smith followed Neil Kinnock as Opposition Leader. He had a more relaxed and confident style than his predecessor and a more satirical touch than the PM. After the events of Black Wednesday in September, Parliament was recalled for a two day emergency debate and all the Government Whips were called to 12 Downing Street as soon as the announcement was made. At the time, I was visiting Normandy with a friend who I had first met a few years before. Teresa, a Chilean who had been in our country since 1979, and I had reached Honfleur after driving from Amsterdam. When I got the telephone message we had to dine hurriedly and then drive to Calais arriving for the 4am cross channel boat. I arrived at the meeting just in time and a few days later at the start of the debate, Smith made a brilliant speech, albeit on an easy wicket, referring to the "total destruction of the Government's economic and political strategy." The phrase struck a chord outside as well as inside Westminster.

House of Commons sittings can be unpredictable. Nothing is certain and high drama or low farce can surface at any time. The high drama was to come later – and in spadefuls on the Maastricht Bill - but two instances of the latter emerged early and both involved new Ministers. Hector Munro, a few months short of his seventieth birthday, was appointed Minister of State at the Scottish Office after first joining the Government twenty-two years before. When he came to answer his first Question, warm cheers echoed around the Chamber, broken by one MP shouting "too young." A few days later, Agriculture Questions brought forth Nicholas Soames, a larger and portlier version of his grandfather Winston Churchill. He was greeted with equal amounts of affection and derision on his maiden ministerial outing. In a friendly greeting from a colleague, he was told not to give up his rumoured regular breakfast of grouse and claret. With full majesty he pondered the thought and answered in the well worn words of a Prime Minister's stock reply when asked to visit a constituency: "I have no plans at present to do so." Collapse of House.

A John Major initiative also was in danger of becoming low farce. It was delivered under the banner of "Back to Basics." The PM intended this to be a rallying cry to change our education policy beginning with an emphasis on the "three Rs." Unfortunately public opinion fed by the Press took the slogan to refer to imagined Victorian values and at the first whiff of any ministerial scandal (and there were quite a few) the charge of hypocrisy stuck.

The first and immediate goal of the Government was to get the Maastricht Bill through the House. Labour were opposed to it because of the two opt outs negotiated while the Liberals were not prepared to support us after 10pm. Given the fragility of our majority due to Conservative rebels, slow progress was made. Two days were earmarked for the Second Reading debate with the first day's sitting ending at 7am. The Government survived the Opposition's reasoned amendment (which didn't attract the Tory eurosceptics) and easily won the main motion by 244 votes (as most Labour MPs abstained) even though 22 Tories voted against. Further progress was halted in the following week when the Danes voted "no" in a referendum on the proposed treaty. Later, Ted Heath bitterly complained to me in front of others in the Smoking Room that we should have driven on through day and night to get the Bill before the summer recess. I told him that we did not have a majority to do so and when he disagreed, I had to remind him that when he was our Chief Whip back in the 1950s with a majority of 100, he only secured the Second Reading of the Retail Price Maintenance Bill by one vote. He went sullenly silent but accepted another glass of Glenlivet!

The problem facing the Tories was that we could not agree on a European policy. We were split on the issue, as was Labour, but divisions in the Government are disliked by the public. My own view was that the UK benefitted from being part of a large free trade area, particularly on its doorstep, and that an effective free trade area could not become a reality until there was a single market. What I found hard to accept was that a single market could not become a reality until there was a single currency, especially when nations joining the new market had different economic infrastructures and cycles.

Another and larger nail in the Government's coffin at this time was the continuing recession and the pressure on the pound within the European Exchange Rate mechanism. The climax of this was Black Wednedsday when we pulled out of the ERM. With two million registered unemployed and interest rates already at 10 per cent, there was a sudden run on Sterling. Interest rates were increased to 12 per cent and then 15 per cent. These arbitrary decisions were then reversed and we left the ERM, reducing the borrowing rate to a sensible level. This spurred our economic recovery but left Ministers humiliated and the Government's economic strategy in tatters.

In December the Committee Stage of the Maastricht Bill finally started on the floor of the House (after a majority of only three on an important procedural vote). Tory rebels indulged in a filibuster with Labour eurosceptics egging them on. The Committee and Report Stage of the Bill took up 25 days and the Third Reading was only secured in late May. When the measure returned from the Lords, another vote had to be held about whether the Social Chapter should be included before the Treaty was ratified. The Government motion merely asked the House to note their policy which was not to agree. The Opposition amendment asserted that the Treaty should not be ratified until the Government said it intended to include the Social Chapter. In a scene of high drama, I had to announce the result of the vote – a tie: 317 to 317. I milked the occasion as much as I could by slowly saying: "Ayes to the Right three hundred and seventeen. Noes to the Left three hundred and seven (dramatic pause) teen." MPs thought the Government had won as one of its own made the announcement. In fact we did, as The Speaker, in accordance with precedent, cast her vote to maintain the status quo. The other Government teller, Irvine Patnick, had over-counted the Opposition vote by one, so we should have won. Irvine reported privately that he had been harassed by some Labour MPs alleging that he had failed to count one of their colleagues and under pressure and protest he had relented and added one to his tally. Fifteen Tories had voted for the amendment and a further eight abstained. Drama indeed, but this was followed by the vote on the main motion when the Government was defeated by 324 to 316, only one MP being absent. Twenty three Conservatives voted against. The PM immediately announced that there would be a vote of confidence the next day and with the aid of nine Ulster MPs and the support of Conservative rebels (surely a case of Tory turkeys not voting for an early Christmas) the Government survived.

Some time before all this, I was asked to represent the Government at the inauguration of the President of the Seychelles. There was doubt about the exact timing of the visit due to the outcome of the Masstricht Bill and whether a presidential candidate would secure over 50 per cent of the popular vote on the first round. Albert Rene, who came to power after a coup in 1977 in which he displaced the first President James Manchan, was re-elected President for the fourth time on the first round with almost 60 per cent of the vote in a three-cornered fight. James Manchan remained leader of the Opposition. Our High Commissioner, John Sharland, was only then able to finalise the arrangements. His first words on the phone to me were to apologise profusely for my having to stay on the island for three days before I could catch a plane back after the inaugural ceremony. I told him that I would try and bear this inconvenience stoically and, encouraged, he invited me to stay longer as his guest at the residency if I wished. I did very much and wanted to stay much longer than five days but had to return to take the family on our annual summer sojourn in Spain. John and his wife Susan looked after me very well and at a busy time for them, with their four daughters returning home from their schools in England.

The Seychelles consist of over one hundred islands in the Indian Ocean just below the equator and it was to be the first time that I had crossed this imaginary line. The three principal islands are all within reasonable distance of each other and contain 90 per cent of the 75,000 population. With an electorate of 50,000, the country had fewer voters than the average English constituency. The islands are surrounded by abundant tuna fishing grounds and the main crop is coconuts. The staple diet is rice which has to be imported and while there I met an Australian who imported potatoes from Perth, over four thousand miles away. After the inauguration, I carried out a number of engagements including a speech to the local Rotary Club and visited the island of Praslin to see the unique coco-de-mer, a double coconut which resembled a rear part of the female anatomy. The Islands' attractive Environment Minister, Dannielle de St.Jorre, presented one to me and it rarely fails to attract the attention of visitors when it sits innocuously in my living room.

After this tropical divertissement, I was ready for a rest, if only to get out of the heat of the Government Whips' kitchen after the first extraordinary session of the 1992 Parliament.

16

SOME POLITICAL
PERSONALITIES

The House of Commons has its fair share of characters although MPs may dispute among themselves who are the genuine cards and who are the poseurs. There were differing views also about whom we admired or simply liked and friendships reached across the Chamber while relations could at times be less than smooth among some colleagues. In my case, a few examples of the former included Arthur Bottomley, Brian Walden, Dennis Howell and George Thomas in my first Parliament and Neil Kinnock, Jack Cunningham, Clare Short, Estelle Morris and Charles Kennedy in later ones. I soon found myself writing personal pen portraits of a number of my contemporaries, for the most part unknown to the wider public when I first wrote them.

At the start of the 1992 Parliament, apart from John Smith, there were three Labour front bench spokesmen who, each in their own way, were impressive. Robin Cook, then forty-six, had been an MP since 1974 and a member of the Shadow Cabinet since 1983. He had just been appointed to the Trade & Industry portfolio. Small in stature, he was clever, articulate and supremely self-assured, standing immobile at the Dispatch Box with ramrod back and puffed out chest, resembling a cross between a Victorian philantropist's statue and a garden gnome. A good debater and accomplished at dealing with interventions, his razor-sharp mind could cut through reams of trivia to find the root of an argument. An instance of this was when he responded with devastating effect to

172

the statement on the Scott Inquiry (into sales of arms to Iraq) with only an hour to examine the voluminous report.

Gordon Brown, forty-one and elected in 1983, had just become Shadow Chancellor. He was sturdier in countenance but with the same singular commitment to politics. This heavy jowled, unsmiling character with overworked jaw positively personified gloom and doom and was perfectly moulded as the spokesman for impending industrial and economic Armageddon. His speeches were always well crafted though delivered with ill-grace and I remember only one glaring misjudgement: to assert after the 1993 Budget that unemployment would rise "month after month after month" when the opposite happened.

The junior of them both was Tony Blair, still under forty when he became Shadow Home Secretary in 1992. He had also entered the House in 1983 and I described him as "a rising mega-star in the Labour firmament... young, good looking and speaking with an intense physical energy which verges on the over-theatrical... assured and able, he is both smart and slippery in dealing with interventions." Always well briefed, he was astute enough to realise when a situation was not as bleak as the Opposition initially hoped and quickly changed tack. Full of facts and figures, memorable phrases rolled off his silver tongue. The barrister in him could argue that black is white, while his earnest and youthful sincerity and smile could sway the most hardbitten audience. By far the most interesting parliamentary duels were between him and Home Secretary Ken Clarke, who once referred to his telegenic shadow as "the tabloid politician." To this observing outsider, Blair, Brown and Cook seemed mutually to loath each other but I was never quite sure about the relationship between Cook and Blair.

There were characters aplenty in the House around this time and I remember some Tory and Labour MPs who stood out starkly from their more grey suited colleagues.

David Evans (Welwyn-Hatfield) was a self-made millionaire via his own office and street cleaning business. He had been a professional cricketer and footballer and was chairman of Luton Town Football Club when he was first elected. Relatively small in stature, what marked him out particularly on his own benches was his voice which could best be described as unreconstructed Cockney. Whenever he was called to speak, those in the Public Gallery instinctively looked towards the Labour benches to see who it was. His accent obviously did not come from the Hatfield House end of his constituency. He was the epitome of a no-nonsense Tory who said what he thought in down-to-earth language and always referred to his political opponents across the Chamber as "that lot over there." Every Commons sitting finishes with a half-hour adjournment debate when a backbencher can a raise any issue. Our Dave was granted one at a time when John Major's pet project was beginning to back-fire on him and chose as his subject "Back to Basics in Welwyn-Hatfield." Normally only the Member raising the issue and the appropriate Minister replying are in the Chamber but on this occasion there were 120 MPs including 11 Cabinet Ministers present. They were not to be disappointed.

Dave's "Declaration" took the form of the Ten Commandments. My hand visibly shook with excitement as my pen recorded his modern version of the tablets of received wisdom. The first was when to say "please" and "thank you." The second was when to raise your hat to a lady and offer her your seat. The third was when to help an elderly person cross the road and the fourth: how to wait your turn in a queue. These were clearly instructive, but the next five were more forbidding: drinking and driving was wrong, as was stealing, rape, murder and adultery. The tenth and final Commandment took the form of a homily on the importance of parental guidance. The decalogue had been delivered and the audience was transfixed. Coveting, bearing false witness, making graven images, keeping the Sabbath and taking

God in vain may have been discarded but few noticed or cared. We all remained in a state of suspended spiritual animation for the rest of the day.

Another *tour-de-force* was a speech on a Ten Minute Rule Bill (a device for raising an issue before the main business of the day twice a week) by another Conservative backbencher, Anthony Steen (South Hams), a tall, silvery haired, leathery faced barrister who billed himself as a youth leader and social worker. Steen was a bundle of energy devoted to the battle against the reddest tape of bureaucracy. On this particular occasion he was incensed at the French National Assembly which had recently passed a Bill, instigated by their Culture Minister, forbidding the use of English words such as "T-shirt", "software" and "weekend." His answer was to introduce a retaliatory measure to prohibit the use of French words in written and spoken English. Our ham from South Hams played to the gallery superbly, claiming that the French Bill was the *raison d'etre* for his measure as it would rip apart the very fabric of the *entente cordiale*. He did not want to be thought of as a *chauvinist* and he was certainly no *enfant terrible*. When Anthony's Bill received the Royal Assent, its provisions would be operated by an additional duty imposed on traffic wardens: to keep their ears open for French words. Those uttering them were to be given an on-the-spot fine of £10. He conceded life might be difficult for some people (I immediately thought of Gallic tourists) but supercharged Steen had a more vivid imagination, suggesting that the inability to refer to a *negligee* might make an *affaire dangereuse* a little more *risque*. There were many more *bon mots* in his peroration which was the *piece de resistance* of the parliamentary day. Before he spoke, Labour MP Gerald Kaufman raised the legality of Steen's Bill given the usage of 14th century Norman French in our parliamentary proceedings. If the Clerk of the Parliaments could not use such a phrase as "*La Reine le veult*", he opined with dead pan face, the Bill could undermine the Royal Prerogative. Madam Speaker was equal to the occasion. She ruled that Court French would still be permissable. However, on this occasion the House was not in a francophobic mood and rejected the Steen initiative. It was with relief that I was able to advise The Queen that her motto "*Honi soit qui mal y pense*" remained politically correct.

Our third card carrying Conservative character was Harry Greenway (Ealing North) who had a greater initial success with his Horses (Protective Headgear for Young Riders) (Amendment) Bill. Harry, a slighter version of Steen stood at just over sixteen-and-a-half hands but had the same silvery mane. He was a former headmaster and amateur riding instructor and the Amendment in his measure was pretty sweeping: requiring everyone to wear protective headgear when riding a horse on a highway or byway. Our Ealing equestrian *extraordinaire* used his ten minutes to deliver a paean for "this noble creature." At first his colleagues thought that he was talking about himself but no, he was giving a homily on the horse and a brief history of equine transport. He was full of nostalgia for the days when there was "manure in plenty on our streets" and for him civilisation had taken a backward step with the introduction of the internal combustion engine. Concern for his fellow equestrians led him to inform his parliamentary pedestrians that thirty-two thousand riders a year had to visit hospital casualty departments. He was given leave to introduce his measure and as he formally presented it to the Clerk and passed me on the front bench felt moved to whisper: "don't worry, this wont affect Her Majesty; she never rides on our roads."

Another memorable Ten Minute Rule Bill was introduced by a new Labour backbench MP, Jon Owen Jones (Cardiff Central). Fate decreed that he did so on his fortieth birthday and the subject he chose was Public Conveniences. Jones is a small, ginger-haired, wizened Welshman with a goatee beard. Few would suggest, perhaps not even himself, that he looked like a hero to the fairer sex but his measure was designed to remove discrimination on grounds of gender in the provision of public toilets and to provide a minimum number of them in every local authority, to which he had added to its short title "and for connected purposes." Equally apposite, his Bill was printed under the title: "Notice of Motion" and with a deadly seriousness and dedication to the job in hand he spared no word, phrase, statistic or blush in putting his case before a sparsely filled chamber which had just flushed itself out after Prime Minister's Questions. After referring to the recently held Incontinence Week, he came out of his closet to tell us that women's needs were greater than men's, yet the facilities provided for men were more prevalent. He demanded more toilets for both sexes. My jaw sagged when he went on to aver that there must be at least one unisex toilet, apparently so that parents could escort their children to spend their pennies - except that they would not need to spend them as he wanted turnstiles to toilets to be outlawed. Our Welsh waterworks wizard made a scathing attack on previous legislation which laid down that local councils couldn't charge for the use of urinals, only for closets. There was no opposition to his measure and the House went on to the next business, spending more than pennies on the Finance Bill.

Then there was the clever and amusing Gyles Brandreth (Chester) who clearly enjoyed being in the House and infectiously spread this happy state among his colleagues, though alas for only one Parliament. He made a particularly witty and adroit maiden speech and at one Question Time spoke about all the good news emanating from his fair city and asked John Major: "to what or to whom does the Prime Minister attribute this encouraging state of affairs?" He didn't quite get the name he was expecting.

Tony Banks (West Ham) was a regular performer who promoted himself from the backbenches with some witty one-liners as well as a number of Ten Minute Rule Bills. His speciality was the rude personal insult. On one occasion he wanted to promote British vegetables, with the exception (as he put it) of those sitting on the Conservative benches. It was at a time when the Government was indeed promoting native produce with cartoon characters such as Sargeant Strawberry and Corporal Carrot (ugh!) and Minister Michael Jack said Banks should volunteer as private Beetroot as "he was red all the way through." The House laughed but even more when the Speaker immediately called Mr (Eric) Pickles.

More recently another Labour MP who immensely enjoys the Chamber is Mr Punch's look-alike Stephen Pound (also from Ealing North) who clearly had self preservation in mind when his declared interests included collecting comics. Sedentary barbs at his opponents were leavened with outbursts of self-deprecation. Like Tony Banks, he could display a short fuse at times but this duo added a welcome irreverence to our proceedings though never at inappropriate times.

Finally, two more Tories. Vying for a place among the seasoned card holders was Toby Jessel (Twickenham). Toby is a virtuoso concert pianist and I have heard him play Mozart's *21st Piano Concerto* with artistic aplomb. A talented musician indeed but with a definite degree of detachment. On one occasion he was found locked in a toilet off the wrong division lobby during a crucial vote. On another, when a guest of the French Ambassador, he bade him *au revoir* in good time to return for a vote. Finding his car blocked, he took some time negotiating it over a high pavement and then made hastily for Westminster, unfortunately attracting the attention of the local constabulary who followed in hot pursuit. All came to a grinding halt in front of Carriage Gates with Mr J. refusing to be breathalysed, claiming some sort of immunity and the need to vote. The upshot was inevitable: he was banned from driving but the strong rumour had it that he was decidedly under the limit. A short time after, when travelling by train from home to work, an imperious elderly lady peered at him over her paper through her *lorgnette* and enquired of him: "are you my MP Mr Toby Jessel?" He said rather nervously that he was, to which she replied: "Splendid. I like a man with spunk." Toby was wont to sport from time to time a grey three-piece suit woven from poodle hairs. This had been made some years before from clippings bequeathed by his grandmother who bred the particular dog. "It is very woolly" he once confided to me, "it tickles behind the knees and the wind blows straight through it." Toby and wife Eira live in the house built and occupied by Christopher Wren when he was commissioned to extend nearby Hampton Court Palace and Eira swears to me that she had conversed with a ghost when she first took up residence there.

"They don't make them like that, anymore" is a regular refrain when discussing the old eccentrics of any institution but the father of them all must be Sir Nicholas Fairbairn (Perth & Kinross) who died in 1995. At his best Nicholas had a devastating wit but in later years we were not witnesses to much of it. More usually, we had to suffer interminable monologues which were memorable more for verbal rudeness which was vituperative, vulgar or more likely both. But he was a character, flamboyant in manner, word and dress. The earliest tale recalled about him was when he was eleven and Labour was enjoying its 1945 Election landslide. A gardener at the exclusive preparatory school making best efforts to educate its precocious charge, aggressively told the young Nicholas that socialism was going to wipe out the likes of him. This made him hugely resentful, or so he told me, and was the catalyst which decided him on a career in politics. He picked up his catapult and put out every window in the local Co-op. This, I thought to myself, was probably his main contribution to the destruction of socialism. The problem with such eccentrics is that in exciting attention they instinctively incite mistrust or worse among at least some of their constituents, often reducing or wiping out their majorities.

Exuberance of language in the House of Commons is limited by convention and often the Speaker has to intervene. After an opposition front bench spokesman called a minister a 'nitwit,' Betty Boothroyd felt impelled to make a carefully crafted statement reprimanding us all. In her first three years as Speaker, she had had to make seventy separate rulings about unacceptable words and phrases. She quoted:

> "Good temper and moderation are the charact-
> eristics of parliamentary language ... we must
> use the richness of the English language to select
> elegant phrases that express their meaning
> without causing offence to others."

The problem for the parliamentary wordsmith is to find exactly where the boundary line is, not least when new words enter the dictionary. Traditionally the word 'liar' is out of order and its variations of 'peddling an untruth', 'duplicity', 'dishonesty', 'falsehood' and 'intended deception.' Describing our colleagues as animals is definitely frowned upon. A 'demented hyena,' 'rat', 'stool pigeon', 'frazzled cat', 'cheeky little pup' and 'twerp' have all recently found disfavour with the Chair. To accuse a Member of being drunk is strictly forbidden and Clare Short was pulled up not so long ago for referring to another MP as being "usually associated with a stronger drink than water." There have been some unsuccessful attempts to insult by resurrecting an unpopular person from the past. I recall two Cabinet Ministers being likened to Lord Haw-Haw and Herr Himmler, while there was a more direct reference to a peeress as Baroness Bonkers (Tony Banks on Margaret). I've also heard ministers referred to as 'little squirts', 'clever little sods' and 'unctuous slobs', while among the epithets earned by backbenchers were 'berk,' 'shyster' and 'lickspittle.' I soon found it prudent to take my smelling salts into the Chamber.

In the late Spring of 1994, fate intervened with a shock to the whole body politic when the Leader of the Opposition died suddenly, aged fifty-five. John Smith was in the midst of a distinguished political career. He had first fought a parliamentary seat at the age of twenty-two, had become an MP at thirty-one, minister at thirty-five and entered the Cabinet just forty years old in 1978. He had been elected leader of his Party less than two years before and was now to be denied the highest political accolade. A talented and much respected man, his personal popularity overflowed beyond the boundaries of his Party. When the House convened on the day of his death, John Major spoke of his rare abilities and the affection in which he was held, while deputy Opposition Leader Margaret Beckett mentioned his "highest ethics and staunchest integrity." The Liberal leader Paddy Ashdown talked about "a thoroughly decent and deeply committed man with a prodigious talent" and Neil Kinnock attested to "his conviction without obsession and the glow of his humour." On behalf of Scottish MPs, Menzies Campbell observed that John Smith had "all the virtues of a Scottish Presbyterian, but none of the vices." In adjourning the Commons for the rest of the day Madam Speaker referred to our sadly departed and much revered colleague as a "dedicated politician without malice."

I have seen anger in the House and been surrounded by angst. I have witnessed hate and hilarity in equal measures. But never before nor since have I felt and seen such sadness as I did on the afternoon of Thursday 12 May 1994.

17

PRELUDE TO ELECTORAL
DISASTER

John Major's flagship was the Citizen's Charter. This was his personal initiative and had one simple aim: to provide better and more accountable public services. When first announced, the Labour benches scoffed with derision but their parliamentary leadership soon realised that John had touched a chord with the public and quickly performed a U-turn. Knee-jerk criticism of the concept soon turned into complaints that the initiative did not go far enough and there were calls for more charters and performance indicators.

Having hoisted his flag, he appointed William Waldegrave as Cabinet Minister responsible with Robert Jackson in support. My first instinct was to wonder whether he could have chosen a more appropriate duo to promote the interests of the proverbial man on the Clapham omnibus as they were both Fellows of All Souls, but this proved to be an unworthy thought. There was another interesting initiative at this time, the National Lottery Bill, which found support on both sides of the House and I realised at an early stage the opportunity it could bring to my erstwhile profession. Owen Luder, the then President of the Royal Institute of British Architects, had invited me to lunch. We had been friends since I was first elected to the RIBA Council over twenty years before. At the Institute's HQ in Portland Place, the conversation at the small lunch party inevitably centred on the profession's reputation with the public, which in all my working life had not been very high. It didn't need the Citizen's Charter to reveal that most Brits didn't like much of the modern architecture they saw, not least the tall, soulless concrete tower blocks which were blots on too many urban landscapes. There were many reasons for these municipal monstrosities: from the desperate need to replace the slums and bomb damaged buildings after the war to the development of industrial prefabricated building systems which offered a reasonably quick and economic solution in terms of cost and effective use of land. My judgement was that funding from the National Lottery would give the opportunity for far more innovative designs for a greater range of buildings and this became a reality with new museums, art galleries and other landmark cultural institutions appearing. I feel that it is these new, hitherto unexpected, projects which have aroused public interest and brought about a better understanding and less disliking of modern architecture. This is not entirely due to funding from the National Lottery – new football stadia have also spearheaded the renewed interest – but it has, in my opinion, been the crucial turning point.

Owen Luder may not be among the best known British architects, but he has achieved something unique: he is the only person to have been President of the RIBA twice. His sartorial trademark is a gaudy bow tie which deflects from a very agreeable person with robust views – he once criticised Prince Charles for referring to a planned extension of the National Gallery as a carbuncle.

Back in the Commons, whatever initiatives the Government took, John Major's administration remained deeply unpopular. Half way through the Parliament the Conservatives had already been pummelled in the opinion polls for a record length of time and were now thirty points behind Labour who were riding high above 60 per cent. The Liberals generally gain in popularity when a Conservative government is in the doldrums but at this time even Paddy Ashdown's Party was struggling to stay in double figures. Little wonder that even the most sanguine Tory began to weigh up his prospects for the next General Election and the possibility of a landslide defeat of the sort Labour had suffered in 1931. The reason for the Government's unpopularity was fourfold: the length and depth of the recession and the painfully slow recovery from it; the lack of a feel good factor in spite of improving economic indicators (an almost unprecedented combination of growth with low inflation); a feeling of betrayal, particularly among middle England, of what was perceived to be broken promises and higher taxation; and a Party seen to be deeply divided at Westminster. The lack of the feel good factor was fuelled by the lack of security in almost every job. Hitherto, getting a degree at University virtually guaranteed employment for life, as did a diploma or certificate at College, but no longer. Even the most able person could suddenly find he was made redundant for reasons ranging from take-overs to advancing technology. This was but one factor that led to the overall impression of a Government not in control and having no sense of direction. John Major was regarded as a nice person but unable to display effective leadership. His Ministers collectively (and I was one of them) were deemed to be arrogant, incompetent and sleaze-ridden.

But something else was happening. After the shock of the leader of the opposition's untimely death the coronation of Tony Blair took place. In John Smith's wake, he moved effortlessly and serenely to the leadership of his Party. At the mere batting of an eyelid, a fresh and engaging face was to captivate the public and even mesmerise the left in his Party. While the Tories looked tired and ill-tempered, Labour suddenly appeared with a fetching face-lift and Blair's political honeymoon went on and on and on. What many of us didn't appreciate at the time was that when 'Bambi' Blair entered the political stage from the left, he kept on walking to the right and stole most of Maggie and Major's wardrobe. Ditching his own Party's Clause 4, he set about reassuring the aggrieved Tory voters that privatisation would not be reversed, nor the new Trade Union legislation, nor the free market reforms; while Education and the Health Service would be improved without income tax being increased. It was an irresistible manifesto and was combined with an incessant attack on the integrity of Ministers and the disputing of any good news. Thus it was claimed that the lower inflation figures had been rigged, unemployment was rising not falling and any popular initiative introduced by ministers was only carrying out what Labour had long espoused and was too little and too late.

Whatever the general view of Ministers, there were many who impressed in the Commons. First and foremost was Foreign Secretary Douglas Hurd. Competent and courteous, he was always in complete control at the Dispatch Box. Perhaps his most difficult problem was to prevent precipitate military action against the Serbs when they were committing atrocities against the Bosnians. The "something must be done" reaction from all quarters of the House had to be balanced with the reality that it would have needed thousands of troops occupying unfamiliar and unfriendly terrain with little prospect of success and no help from the United States. His diplomatic skills combined with a political sensitivity paid off. He had made it known that he would like to retire when the Prime Minister next decided on a ministerial reshuffle and when the occasion arose John Major paid him a thoroughly justified tribute. He said that Douglas's "deep knowledge and calm authority have earned great credit for this country." He had just attended his 16th and last European Council as Foreign Secretary and had devoted forty-three years of unbroken service as a diplomat, politician and minister. He also had a good team supporting him which included Douglas Hogg, son of Quintin, with a considerable mind masked by a somewhat unconventional manner, who answered supplementary questions without a note.

Patrick Mayhew was another minister with gravitas and sense of occasion. Relaxed but authoritative, the Northern Ireland Secretary oozed commonsense and was reasonableness personified, the exact ingredients necessary in what was then thought to be the insoluble problem of Ulster until the initiative of the "Downing Street Declaration" at the end of 1993.

And then there was Michael Heseltine, the master political orator and operator. At this time he was a young looking sexagenarian who towered at the Dispatch Box with the whiff of a yet-to-fade matinee idol. He gave unorthodox performances with colossal self assurance. When debating in the House, "Tarzan's" technique was to pick up some of his opponents' points and, one by one, manipulate, massacre or misinterpret them before introducing his own agenda. A classic example was an opposition day debate on the state of Britain's manufacturing industry. Robin Cook had made a very good speech, stressing the importance of the steel, car and airframe industries which "could not be allowed to fail if Britain was to remain an advanced economy." He said that these industries were failing because of continued redundancies and the acquisition of Rover by BMW. Cook proclaimed that Labour wanted "an industrial strategy to achieve competitiveness through a high-tech, high investment manufacturing base." Heseltine's line was to assert that these three industries had survived because they had been privatised; that an industrial strategy would lead to politicians and civil servants meddling and telling experts how to run their businesses; and competitiveness depended upon "inflation, now at an all-time low ... exports, now at an all-time high ... and good industrial relations, now the best for a century." He spoke with a kind of messianic fervour, not completely dissimilar in style, looks and demeanour, I thought through half-closed eyes, to Dr Billy Graham at one of his religious rallies, though perhaps without the godliness and gracefulness.

In stark contrast was Tony Newton. The Leader of the House is one of the most visible ministers in the Chamber but perhaps the least known to the public. He is the face of the Government in the Commons and a certain knowledge of MPs' individual pet projects and prejudices is essential. Tony Newton was no matinee idol but a chainsmoker and workaholic with a careworn face. He was courteous and well informed who did his parliamentary homework assiduously and stood in for the Prime Minister in the Commons when he was abroad. If he lacked charisma, he thrived on competence and was impressive precisely because he did not try to be.

Ken Clarke, in the Cabinet since 1985 succesively as Paymaster General, Trade & Industry Minister, Health Secretary, Education Secretary and Home Secretary before becoming Chancellor in 1993, is a parliamentarian to his finger tips and is the most agreeable company. It is impossible not to be relaxed in his presence and he is completely at ease at the dispatch box, elegant in phrase yet forceful in argument. On one occasion he and wife Gillian invited me to no. 11. After I accepted, I had a call from Reggie Maudling's daughter, Caroline, and arranged to meet her the same evening. I asked Ken if I could bring Caroline and he enthusiastically agreed. When we arrived, Caroline was shown around every room in the building which had been her home thirty years before when Reggie was Chancellor. She never thought she would see the place again.

Like a bolt from the blue, in the midsummer of 1995, John Major announced he was resigning the leadership of his Party and would immediately stand again, inviting any other colleague to apply for the post. As he couldn't temporarily resign as Prime Minister, it was a pre-emptive strike to try and clear the air and so decide who was to lead the Party into the next General Election. John Redwood (the third ministerial Fellow of All Souls) resigned as Welsh Sercretary and declared himself a candidate. This ensured a ballot with a serious candidate who could in no way be described as a stalking horse. When by chance I met him in the Tea Room shortly after his announcement, I innocently enquired if he was missing his ministerial salary. He replied that this was more than compensated for by now being able to put down Parliamentary Questions to Michael Portillo. By now I had mastered the complex electoral system which operated. The successful candidate had to secure 50 per cent of those entitled to vote and be 15 per cent ahead of the nearest rival. There were 328 Conservative MPs and therefore Major had to secure at least 164 votes or 190 votes if every MP voted for either of the two candidates. In effect, there was a third candidate, the abstainer or spoiler who would still be able to register a protest against the PM without declaring for Redwood.

I calculated that there were three tents pitched on the Conservative field. There was the Right who put the preservation of Westminster sovereignty above all else and wanted a reduction in public spending as a proportion of GDP. Their two most visible leaders were Redwood and Portillo. Then there was the Left who saw Britain's best, if not only, future in Europe if we were to compete successfully in the mega markets of the globe, while not being averse to more interventionist policies if necessary at home. Michael Heseltine and Ken Clarke were their standard bearers. Finally the Centre, who wanted to keep all the European options open (without a single currency) and wanted to cut direct taxes but not at the expense of harming the essential public services. John Major and most of the Cabinet were in this tent, as I was and I described once our view on Europe as being that of 'on the continent but not incontinent'. My calculation was that the Centre would beat the Right, but could not do so decisively without the support of the Left. The dilemma for the Left was whether to ensure the outright defeat of the Right by voting for Major; or abstain, giving itself a chance in any second round contest (when new candidates could enter). On the eve of the vote, I made a forecast: John Major would get 210; John Redwood just fail to get 100 and a score of colleagues would abstain. In the event, Major got 218, Redwood 89 with a dozen spoilt papers and eight abstentions. The air was cleared, if only for a short time, and the following day Major had a major reshuffle. Hurd retired and was replaced by Malcolm Rifkind. Richard Ryder had also arranged to retire at this time and was succeeded by Alastair Goodlad as Chief Whip.

Later that evening, I was in the Smoking Room when the telephone rang. One of the staff came across and said it was for me. My heart missed a beat as I assumed it must be an emergency call - perhaps an accident or worse in the family. Never before had this happened and clearly the Whips Office had immediately re-directed the call to the place where I had for long concluded was the best venue for getting a feel for the views of colleagues. Fortunately it was a lady at no. 10 saying that the Prime Minister would like to see me. "When?" I asked, thinking that an appointment would be made for the following morning. "Immediately" was the reply. I asked if fifteen minutes time would be acceptable as I would have to walk there. It was and I hastened to meet the First Lord of the Treasury. By the time I entered Downing Street cameramen were putting away their paraphernalia after the comings and goings earlier in the day and I convinced myself that promotion was in the air, especially as there were still a number of ministerial positions to be filled. Only the major changes had been announced and I still had my eye on the eponymous junior portfolio in the Environment Department. I walked purposefully through the doorway and was greeted by the Chief Whip's delightful Secretary, Shana Hole, who immediately wheeled me left into No.12 to take a phone call from Alastair Goodlad. "Just thought I would let you know before you see the PM that we've decided to make some changes in the Whips' Office so you and David Lighbown are being asked to resign." I was then escorted back and entered the Cabinet Room with a solitary John Major sitting at the large, suitably coffin-shaped, table. "Sydney, I just wanted to thank you for all you have done in the Whips' Office and to say that, as you know, Her Majesty is in Scotland but is delighted to honour you with an immediate Knighthood." This came as a genuine surprise, not least as I was always told that the recipient of any award was given the option of declining the honour and, in any case, they are usually made in the twice yearly (Queen's Birthday and New Year's) Honours' Lists . It seemed that I had no choice, not that I would have been among the alleged 1 per cent who refuse. We talked for five minutes and then there was a knock on the door and an official entered to remind the PM about his next engagement. Twice he had to tell her that he would like more time with me before the lady left. I thought to myself that this intervention was the pre-arranged way in which he could finish a conversation with any minister who cut up rough at such a time. We had another five minutes of friendly chat and finally bade each other farewell. As I had only myself to talk to on my longest walk back to the House, I briefly contemplated my post-ministerial future. My desk in the Government Whips' Office at Westminster seemed far away, but not as distant as the Environment Department.

I decided that the first priority was to clear my desk. I had been in the office for six-and-a-half years. It is easy to conclude that the Whips are some sort of secret society who practice the black arts and are forever threatening their colleagues with exposure of their misdemeanours or worse if they do not toe the Party line. Not so, but perhaps on the rare occasion some of us may have wished this was the case when the odd colleague had been behaving disingenuously. At the time of the crucial Maastricht debates, one such MP announced to the world on radio that she would be supporting the Government on a crucial issue, only to go into the other division lobby when the said issue was voted on a few hours later.

Then there is the Whips' infamous "black book" wherein it is alleged that all the peccadillos or worse of our colleagues are carefully recorded for possible use at a later date. Again, not so. Apart from the stupidity of committing to paper in this day and age whatever sensitive information any Whip might have, we met every day so reports, if there were any, of such carnal indiscretions or financial improprieties would have been communicated by mouth. But there was a black book, though its cover was blue, for recording domestic information gleaned which would be of interest to the other Whips but which did not need discussing at our meetings. A typical example was when the young son of one of my "flock" was shaken but not seriously injured in a road accident. When I was told this by the father, John Wilkinson, I put the salient details in the book so that other Whips would know and could express concern when they next saw him.

I had been the Vice-Chamberlain for exactly half the time I was in ministerial office. I had written nearly four hundred Messages to Her Majesty. They varied in length, a couple of little more than two hundred words while the longest was over eleven hundred. The vast majority of them were about seven hundred words and so Her Majesty had to suffer well over one-quarter-of-a-million words from me over the forty month period. As previously mentioned, my messages were handwritten and there was time for only a cursory check before dispatch. Only later could the copy I always made be checked for grammar and spelling. I was horrified to discover that in two of my earlier offerings I had spelt the word 'hypocrisy' as 'hypocracy' (presumably the word had been written in the context of 'democracy and literacy'). I blush to think of other etymological gaffes written and read.

In addition I had talked to The Queen privately on a score of occasions and seen her briefly at a few functions such as the three Garden Parties at Buckingham Palace every July. I was expected to attend these, wand in hand, before joining a select group for tea in the Royal Enclosure. On one occasion, she asked me in front of a brace of Cabinet Ministers about matters in the House. I observed that the Tory Party ill at ease with itself was not a pretty sight. She laughed but I noticed that my ministerial colleagues looked somewhat askance. In suffering me for so long I reflected that she really did have to work at times beyond the call of duty.

Shortly after leaving the Government I had to surrender my wand to her at a formal but private ceremony and I was dubbed at Buckingham Palace by Prince Charles a few months later (as The Queen was on a State Visit to Australia). Two others were 'knighted' with me: Martin Gilbert, Churchill's biographer, and Joyce Anelay who later went to the Lords and became one of our shadow ministers.

After all this, I was sliding effortlessly down the greasy political pole with another poll looming.

For this NEW Britain, a NEW man

Your Conservative Candidate, Sydney

CHAPMAN

Some election campaigns

Handsworth Division General Election 1970
JUNE 18th

Sydney
CHAPMAN
CONSERVATIVE
Candidate

Sydney
Chapman

CONSERVATIVE

C

WANTED

SYDNEY
CHAPMAN
for the next
PARLIAMENT
to continue as our local M.P.

SYDNEY
CHAPMAN

WHEN IT COMES TO EXPERIENCE

IT HAS TO BE SYDNEY CHAPMAN

18

INTO THE ABYSS

On leaving the Whips' Office, David Lightbown and I were allocated a handsome room towards the House of Lords end of the Palace. He had been a Minister for nine years and it was generally expected that he would have retired at the first reshuffle after the 1992 election. Shuffles came and went but he remained in post and after each one would announce to all and sundry that "Sydney and I will retire at the next one." As new colleagues came into the office we must have been regarded as the part of the furniture and became known as 'Little and Large' (though I am six foot tall). Given 'Large's' dimensions, even the widest corridors had difficulty in containing both of us side by side when others approached. At such times I would disappear behind him while he would jocularly shout some insult at the oncoming colleagues. After being verbally abused, I would appear from behind his bulk to assure those assailed not to worry as I was the community caring whip.

His eccentricities were verbal as well as physical. He had great difficulty saying certain words. For instance, he referred to Michael Portillo as "Portillio" and at the table he was continually ordering "patio" instead of pate. I warmed to him even more when we shared our new office, which he had apparently sequestrated from the Upper House when he was the Accommodation Whip in anticipation of his eventual return to the backbenches. He got himself (and me) appointed to the Accommodation & Works Committee, presumably to ensure that the Lords would not reclaim our new found demi-paradise. Early in December, he told me not to expect him the next day as he was off to the Oxford-Cambridge rugby match at Twickenham. I was deeply shocked when told that he had collapsed and died there. Thereafter our room seemed larger and emptier.

On returning to the backbenches I did enjoy one unusual experience – steering a Private Member's Bill through all its stages in five minutes. The Party Wall etc Bill had been introduced in the Lords by a hereditary Peer, James Lytton, a Chartered Surveyor. Unfortunately by the time it reached the Commons there was no time left for consideration. The only possibility was for it to be presented and passed on the last Friday for consideration of such a Bill. I was asked to try and get it through, knowing that the Deputy Speaker, Dame Janet Fookes, was opposed to this sort of procedure. All Bills, she rightly oberved, should be debated and it was quite wrong for a measure to reach the Statute Book without a word being spoken. I agreed with her but said that this one was an exception: the Government and all other Parties agreed with its provisions; the Bill had been exhaustively discussed and amended in the Lords to meet all points of view; and if it did not pass through the Commons at this last opportunity, its hard won acceptance would count for nothing and the Bill would be lost. Janet accepted my plea and said she would allow me to try but warned me that it would only need one MP to say 'no' at any stage and my efforts would be doomed.

I sat nervously in the Chamber looking across and around me to see who I might have offended over the years. As my very last item of business was called, I moved Second Reading (accepted); "that the Bill be committed to a committee of this House" (no objection) and "that the Bill be now considered" (agreed). The Sarjeant-at-Arms advanced, put the mace under the table and retreated. I then reported that no amendments had been tabled and that the Bill be reported to the House (none demurred). The Sarjeant then replaced the mace and I reported that the committee had considered the Bill without amendment. I then moved the Third Reading and there was no objection. It was through and on its way for Royal Assent. It was the most productive five minutes in my political career. For the record I should add that its twenty-two clauses extended to England & Wales what originally applied to only Inner London and dealt with the rights between neighbours when one of them wished to develop his land or premises when adjoining the boundary line of the other.

Back to more conventional parliamentary business and whatever initiatives John Major took, the stock of the Government fell, three of our backbenchers defected, more Ministers were forced to resign and eventually our fragile majority disappeared. David Lightbown's seat in Staffordshire fell to Labour with a 22 per cent swing and in the last by-election of the Parliament my only other namesake in all my years in the Commons arrived when Ben Chapman won Wirral South for Labour with a 17 per cent swing. In the year before, the Scott Report into the sale of arms to Iraq damaged the Government's standing further, as did the outbreak of the "mad cow" disease with the EU banning all British beef exports. When the Government promised a referendum if it ever recommended entry into the single currency, Labour responded similarly. Truly it was all gloom and doom for the Tories as time ran out. Eventually the Prime Minister dissolved Parliament in mid-March and called the election for May Day. A distress signal indeed.

At the start of the campaign opinion polls put Labour on 50 per cent of the vote, Conservatives with just under 30 and the Liberal Democrats hovering around ten. The prospect of six weeks campaigning put a chill down the spine of most candidates and much of the electorate whose boredom was clearly evident to canvassers. The opinion polls reported little shift in allegiances except support for the Lib-Dems moving up to 15 per cent.

In Chipping Barnet, the omens were not good with six other candidates standing, including a self-made millionaire friend who decided to stand as a Looney. Of his twelve nominators, I knew six of them personally and the other fringe candidates came from the Referendum,

196

Pro-Life and Natural Law Parties. My main opponents were Geoff Cooke for Labour, a forty-nine-year-old software engineer who had been a Barnet councillor for eight years and Sean Hooker for the Lib-Dems, a thirty-one-year-old insurance underwriter. They were both thoroughly decent people and, as usual, we were left alone by the national media as we were not expected to hit the headlines. Recent boundary changes had reduced the seats in Barnet Borough from four to three, resulting in my electorate increasing by over 12,000. However, the effect was minimal: the psephologists calculated that there was only a 1 per cent disadvantage to me while my majority (due to the increased electorate) would increse by a notional 2000. With the opinion polls suggesting a Labour lead over the Tories of about 20 per cent compared with a 7.5 per cent Tory lead at the previous election, the prospect was a swing to Labour of nearly 14 per cent. Statistically, it needed only a further 1 per cent swing to get me out.

As soon as I started my door-to-door canvassing, I could feel the wind of change. Very few Barnetonians were explicitly telling me that they would no longer support me, just that they "had yet to decide" or they could understand others saying "it was time for a change." What might be working for me, I optimistically hoped, was the level of recognition and friendliness I encountered (doubtless the feeling of any long established MP) combined with the hope that, since we were going to lose the election, some might still vote for me in order to avoid a massive majority for Labour (the opposite of my fear in the 1983 campaign). In the last week I was saying discreetly to some wavering supporters that "if the gap is still the same come polling day, Labour is going to win in any case but do you want me out as well?" I knew the result would be bad but self delusion had again set in and my calculation was that I would survive with a majority halved or, at worst, of 5,000. My new agent Stephen Payne, already a veteran of local and national elections, had methodically plotted where and when I should canvass as well as the literature to be distributed. He had also encouraged me to lead our team of supporters in mutual help to my colleague Ian Twinn in his wafer-thin marginal of Edmonton on five occasions as well as my taking a weekend off to help David Lightbown's widow Ann fight Tamworth and fellow ex-Whip Irvine Patnick in Sheffield Hallam. Stephen clearly knew our result would be very close when he asked me to deliver personally signed letters to targetted voters late on the eve of poll and suggested that I personally telephoned known supporters on election day instead of visiting polling stations.

There was a new venue for counting the votes in the Borough: a recently built Sports Centre in Hendon, across the South Circular road from Brent Cross Shopping Centre. This provided more spacious accommodation than the Town Hall and easier access between all three counts. And so it was that I saw with mounting horror my colleagues John Marshall losing Finchley & Golders Green with a swing of 15 per cent, followed by John Gorst being thrown out of Hendon with a swing of over 16 per cent. At my count, the Conservative and Labour rows of ballot papers lying on the table were pretty evenly matched throughout but with mine holding a slight edge. Finally the Chief Executive of the Borough, Leo Boland, acting as Returning Officer in the absence of the Mayor Pam Coleman attending her son Iain's triumph in Hammersmith & Fulham, spoke to our agents to tell them the result before publicly announcing it. Immediately Labour's agent, a youngish girl, demanded a recount. I saw Leo looking slightly surprised, giving the impression that a recount was unnecessary. However, presumably not wanting to to be at the centre of any political row, he ordered that all the hundred vote bundles of ballot papers be re-checked. A very long half-hour later it turned out that one bundle had a vote cast for the Labour candidate on top with the ninety-nine underneath for me. This meant that the original count had reduced my majority by 198 and it was now 1,035 instead of 837. I reckon the

Labour agent learnt a counting lesson that night: leave well alone, especially when her Party could have boasted that they had cut my hitherto five figure majority to a meagre three.

The turnout in Chipping Barnet was down by over 7 per cent and my vote was reduced to 21,000. The Referendum Party candidate received nearly 1,200 votes (more than my majority) and the other three candidates mustered 650 between them (the Loony candidate claiming 250). I returned home at about 5am to the dawn of a new morning with the first flowering of the climbing plant outside my front door: it was a red rose. I had been very lucky. The swing against me was 14 per cent but I was surrounded by four other Conservative seats which had all been lost by swings of well over 15 per cent; in one it was almost 19 per cent. The number of Tory seats in London fell from 48 to 11.

The epicentre of this political earthquake had been in the suburbs around the main cities and the number of Tory seats was halved. Labour won two-thirds of all the constituencies with an overall majority of 178. The Lib-Dems more than doubled their representation in the Commons to 46 even though their vote declined by 750,000 (for once the electoral system moved in their direction). Labour's vote increased by nearly 2 million while the Tories fell by almost 4,500,000. The final polls had slightly underestimated the Tory support and less slightly overestimated Labour's strength. Even so, few expected such a huge Labour majority. Anji Hunter, Tony Blair's new gatekeeper at No. 10 whom I had known for some years, told me that they were hoping at best for an overall majority of 70 to 80. Seven Cabinet ministers were defeated, including Michael Portillo in next door Southgate, Malcolm Rifkind and Tony Newton.

The new House of Commons was, of course, vastly different. In addition to the defeated Tory MPs, over 70 had retired and among the record number of Labour MPs elected were over one hundred women. When the House met, I found myself on the Opposition benches for the first time and witnessed the new Labour MPs applauding instead of shouting the customary "hear, hear." Profound changes were being planned by the new Government. First, Tony Blair arbitrarily decided to answer PM's Questions only once a week for half-an-hour on Wednesdays instead of fifteen minutes on Tuesdays and Thursdays. To the outsider it is difficult to convey the disadvantage to the Opposition of such a change. Then there was to be a radical reform of the procedures and business of the House, imposed by the brute strength of the Government's majority. It would be churlish to pretend that all the changes were for the worse. For example, I had long advocated the sensible time tabling of all Bills in Committee and this was at last introduced. What was wrong was the brief and insufficient time allotted to examining the more controversial and far-reaching measures, with whole swathes of Clauses undebated when sent to the Lords. Never had the Upper House had such a crucial role to perform and its hours of sitting expanded in consequence, often exceeding those of the Commons.

This was because another major change was made in our hours of sitting. The business of the House was curtailed after 10 o'clock. This had the deleterious effect of reducing backbenchers' rights to speak. Matters which hitherto had been discussed after the new deadline were "taken as read" and voted on by ballot in the Division Lobbies immediately after Prime Minister's Questions (judged to be the time most MPs would be around). Eventually it was decided to have morning sittings on Tuesdays, Wednesdays and Thursdays so that the business could be concluded by seven in the evening. This was clearly more convenient to the 'Blair Babes' with more friendly family hours. Added to all this was the propensity of Ministers to make important announcements to the media before Parliament, a practice which was denounced by Madam Speaker (Betty had been unanimously re-elected).

An additional problem facing the Tories was quite simply one of numbers. When Labour had its nadir in 1983, it still won over 200 seats and I always thought that this was the minimum necessary for the Official Opposition to be an effective force. Here we were, sparsely covering the green leather, while the Government benches truly overflowed. There was also the factor of the Lib-Dems, now more than one-quarter of the Tories. They began to realise the need for a collective and planned strategy instead of the scatter gun approach when they had relatively few Members. It was essential for all the Tory hands to be seen on deck and the real problem was in major debates when often there were less than half a dozen on our side after the front bench opening speeches. So much had to be done in Committees outside the Chamber and there was to be the new Westminster Hall debates which restored some of the lost "post 10 o'clock" business (without voting) and provided additional hours of sitting so that the Government could claim that debating time had not been curtailed. This was so, but sometimes sittings were in both places at the same time. With all these alternative calls on MPs' time, it became less likely to find us being prepared to wait for hours to speak. Luckily for us, the inexperience on the government backbenchers was such that many of them deserted the Chamber during the more humdrum business and we were rarely embarrassingly outnumbered. But we did have the additional problem of former Ministers. Over a third of the previous administration had lost their seats apart from those who had retired and therefore experience was at a premium on the Opposition front bench. There was some consolation in having lost so badly, but it was pretty thin gruel: a better chance of being called to speak or ask a supplementary Question, given the tradition of the Speaker calling Members alternatively from each side of the House; while voting in the Division Lobbies became an infinitely more comfortable experience for us, as if we were strolling in Hyde Park instead of resembling sheep going through a dip.

Back in Chipping Barnet, Phase 1 of the new Barnet General had opened the month before the General Election but this clearly hadn't help me electorally. In the summer of 1998 new trains at long last surfaced on the Northern Line but this resulted in complaints that there were fewer trains because all of the forty year old rolling stock had been withdrawn. "Short term pain for long term gain" was the recycled message from the Managing Director of London Underground, Denis (now Lord) Tunnicliffe. The latest threats to the Green Belt included a proposal to build a park-and-ride station between Barnet and Potters Bar which would have severed the remaining open space between the metropolis and the Hertfordshire town. I campaigned with the new Labour MP for Southgate, Stephen Twigg, against the proposal and soon found myself cooperating with the two new Barnet MPs, Rudi Vis (Finchley) and Andrew Dismore (Hendon) promoting our Borough's interests in Parliament.

The Labour-Liberal coalition on the Council just kept its majority at the May 1998 local elections and Geoff Cooke, my Labour opponent a year before, won a seat from us in the Brunswick Park Ward while a new twenty-five year old Conservative candidate, James Chapman, topped the poll in the safe Friern Barnet Ward, ahead of the two veteran Tory councillors. I like to think that his surname was the reason for this! After these elections my Association's secretary retired after twenty-one years' service to my three agents. Pam Carpenter had been appointed in 1977 and had become a fixed beacon and much liked person in an ever changing office. On the family front Laura was enjoying some academic success. She had sung a solo at the annual schools concert in the Royal Albert Hall and became head girl at Haberdashers' Aske's in 1996. She then went on to Homerton College Cambridge and took the four year B.Ed. course. In her last year she became engaged to a tree surgeon with the appropriate name of Andy Woods. Michael had been at Queen Elizabeth's, a former grammar and now grant maintained school, just round the corner and was to begin a four year course (with an additional gap year after the third) in computer design technology at Oxford Brookes University. The 1999 University academic year, Laura's last and Michael's first, was to prove a very expensive one for their father, making a sizeable hole in his net parliamentary income, although Laura had escaped the newly imposed £1,000 tuition fee as her course had commenced before its introduction.

When the new Government introduced tuition fees, I put this barbed point to Education Secretary David Blunkett: "In a quiet moment of contemplation, does not the Right Honourable Gentlement think it ironic that it is a Labour Government which is responsible for our education system no longer being free to all students at the point of delivery?" He was not best pleased; indeed, he was incandescent with rage. I had obviously struck a sensitive chord as I did with Environment Secretary John Prescott when he was attending a conference abroad which clashed with his Question Time. Normally the minister answering the first question would apologise for the absence of his senior colleague, explaining the reason. This did not happen and I raised the matter on a point of order with The Speaker. When I next saw John after his return, he bitterly complained about what I had done, but it was his junior minister's fault in not courteously observing the convention of the House.

The new Government basked in the beam of public approval while Tony Blair determined to show that his ministers were competent in the economic management of the country and could win a second full term of office, both of which previous socialist administrations had failed to achieve. The Cabinet was downgraded from decision-taking and the Whips' Office was thrown out of 12 Downing Street to make way for Alistair Campbell. Presidential government was strengthened. There was a vast increase in political appointments in the Civil Service with dual leadership at the top. Gordon Brown apparently had a veto on much of the domestic agenda as well as complete control in the Treasury. It was rumoured that Blair had no inkling of what was to be in Brown's first Budget until the day before it was delivered and it was the Chancellor who decided and announced what the five economic tests would be before Britain might join the Euro.

The Prime Minister strutted his stuff on the world stage, committing troops in Sierra Leone, bombing Iraq to enforce the no-fly zone and urging a reluctant President Clinton to launch NATO air attacks on Serbia in the Spring of 1999. He put considerable effort and risk into securing the Good Friday agreement in Northern Ireland (without the Democratic Unionists) and set about constitutional reform with the new Scottish Parliament, Welsh Assembly and Greater London Authority and Mayor with new PR systems for all of them and the European elections. The European Court of Human Rights pronouncements were incorporated into UK law and a Freedom of Information Act introduced. I served on the Standing Committee examining the GLA Bill and was dismayed to see the word 'chair' instead of 'chairman' introduced. I railed against this, observing that my name was Chapman, not Chap, and the chairman was no inanimate object. I asked if I should change my name to Person-Person, pointing out that even the last syllable was suspect.

Gordon Brown initially stuck to the public expenditure plans announced by the previous Conservative Chancellor, Ken Clarke. He imposed a £5 billion windfall tax on the privatised utilities and then taxed dividends received by pension funds which brought in much more. National Insurance contributions were increased and other "stealth taxes" introduced. All this led to a sizeable Budget surplus and when the new triennial expenditure plans were announced in 1998 they showed a £40 billion rise in spending, mostly on education and the NHS. When boasting about this increased spending, Brown introduced the concept of triple counting adding together the rises for each of the three years. Thus the announcement of a £18 billion increase in education meant a £3 billion rise in each year which Brown calculated as £3 billion the first year, £3 billion plus £3 billion the next; and £3 billion plus £3 billion plus £3 billion in the third year. The new Chancellor inherited a good legacy: economic growth had started five years before with inflation firmly under control, unemployment falling and interest rates dropping. This trend continued, Brown's reputation grew as a prudent Chancellor and the popularity of the Government remained high in spite of charges of sleaze when the ban on tobacco adverts on Formula One car racing was delayed after Bernie Ecclestone's £1 million donation to the Labour Party.

At the beginning of the Parliament I had been elected a member of the Executive of the Conservative MPs 1922 Committee under the chairmanship of Sir Archie Hamilton, the former Defence Minister, thus becoming one of the men in grey suits who oversaw the running of the Party in the Commons. An early responsibility for the Committee was to oversee the election of a new leader following John Major's immediate resignation. Five candidates stood in the first round with Ken Clarke having the support of forty-eight colleagues, William Hague forty-one, John Redwood twenty-seven, Peter Lilley twenty-four and Michael Howard twenty-three. In round two Ken was still just ahead of William but when Redwood was eliminated the final result was Hague with 92 to Clarke's 72. Our new leader was a mature thirty-six year old Yorkshire lad who had become an MP only eight years before and a Cabinet Minister aged thirty-four. I voted for William principally because I felt we needed a new start led by a younger MP. But even with our Party being led by someone more youthful than Tony Blair himself, it was a bleak and unpromising political future which faced my Party as 2000 approached. On the eve of each new year, MPs are usually asked to send a message to their constituents via the local media but I felt the approach of the new millennium deserved more than merely wishing them a merry Christmas and a healthy, happy and prosperous new year. I sent a more meaningful but uncharacteristically apocalyptic message:

> "When Jesus Christ was born, an estimated 133 million people inhabited the earth. It took 1830 years for the world's population to reach 1 billion and then only a further hundred to reach 2 billion. Today, over 6 billion occupy mother earth; a figure expected to grow to 10 billion by 2050 AD.
>
> Today, one-quarter of the globe's inhabitants are over-nourished while the other three-quarters suffer malnutrition. The world's demand for water has increased by 50% in the last twenty years, yet fresh water is limited. We have destroyed 70% of our forests and if we continue to chop down our rain forests all of them will have disappeared by 2027. In the last twenty-five years, over 700 million acres of land has been lost to desert and the same amount to urbanisation. The area of land for food per person has been halved in the last quarter of this departing century.
>
> We are polluting our seas, lakes and rivers with a vengeance. The oceans and seas cannot provide more food because if overfishing continues, stocks will decline still further...
>
> The future for mankind looks bleak unless decisive action is taken urgently and international co-operation dramatically improved. Fertilisers and pesticides have helped to provide more food but the changing chemical composition of the atmosphere ...has resulted in acid rain destroying forests, plants and water creatures. We have to develop new products which reduce risks to and help sustain our environment... Achieving sustainable development world-wide will require rich nations to give practical and financial aid to poorer ones...
>
> Should we be optimistic or pessimistic? I leave you with this thought. History is redolent with Jeremiahs thinking the worst but the human

spirit and science and technology have repeatedly
proved them wrong.
I put my hope and trust in the faith, imagination,
innovation and enterprise of the human race."

The last fifty words of hope were added to minimise the
risk of an editor heralding the message with the headline:
"Approaching Armageddon" but I need not have feared.
The article was not published by any local newspaper
but belatedly saw the light of day in the Spring 2000
edition of *Science in Parliament*.

The first week of the new millennium would see me
moving into a more modest house in Chipping Barnet,
downsizing after the children had flown the family nest,
and the first year would see me reaching pensionable
age and Laura getting married. Not long after there
would have to be another general election with my
Party's fortunes still in the doldrums. A changing and
challenging time was in prospect.

19

PORTCULLIS & EUROPE

U pon returning to Westminster after the 1997 Election Patrick McLoughlin, the Opposition Pairing Whip and no.3 in the pared down office, asked to see me. He had become an MP at the age of twenty-nine in 1986, holding West Derbyshire in the by-election caused by Matthew Parris's departure to ITV. Patrick was our only ex-miner and Margaret made him a junior minister three years later. However, he seemed much more comfortable in Government as a Whip and John Major sent him there in 1995. He has flourished in our parliamentary party's engine room ever since. We had become good friends (though we were never Whips together) and I had spoken at a dinner in his constituency wherein my brother had lived.

I offered to come to his room but he insisted on coming to mine, a sure sign that he had a favour to request. He duly asked if I would accept nomination for the chairmanship of the Accommodation & Works Committee so that I would be responsible for overseeing the building of Portcullis House, providing much needed additional accommodation for MPs. "You are the right person as our only architect in the House," he hopefully observed. This must have been one of the shortest straws to draw in the new Parliament with the media ready to pounce on any hiccup in seeing through the construction of the most expensive building per sq. ft. in the country. I would be the fall guy if it was not completed on time and within its very considerable budget. I could already picture the fleets of lorries bringing materials to the site being seen as part of a never ending gravy train feathering the nests of MPs. I accepted this poisoned chalice which included overseeing the Commons end of the Houses of Parliament and other outbuildings on the Parliamentary estate.

The go-ahead for the building had been given in 1992 by the then Housing Minister Sir George Young and was costed at £165 million. Designed by Sir Michael Hopkins, it covered the same ground floor area as Westminster Hall. Construction work could not start until excavation work for the Jubilee Line extension below the existing Underground Station had been completed. The site was handed over to us at the end of 1997, eleven months late after problems in tunnelling; and, with building inflation costs, further security measures and new statutory health, safety and fire regulations, the revised cost was now £250 million. The reason the building was so expensive was that it had to be constructed over the deepest hole in Europe (as a result of the excavations for the new Jubilee Line station) with more durable materials such as aluminium bronze and natural stone befitting a new building next to the Palace of Westminster. The accommodation included over two hundred offices for MPs, nearly two hundred desk spaces for their staff; fifteen Committee Rooms, refreshment facilities and shops for the public. The six largest committee rooms were to be given names and it was agreed that one of them should be called The Boothroyd Room after Madam Speaker. I suggested that the Labour and Conservative Parties should choose the names of two each and the Liberals the other one, offering the Government Party the largest. Happily, all the names which emerged related to statesmen from the second half of the twentieth century: Attlee, Wilson, Macmillan, Thatcher and Grimond (Churchill's name had already been allocated to a House of Commons dining room). There was to be a direct underground pedestrian link from the Palace and the new building would be constructed on a vast concrete platform supported over Westminster tube station by six huge columns over one hundred feet deep. The project was to take three years from the handover by London

Underground. This meant that completion was due at the beginning of 2001.

The public prints did not disappoint me. The most frequent charge was that the building cost £1.2 million for each MP. This figure was derived by simply dividing the total cost of the project by the number of MPs' offices, conveniently forgetting the offices for staff, committee rooms and other accommodation which would be used by all MPs and staff throughout Parliament. Another erroneous assertion was that £15,000 was to be spent on furniture in each office – the figure was about £2,000 – and, unlike most new parliamentary buildings overseas, there was no provision for a bed or individual washing facilities.

I prepared myself for further onslaught from our fourth estate. My first line of defence would be to emphasise the unavoidable costs of the underground works and the stark fact that the alternative to the project would be no building at all on the site. If this failed to assuage the tabloids, I would pull up the metaphorical drawbridge of Portcullis House and talk about the need for a permanent edifice befitting its next door neighbour, one of the best known buildings in the world. If this argument failed I would retire into my keep, admit that the project was very expensive and refer obliquely to the security costs involving bomb shields and special windows. Finally, if all else failed, I would desperately observe from my dungeon that the building was indeed horrendously expensive but would cost a mere one-third of the Millennium Dome and would likely last much longer.

Progress on construction was good, not least because each different prefabricated section had been tested and fitted to its neighbour before being taken to the site and assembled. An independent assessment of the project half way during construction was favourable and Portcullis House was completed three months ahead of schedule costing £234 million, more than £15 million less than estimated. Nonetheless, this didn't stop the media complaining about the imagined overspend and delay. We were even criticised for the cost and species of trees to be put in the new courtyard, at first complaining that we had not chosen a native specimen – we couldn't because only a sub-tropical tree could survive under its glazed roof – and then the cost of them. We had decided to rent the trees so that, if any of them didn't flourish, they would be replaced without cost. In the BBC Radio 4's *Today* programme, John Humphreys (luckily for me in one of his more kindly moods) observed that he could buy a tree from his local garden centre for ten quid. Having explained the sub-tropical point, I chanced my arm and told him that if he could buy the more than twenty foot high fig trees for a tenner each in his local outlet, I would personally eat all the figs on them. I never told him nor anyone else that the species – recommended to us by Kew Gardens – was called a *weeping* fig.

The foundation stone was laid by Speaker Boothroyd in 1998 and the topping out ceremony took place in July 1999 when, as chairman of the committee, I was presented with a heavy brass cross with appropriate words on it (I appreciated the meaning of this gesture without the need for any inscription). Another renewal of my acquaintance with Her Majesty took place when she formally opened Portcullis House at the beginning of 2001, after MPs had started moving there in the autumn before. Only upon completion of the project was it possible for every MP to have his own office though some of them in the Palace remain very small. I was approached to see which one I would like to occupy in the new building but utter propriety overwhelmed me and I declined the invitation. In truth, I preferred to stay where I was - close to the Chamber. The public's initial perception of the building was mixed but I am confident that in time it will be admired. Michael Hopkins had worked hard on a design that would fit in with its illustrious neighbour without having to sacrifice a modern style to replicate the character of its 'big brother.' My only concern was that the fourteen huge 'funnels' which draw in fresh and expel stale air would be too dominant, while the completed building was darker than I anticipated. It was soon dubbed the 'Titanic' by some and an 'upturned table' by others but I consoled myself with the thought that the beautiful King's College Chapel Cambridge is affectionately known as 'the upturned sow.'

*   *   *

Not long after leaving the Government in 1995 I was approached about being appointed to the Council of Europe. After my brief encounter with one of their get togethers on housing standards in Stockholm in the early 1970s, I politely declined. A year later I was prevailed upon again to let my name go forward on the understanding that a General Election was not far away and, if I didn't like the experience, I could back out in the new Parliament. I reluctantly agreed and set out to learn more about this little known organisation which hardly registers on the public radar screen.

The Council of Europe was founded in 1949, predating the EEC. In the aftermath of World War II it had been set up to promote greater unity among countries which subscribed to democracy, human rights and the rule of law. Depending upon exactly where the Continent ends and Asia begins, there are forty-seven countries in Europe and, today, forty-six of them are CoE members (the odd one excluded is Belarus). In case you have difficulty in finding all the countries I should add they include Andorra, Liechtenstein, Monaco and San Marino. The two parts of the CoE are the Council of Ministers (the Foreign Ministers of each country) and the Parliamentary Assembly (PACE) with numbers from each country roughly in proportion to their populations but with a minimum of four and a maximum of thirty-six. Representatives are appointed from their national parliaments: half of them are members and the others substitutes, who can attend but only vote when recorded as the substitute for an absent member. There were about 280 members when I first attended (now 315). The thirty-six UK representatives were appointed in strict proportion to Party numbers.

PACE meets four times a year in Strasbourg but it begets a number of committees which convene during the week-long quarterly sessions and sometimes in between. There were two contrary views about the Council. The first was to echo Winston Churchill's dictum that "to jaw-jaw is always better than to war-war" and realise that the CoE was set up after our Continent had been involved in internecine warfare three times in the previous eighty years. If parliamentarians could meet and talk, this would make us all more understanding of each other. The other view was that the Council was a complete waste of time and money. I soon realised that both views were valid but since the Council costs little money, I reckon Winston's point prevailed. A considerable achievement of the Council was setting up the European Convention on Human Rights in 1950 under which the Commission and Court of Human Rights was established.

Having been officially appointed by the Prime Minister, I was unable to attend the January 1997 session of the Assembly as I had Commons and Constituency engagements already accepted and it turned out that none of us attended the April session (except retiring MPs) as this was in the middle of our General Election campaign. My first appearance in Strasbourg was in June, which was the last meeting of the old delegation - it was a few months before Mr Blair confirmed the new representatives. When this was done, there were 29 Labour MPs appointed, nine Conservatives, three Liberals and an Ulster Unionist. David Atkinson (a former YC National Chairman) was our Party leader (following Sir Anthony Durant in the previous Parliament, who had been national organising secretary of the YCs when I was the chairman). David cornered me early on to ask if I would agree to be our Whip, citing my long experience in this office at Westminster. I kept a straight face and said I would on one condition: that I could call myself the "Chief Whip." The deal was done. My title was a sinecure as only four of our nine representatives had votes. The new leader of the UK delegation was Terry Davis, a Birmingham MP, who was to be elected the Secretary-General of the organisation in 2003.

One of the agreeable side effects of being a parliamentary member of CoE was to meet the spouses of colleagues who could come along at their own expense. Many did (at least to some of the sessions) and so I met such people as Anne Davis, Jacqui Vis, Laura Wray (wife of Jimmy) Phyllis Rapson (wife of Sydney) and Lynda Malins, wife of Humfrey. Her husband is, in my opinion, one of my most underrated colleagues and has sat only intermittently on our front bench. Another colleague, alas no more, was Michael Colvin who was frequently accompanied by his wife Nicola, the life and soul of any gathering. Michael seemed never to be parted from his sketchbook and had a rare talent for quickly drawing and water colouring street scenes and landscapes as he saw them. Sometimes they resembled upmarket cartoons but he had an enviable gift (in the genre of Nicholas Ridley). Shortly after I had spoken at his Romsey constituency dinner and stayed the night in their beautiful home, they died when it was consumed in flames one night at the beginning of the millennium.

While few very well known MPs, such as former Ministers, become British representatives, this is not so with many other countries. In my time, former Prime Ministers who subsequently became members of the Assembly included Silvio Berlesconi of Italy and John Bruton of Ireland, while four colleagues went on to become Presidents of their countries including Abdullah Gul in Turkey and Mikheil Saakashvili in Georgia.

David Atkinson first became a member of PACE in 1979 and served us almost continuously thereafter. He has devoted much of his political career to human rights' issues and probably knows more about the Council of Europe and its personalities than anyone else. He became chairman of the European Democrat Group on PACE in which British Conservative members invariably took a leading role, including the redoubtable Baroness (Jill) Knight, the former Birmingham MP who is a bundle of energy and a consummate teller of some extremely funny stories.

UK MPs appointed to PACE are also put on the Defence and Security organisation, the Western European Union. Originally the Brussels Treaty Organisation, it was founded by Britain, France and the Benelux countries in 1948 to provide collective self defence and economic and social collaboration. This became the WEU in 1954 with the addition of Italy and West Germany and now has twenty-eight countries in various forms of attachment. In 1999, the European Union and NATO wanted to establish a direct relationship on conflict prevention and crisis management but co-operation between the two always seemed flawed to me as not all NATO members belong to the EU, such as Turkey, Norway and Iceland, while some EU members are not part of NATO. The WEU Assembly, with fewer members than PACE, meets for three days in Paris biannually, with interim committee meetings held mainly there or in Brussels. Sir Dudley Smith, a great friend and parliamentary colleague for many years, was President of the Assembly just before I became a member.

*　　*　　*

Back at Westminster, the new millennium confirmed the continuing popularity of the Government, even though Labour had been beaten badly in the 1999 European elections and sleaze was rearing its ugly head in the new administration. At the end of February 2000, the ballot for Prime Minister's Questions smiled upon me (it had done so only twice before since Mr Blair answered) and I found myself waiting impatiently to be called. Just before the moment came, I received a scribbled note from The Speaker asking if I would refer to an exceptional anniversary: fifty years since Edward Heath became an MP. The Father of the House had served continuously for half-a-century and neither Blair nor William Hague had referred to this achievement. Keyed up though I was to put a hopefully pertinent point to the PM, I knew that Betty would not cut me short if I spoke too long, so I was able to preface my question by inviting "the Prime Minister and the House to join with me in congratulating my Right Honourable Friend the Member for Old Bexley & Sidcup on being first elected to this House on this very day fifty years ago and continuously serving his constituents with distinction since then ..." It was only later that a colleague told me that someone on our side of the House had muttered "creep" and even Ted didn't show any sign of acknowledgement. Nevertheless, Mr Blair responded appropriately and I consoled myself by concluding that you can't win them all.

A happier occasion was the election of my agent, Stephen Payne, to the chairmanship of the National Association of Conservative Agents with its annual dinner on the eve of the Party Conference attended by the leader. Traditionally, the agent's MP gives the vote of thanks and it so happened that the 2000 dinner was on the final day of the Sydney Olympics. I introduced myself as unique among all politicians in that I was the only one with an Olympic Games named after him. I was reminded later by William Hague that this was not true: Lord Melbourne, Queen Victoria's first Prime Minister, had the 1956 Games but he told me that Ffion and he had found the remark very funny. I returned the compliment by promising William that I would actively support The Hague for the site of the next Games.

Although Labour got a drubbing in the May local elections and Peter Mandelson was forced to resign from the Cabinet for the second time at the beginning of 2001, such events appeared to have little effect on the opinion polls which had given the Government a consistent double figure lead throughout the Parliament with the exception of a nine-day wonder in the autumn of 2000 when the Tories went ahead after protests erupted about high fuel prices and road blockades had been set up by some farmers and road hauliers. There seemed to be two certainties about the impending election: that it would be held on 3 May and Labour would win with another landslide. One of these predictions proved wrong – the date. An outbreak of foot and mouth caused the poll to be delayed by a month.

Back in Chipping Barnet, I prepared for my sixth election campaign in the constituency and ninth in the country. This one was to be different: for the first time I was targeted by Labour, who were hoping to win the seat after in-depth polls suggested that professionals were deserting the Tories in droves and my patch was identified as one with a heavy percentage of them. *The Times* followed this line up when a senior reporter with photographer was sent to interview me. It was a rain-sodden day but this didn't prevent dozens of photos being taken and the one selected in next day's paper showed the back of a wind-swept, head bent Conservative candidate engaging a grim faced widow on her doorstep. The caption underneath proclaimed: "Managers on verge of sacking their knight" and the article confirmed the apparent psephological trend. I was slightly miffed (how thin-skinned and sensitive you can get during a campaign) when my description of Chipping Barnet as "the place where London meets Hertfordshire and the metropolis meets the countryside" was quoted in the article but unattributed. We were duly battening down the political hatches when a small piece of good fortune came to hand. The month's delay in calling the election meant son David becoming a father a few days before the campaign commenced. Agent Stephen Payne sent me hot foot to the Queen Elizabeth Hospital in Welwyn to be photographed with my first grandchild with mother Lindsay and this was printed in my introductory leaflet. The two most frequent remarks made to me when I went canvassing were: "we hadn't realised that you may lose the seat" and "by the way, congratulations on becoming a grandfather," whereupon I feigned modesty, mumbling that it was easy when you knew how.

I had only two opponents this time. Damien Welfare, forty-three, the Labour candidate hailing from Islington and a seasoned politician, having fought Spelthorne fourteen years before. He was described in the local press as "a full-time student completing his training to become a barrister" and he had beaten my previous opponent Geof Cooke to win the nomination. I was suitably impressed by his surname, more so than that of Sean Hooker standing again for the Lib-Dems and fortified by winning a seat on the Council for the nearby Mill Hill ward in the previous year's local elections.

Come polling day and again I continued to canvas support and visited only a few of the polling stations in the evening. Although we felt that there had been a small swing to us since 1997, I came to the count forearmed in my mind with two speeches: one thanking the good people for again re-electing me and the other resignedly dusting down my "back to the drawing board" comment which I reckoned would have been forgotten in the mists of time.

The shocking event of the day was the low turnout, down from nearly 72 per cent to just over 60 per cent in Barnet and to less than that in the country. While I was relieved to have held the seat with a swing of just under 2 per cent and a majority of 2,700, my vote was down by 1,600 and the turnout down by 7,000. There were 3,000 fewer Labour votes and Sean Hooker was again a distant third. The media had been waiting patiently for an upset but TV cameras were switched off as soon as the result became known when I stood on the right of the Returning Officer. After the short speeches following the declaration, I left the platform and was immediately accosted by a reporter from *The Times* to be asked if I was going to retire. I told him with an edge of feeling that I hadn't fought a hard campaign just to resign.

In the country, the result was almost a carbon copy of 1997. Labour lost only six seats (overall), the Lib-Dems gained six while we managed to increase our number by a massive one. As a socialist seer stated: "given an election on average every four years, the Tories can expect to be back in power in six hundred years time." In all, only 25 seats changed hands and 6 of these were in Northern Ireland which is always a political law unto itself. The overall vote was down by almost 5 million and in the overwhelming majority of constituencies sitting MPs (of whatever Party) seemed to have a slight edge in attracting a few extra votes from unenthusiastic supporters who otherwise would have joined the more than 18 million voters staying at home. It was with equal measures of personal relief and political concern that I returned to Westminster.

20

DINNERS IN THE HOUSE

Any event in the House has to be sponsored by an MP and many take place each week – on sitting days, Saturdays and during parliamentary recesses. Usually receptions and meals are under the jurisdiction of the Refreshment Department. I was unable to sponsor many events when I was a Birmingham MP because I was not in London on non-sitting days. However, I did arrange a 'twenty years after' dinner to mark the 1953 intake of fellow architectural students at Manchester University. On a Saturday evening in the autumn of 1973 more than forty of us sat down in an agreeable ambience, nostalgically and convivially recalling our student days. The timing of this reunion was both accurate and wise as I was no longer able to sponsor such events when I lost my seat less than six months later.

It was only when I became Chipping Barnet's MP that I could sponsor events more frequently and nearly all of them were in response to requests from others rather than initiatives by myself. The first was to be the host at the annual Faculty of Building Dinners which hitherto had been sponsored by Sir Graham Page, the Housing, Local Government & Development Minister in the Heath administration, who had died in 1981. Graham had been an intensely hardworking and competent minister who mastered the contents of any Bill with a solicitor's eagle eye for the small print. The Faculty of Building had been founded by the legendary Sir Alfred Bossom, born in 1881, who had trained as an architect, emigrated to New York, married the daughter of an oil magnate and enjoyed a career as a designer of banks and skyscrapers. He then returned to England at the age of forty-five and became the MP for Maidstone in 1931; a seat he held until 1959. Bossom was a generous host and at one time was Chairman of the Royal Society for the Arts, eventually receiving a Life Peerage. It was of his surname that Churchill mischevously remarked: "neither one thing nor the other." After Graham died, the Faculty, consisting of professionals throughout the construction industry, clearly chanced its arm in asking a far lesser known MP to be the sponsor. I hosted this perennial banquet in the large Members Dining Room for many years and was honoured to be made a Fellow of the Faculty in 1980, an Honorary Fellow in 1988 and President in the millennium year.

Not long after losing my Handsworth seat, I was asked by a person who had been Chairman of Aston University Conservatives and helped me in my two Birmingham election campaigns to be his guest at the annual dinner of the Sherlock Holmes Society of London. He was Philip Porter, then aged twenty-five, of lean countenance with a profusion of black hair flowing in all directions. This highlight of the Society's year had always been held in Charing Cross Hotel and I was soon made aware of two things: its members' profound knowledge of the works of Sir Arthur Conan Doyle and the genuine eccentricity of most of them, expressed in both sartorial appearance and the imagination of their minds. Philip was no exception but his enthusiasm for all things Sherlockian was matched by other interests, from renovating a Tudor farmhouse in deepest Worcestershire to hot air ballooning. He was also an airship pilot of some repute and is a prolific writer and motor memorabilia maniac who collects vintage cars. He met his match when his eyes alighted on Julie, an actress performing at a Jerome K. Jerome Society meeting, another esoteric literary outfit with which he had been associated for some years. They share their home with several cats which have always chosen to stay with them and been rewarded with names such as Holmes, Watson and Mycroft. Once they had a dog which just had to be named Moriarty.

His generosity extended to asking me to subsequent dinners and when I returned to the Commons and noticed that the size of the hotel's dining room was insufficient to meet demand, enquired if they would like me to sponsor their next dinner at Westminster. They accepted and the first gathering in the Members Dining Room (maximum sitting capacity of one hundred and eighty) was oversusubscribed by fifty and the following two by one hundred. And so the event had to be switched once again to a larger venue. They departed for the Café Royal and then the Langham Hotel but numbers dropped and in 1987 they returned for their Centenary Dinner with Merlyn Rees the former Home Secrtary as their guest of honour. Over the years, others have included P.D.James, Bill (now Lord) Deedes, Colin Dexter, Antony Hopkins and Stephen Fry. Traditionally the dinners were named after one of Conan Doyle's sixty stories and the guest speaker was expected to declaim about it or some aspect of the great detective. Most did so with considerable expertise but a notable exception had been Agatha Christie in 1962, who had politely declined to utter a single word. I enjoyed my few minutes of warming them up with a welcome speech and then relaxing for the rest of the evening but I was gobsmacked to be asked to be their guest of honour and give the main speech in 1996. The chosen adventure was *The Veiled Lodger*, the shortest and the only one in the canon in which Holmes did not appear. I picked on a reference in the opening paragraphs to a politician, a disused lighthouse and a trained cormorant which was never subsequently explained and took it upon myself to provide it in a flight of fancy which owed much to my warped imagination but did little to advance Holmesian research.

Philip Porter was chairman of the Society for some years but had another time-absorbing passion, Jaguar cars. He is the author of about fifteen books (so far) on this icon of the road and was over the moon in his air balloon when I managed to get Margaret Thatcher to write a foreword to one of them in 1986. Inevitably, he became chairman of the XK Club and, guess what, I agreed to sponsor their annual dinner in the Commons. All of them had been attended by Sir Stirling Moss and on one occasion I observed in my welcoming remarks that there must be many engineers in the room and confessed that I was an architect. This was greeted with dutiful jeers before I recited a ditty given to me by an ex-RIBA President Owen Luder:

"Roads and Bridges, Ports and Piers –
That's the stuff of Engineers.
Wine and Women, Drugs and Sex –
That's the scene of Architects."

At these dinners I reflected ruefully that I must have been the only person in the room who didn't own an XK, the opposite of Philip who possesses no less than four including the third one off the production line. He also owns the oldest E-type Jaguar in existence and another which starred in the film *The Italian Job* with Noel Coward and Michael Caine.

An even more eccentric group was the SODS Opera. SODS stood for the Society of Delectable Snufftakers. Goodness knows what Opera referred to but its members seemed to be mainly retired businessmen from the transport world. Sir Marcus Fox, former Chairman of the 1922 Executive, had hosted their annual lunches in the Commons but when he lost his seat in 1997 asked me to take over the sponsorship. I did, little knowing what lay ahead. Its members lunch eight times a year in different hostelries but traditionally have their special lunch with guests at Wesminster. Rumour has it that this used to be in the House of Lords but rowdiness had resulted in a non-renewal of the invitation. When I first arrived at the event, the welcome and hospitality was warm, the drink was flowing and the language truly overflowing. Tradition was that the Sponsor spoke at the end and then answered questions. On my first occasion, I must have been the only one there not in his cups

and when speech time came, I endeavoured to make a
light and witty contribution but I needn't have bothered.
Every point I made was greeted with sustained laughter
and applause (including one I hadn't finished making). I
couldn't believe my luck, until question-time came and
some very pertinent ones were asked concerning the
political situation of the day, including the then abject
state of the Tories. I gave serious answers to these and
everyone seemed satisfied, not least yours truly when
I received a generous cheque for a local charity of my
choice. At subsequent lunches I took the precaution of
clearing my diary of afternoon engagements and speaking
at the beginning, starting with a grace. The first one I
pinched from Marcus Fox (I felt he owed me a favour):

> "God, bless us for this food and wine
> And Lord bless those who sit and dine.
> And if long speech you must endure –
> Pray God you've got a good liqueur."

The following year I judged that a more apposite one was
relevant:

> "God bless this bunch,
> As they munch and crunch their lunch."

One year, my speech had gone down extremely well so
I gave it again the following year and no one seemed to
notice – or care. The members of this little known lunch
club were indeed a generous bunch and I atoned for
my one Friday autumnal afternoon off by ensuring that
a different local charity each year received a generous
donation.

Perhaps the most important political dinners that
I sponsored were in Dining Room "A" (which seated a
maximum of fifty-eight). The United & Cecil Club traces
its antecedents from 1881 (the year Benjamin Disraeli
died) and is reputedly the oldest political dining club
in the world. A group of Conservative barristers had

formed "The United Club" and a number of ex-Ministers and rising stars were the founders of "The Cecil Club," named after the 3rd Marquess of Salisbury who had become leader of the Conservatives upon Disraeli's death. In 1949 Winston Churchill, President of both clubs, arranged the merger and since then the Chairman had always been a senior MP. However, shortly after the centenary celebrations when Nicholas Scott retired, Brian Goswell became the first non-MP to be elected chairman but could not sponsor the dinners. Brian had been a YC but had chosen business ahead of politics. He was a Chartered Surveyor and had worked most of his life for the well known firm of Healey & Baker. I was elected Vice-Chairman and sponsor. Brian was followed by Lord Colnbrook (Sir Humphrey Atkins) in 1985, Sir Marcus Fox in 1989 and Tony Baldry in 2000. In the millennium year, three former PM's dined with the Club: Heath, Thatcher and Major; and on my sixty-fifth birthday William Hague was the guest speaker. Harold Macmillan had been the guest of honour just after his nintieth birthday in 1985. Luckily for the Club, sponsorship did not entail any speeches from me, except introductory ones when Marcus Fox could not be present. On one such occasion, our guest was Robin Ferrers, a distinguished looking long-serving Minister in the Lords. I did my usual pre-dinner research and was astounded to discover that his Lordship, born only six years before me, had first become a Minister in 1962 and had served under five Conservative Prime Ministers, from Macmillan to Major. I majored on this in my introduction: my fellow diners were impressed and the 13th Earl Ferrers was heard with due reverence.

Another political dining club was The Third Term Group, started by Andrew MacKay and Tim Yeo at the outset of the 1979 Parliament. They invited a dozen Tory MPs from across the Party spectrum to informal monthly gatherings, occasionally addressed by a Cabinet Minister. The Group's name was chosen to indicate our optimism for future elections and clearly we understated our success. Other members over the years have included Virginia Bottomley, Steve Norris, William Hague, Tim Boswell, David Heathcoat-Amory and Peter Atkinson.

Occasionally I was able to invite individuals to dinner, not least the officers of my Conservative Association. When I was the Vice-Chamberlain, I invited Sir Robert (now Lord) Fellowes, The Queen's Private Secretary, with his wife Jane. He was my main link with Her Majesty but it was the first time I had met his wife and, engaging in small talk during the first course asked her if she had any brothers or sisters. She replied that indeed she had one brother and sister and to my embarrassment suddenly I realised that they were Earl Spencer and Princess Diana!

Rarely was I able to accept invitations to dine out and then only subject to the business of the House. On one such occasion in the early 1970s, Edward du Cann, then Chairman of the 1922 Committee, invited a small group of us to his London home to have dinner with the former Governor of Texas, John Connally, who had also been shot in the same car when President Kennedy was assassinated in 1963. More recently, Speaker Martin invited me as a guest when he entertained the Chief Rabbi, Sir Jonathan Sacks, to dinner in his State Rooms in the Palace. I was delighted and honoured to find that I had been placed on the immediate right of the guest of honour and had the opportunity to talk to a person whom I had come to admire and respect, not least as leader of the Jewish community in the UK.

All of which leads me to admit that I am not only a unashamed name dropper but also a shame-faced place dropper.

21

MY LAST PARLIAMENT

U pon returning to Westminster at the beginning of the 2001 Parliament, I entered the Chamber and sat staring at more or less the same happy faces on the Government benches. This did little for my self confidence so I turned to see who was new among the Opposition ranks. There was a strangely familiar face among the Lib-Dems and for a moment I was transported back in time to 1970 and the spitting image of a young Christopher Chataway was with us again. I made enquiries and was told that the person in question was David Laws, Paddy Ashdown's successor in Yeovil. I then turned to look for any new colleagues behind me and could not believe my eyes. There was Mr Bean himself sitting among us but on further enquiries this turned out to be Paul Goodman, the new MP for Wycombe. Enough was enough and as soon as it was decent to do so, I repaired to the Tea Room and found myself sitting at a table with some new colleagues. After a few minutes our Chief Whip-to-be, David Maclean, hobbled in with his trade mark shepherd's crook. A few years before, David learnt that he had MS but, undaunted, busied himself about the place stoically bearing periodic outbursts of pain with fortitude. Among the new colleagues with me were David Cameron, just elected for Witney in the place of Sean Woodward - who had defected to Labour in the middle of the previous Parliament – and George Osborne, who followed the Independent Martin Bell in Tatton and had just celebrated his thirtieth birthday. I suddenly realised that I had first become an MP before he was born - just! As Maclean approached our table conversation ceased when he stooped, looked at me and exclaimed: "My god, did you really get re-elected?" Dutiful laughter ensued until the company saw my face feigning unadulterated fury. In an embarrassed silence, I spluttered: "Good heavens, I could have sworn that three years ago I attended your Memorial Service." Further laughter erupted with someone muttering "one-all" and more normal pleasantries continued.

On the day after the election, William Hague had announced his resignation as leader of our Party and his successor had to be chosen under new rules which essentially involved the top two choices of Tory MPs being put to a ballot of all members in the country. William had driven through the new rules as part of his priority to modernise the Party, giving all members a vote for the leadership. This resulted in a longer process than hitherto, not least as we had to elect a new chairman of the 1922 Committee following the retirement of Sir Archie Hamilton. The new occupant would be the returning officer and the first fortnight was taken up with this election. Sir Michael Spicer, a good friend, was chosen and he then set the wheels in motion. Michael Portillo was thought to be the favourite and though he led on the first ballot, obtained only 49 votes from the 166 electorate. Ken Clarke was favoured by the Tory left, Iain Duncan Smith by the right and Michael Ancram and David Davis were the other two contenders. They came equal fourth and so another round with the five candidates ensued. The third and final round resulted in Ken getting 59 votes, Iain 54 and Michael 53. It couldn't have been much closer and my colleagues had clearly sent an indistinct message to the 300,000 Party members who rallied to the more euro-sceptic candidate and returned Iain Duncan Smith with over 60 per cent of the votes. I plumped for Ken and thought it right to tell Iain this when congratulating him and pledging my loyalty. I sensed that he appreciated my frankness.

I was quite resigned to continuing as the Chairman of the Accommodation & Works Committee when Patrick McLoughlin again sought me out and asked if I wished to continue in the job. He hoped that I would but added that if I didn't want to, someone else had expressed a willingness to take over. I was both surprised and pleased, not least because I liked to do something different in each Parliament, so happily stood down and was succeeded by Derek Conway, a former fellow Government Whip who had lost his Shrewsbury seat in 1997 but had just been returned for Ted Heath's patch in Bexley. Nonetheless, I was extremely willing to continue as a member of the Council of Europe and the WEU.

I was now firmly established on the Environment Committee of the Council of Europe and in due course became a deputy chairman. It covered a wide range of responsibilities from the regions and local government to agriculture to the environment and there were three sub-committees to cover them. Given the main committee's name, the sub-committee covering the environment was called Sustainable Development and in due course I was elected its chairman. A happy consequence of this was that I was entitled to attend the World Summit on Sustainable Development held in Johannesburg in August 2002. This 'Earth Summit' was the fourth of its kind, the last one being Kyoto in 1997. These summits are usually disappointing events if only because the media hypes up expectations and Jonannesburg turned out to be no exception, but there was one specific commitment agreed: to halve the number of people without proper sanitation by 2015. We shall see. At a meeting of parliamentarians from all five continents I stressed the need to make plain to people the meaning of sustainable development: "We all talk about sustainable development but did our constituents know what we were on about?" I suggested a short and easy-to-understand definition: "conserving earth's finite resources for future generations." While one expert questioned whether all the globe's finite resources needed saving, I'm still waiting to hear a more apt and equally crisp definition. Also attending the Summit was fellow MP Alan Meale as chairman of PACE's Environment Committee and our Environment Secretary Margaret Beckett and her predecessor and Deputy PM, John Prescott, who seemed to regard me still with deep suspicion. Two things became vividly etched in my mind from the conference: the stark realisation that if any global agreement to save the world's fragile ecosystem was to be successful, tackling poverty, hunger and disease in the world's poorest countries was essential; and the developing countries (led by South Africa's Environment Minister) making it starkly plain that their industrial development was not going to be curtailed by any environmental limitations anymore than the developed world's had been in years gone by.

By far the most dominant and controversial political issue in the new Parliament was the invasion of Iraq in March 2003. After the 9/11 attacks on the twin-towers and the Pentagon in 2001, Tony Blair immediately recognised the significance of them and declared he would stand "shoulder to shoulder" with President Bush. When it became clear in 2002 that Bush was planning to invade Iraq, Blair supported him in spite of deep hostility from many Labour MPs. The British Prime Minister had to build a case for war and in September produced a dossier warning that Saddam Hussein had weapons of mass destruction which could be deployed within the hour. Before any invasion, Blair persuaded Bush to seek the backing of the UN and, back here, promised MPs a debate and vote, which took place in March. Blair was at his best and made a brilliant speech taking many interventions from his anxious backbenchers. He certainly impressed me and I told him so. Although the Government had a comfortable majority, no fewer than 139 Labour MPs voted against – over one-third of their total number. Air strikes started almost immediately and the war was swift, with US forces taking Baghdad within a month.

I agreed that we should actively support the Americans and take the opportunity to rid Iraq and its people of the evil of Saddam Hussein, believing that he did indeed have weapons of mass destruction. I also assumed that while the allies would win the war – and quickly – there would be a carefully thought out plan to win the peace and prevent Iranian insurgents from infiltrating the country. My worry was that the history of Iraq and its neighbours suggested otherwise and when I studied the voting lists it was not the extent of the Labour rebellion which caused me anxiety but the calibre of the sixteen of my colleagues who voted with them, some of whom I deeply admired and respected, including Peter Ainsworth, Tony Baldry, Kenneth Clarke, John Gummer and Humfrey Malins. The rest, as they say, is history but events clearly took their toll on the Prime Minister and relations between him and his increasingly impatient successor-in-waiting took an ugly turn. Mr Blair then made, I thought, a fatal mistake. He announced that he would lead his Party into a third general election (after recovering from a fit of depression which almost led him to give up) but then declared that he would not fight for a fourth term. Putting a time limit on office immediately causes uncertainty which feeds rumour and speculation. And so, I believe, it did. The WMD issue damaged Mr Blair's integrity; the Iraq invasion and aftermath destroyed people's confidence in him and the Hutton Inquiry (although clearing the PM and the Government of all charges) lost him the trust of the people. Although he was to win a third term with a comfortable albeit more than halved majority, I calculated that it was going to be down hill for him from then on.

In my heart I knew that the 2001 election would be my last campaign but my head told me not to make any public declaration too soon. However I felt it would be unfair to my association if I were to back down at the very end of the Parliament. Far better to make the announcment so that my successor could be selected with plenty of time to get around the constituency and be known, whenever the contest came. I made the announcement to my Executive Council early in 2003. I guessed – for once rightly – that the election would be on 5 May 2005 and by that time I would be approaching the biblical age of three score and ten with almost thirty years service as an MP. I knew that I would miss Westminster and my life in the constituency very keenly but I was also aware that it must be in my Party's interests to ensure that a new and younger person should now sit for Chipping Barnet on the green leather benches. After the announcement of my impending retirement, I received an extraordinarily generous letter from Iain Duncan Smith thanking me for my long service to the Party and I suddenly realised that it was fifty years to the day since I had first joined the Young Tories.

The due procedures for choosing a new candidate were put in place and almost two hundred Conservatives applied. About twenty of them were selected for interview, including the seven local candidates who had applied. I told my association that I preferred not to play any part in the selection process, leaving the judgement entirely to the committee and the final approval to all members. Eventually three were chosen to appear before all members. Exceptionally, if not uniquely, the trio were all women, though I was told that originally a man had been included but dropped out. The three were Pamela Chesters, then chairman of the Royal Free Hampstead Hospital NHS Trust who had fought Bristol West at the previous election and had also been leader of the opposition on next door Camden Council; Jane Ellison, a local councillor from Hendon; and Theresa Villiers, who was our no. 1 Greater London MEP. I calculated that Theresa would be the favourite because she was already well known by a large proportion of the selectors; and so it turned out. I had promised to give lunch to the successful candidate and officers of the association and invited the local press who hopefully would record the happy scene. A young reporter, pencil and notepad poised in hand, asked me what I thought my constituents would think of my successor. I speculated that the good people of Chipping Barnet would be excited when they met Theresa. Scribbling this down, he then looked up at me and enquired "why?" "Well," I intoned, "they will have the exciting prospect of voting for a young lady to take over from an old woman." I then turned to my successor and with all the patronising pomp I could muster added: "My dear, over the next two years, you have my full authority, nay my most earnest desire, to personally stalk me." I knew her well and had already discovered that she was almost half my age and much easier on the eye. A few months later, I accidentally overheard two constituents in the High Street discussing our relative merits and one saying to the other that she had nicer legs. I was deeply offended. After all, few people had ever seen my legs and after this incident I made sure that even fewer would.

Towards the end of 2003, dissatisfaction with our new leader led to the requisite number of Tory MPs triggering a no-confidence ballot and Iain failed by 90-75. We had no stomach for another drawn out election and instinctively recognised that Michael Howard must lead us into the next election.

In early 2004, I instituted a short debate in Westminster Hall about arrangements for the sixtieth anniversary commemoration of D-Day. At first the Government appeared half-hearted about any special event to recall the invasion but after the clear wishes of many veterans had been expressed, aided by media interest, the Ministry of Defence fully co-operated and plans were made. Following comments made to me by local members of the British Legion and Cllr Terry Burton who was deeply involved in the Normandy Veterans' Association, I was concerned about some of the arrangements - or lack of them - such as travel facilities for elderly veterans and their ability to actually get to the beaches and ceremonies, given the tight security necessary when world leaders gather. I had no intention of turning the debate into a party political issue but merely recorded a number of points that had been put to me, expressing my confidence that the Government would take them on board and respond positively to ensure a memorable event.

The Minister responsible was Ivor Caplin and he replied with courtesy and concern which reassured me. A few weeks later I was astonished to receive an invitation to attend the various ceremonies as an official representative. I thought a mistake had been made and asked my secretary to ring the Minister's office to say so. But no, Ivor had deliberately asked that I be one of the ten parliamentarians to attend, with the PM, Defence Secretary, the Leader of the Opposition and Shadow Defence Secretary, the Liberal Leader and his spokesman, an Ulster Unionist and the Chairman of the Defence Select Committee. Many years ago a film had been made about D-Day entitled *The Longest Day* and it was certainly a long one for me on 6 June 2004. I had to be at RAF Northolt by 6am. When I arrived, my car was taken from me and alighting from the one in front was Michael Howard and Nicholas Soames. They looked at me and then at each other clearly thinking "what is he doing here?" When they were inside, they discreetly asked me as much. An RAF plane took us to an airfield near Bayeux but we had to spend the best part of an hour circling because the President of the United States was due and security demanded it. This did little for UK/ US relations and even less for our comfort.

When we eventually landed we were first escorted to a cemetery where hundreds of veterans were gathered for the main Commonwealth/French wreath-laying event attended by The Queen and President Chirac. While waiting for them to arrive, I mingled with many of the VIPs including Tony Blair (he gave me the same initial look as had Michael Howard and Nicholas Soames), the Australian PM John Howard, and Winston Churchill's grandson and former colleague in the House. A mild looking, friendly faced man in military attire approached me and asked how I was, venturing that it was some time since we had last met. It was the uniform which threw me but I immediately engaged him in pleasantries about the weather (it was a very hot day) before the penny dropped and, just in time, I was able to introduce the Lib-Dem Defence spokesman Paul Keetch to him. He was HRH The Duke of Gloucester, fellow architect and leader of our Embassy hunt in Moscow nearly twenty years before. After this ceremony we travelled to the beach-head near Arromanches where the main event attended by the heads of fourteen nations (including Germany) was to take place. We waited for the Presidents and Prime Ministers from thirteen of them, including Jacques Chirac, to arrive in a modest coach and the crowd greeted them enthusiastically. We then waited for President Bush and waited for so long that I feared his reception might be distinctly cooler. At last we spotted a police escort leading a large limousine followed by back-up on the horizon but when the cavalcade arrived it continued on, to be immediately followed by another one from which the President finally emerged. I stood transfixed at the sight of such a security spectacle but he was well received and the ceremony proceeded. When it was over, I happened to be walking to the next event with Michael Howard, accompanied by a high-ranking RAF officer, when our progress was temporarily interrupted by the US procession departing. When it had passed, the officer observed that it contained no less than forty-nine vehicles. I couldn't resist saying in front of my Party leader: "Oh, just like my annual visit to Chipping Barnet."

The final event involved us walking down a steep hill at the bottom of which nestled the town square where the final British event was to take place. This was a march past and inspection of the veterans by The Queen, a slightly less formal finale to a memorable day. My two abiding and deeply emotional memories of having the privilege to attend these commemorative events were of the bemedalled veterans standing proudly in the market square (one with seventeen medals and most of them with over ten) and the immaculate rows of hundreds of gravestones in Bayeux Cemetery recording the deaths of young men who had given their lives so that we could live in freedom. There were tears in my eyes as I read the names and ages of many of them, some still in their teens and most of the rest in their twenties.

Later in 2004 I was to make a much longer visit to a much further distant land - Australia - for three weeks in August, first staying a night over in Singapore. This was on a Commonwealth Parliamentary Association delegation and was my first visit to the other side of the world. Our leader was Helen Liddell (former Scottish Secretary) whose appointment as our High Commissioner had just been announced. The other two Labour MPs were Alan Meale (again) and Diana Organ while the other two Tories were Sir John Butterfill and Sir Nicholas Winterton. Andrew Tuggey, the CPA UK Branch Secretary, looked after us and we all met up at Brisbane Airport and spent our first five days in Queensland before going down to Canberra to meet a number of Ministers and see John Howard at his PM's Questions session. Australia's capital (like Washington DC) is planned on a long axis stretching for miles with the new Parliament House at one end, the Old Parliament building in the centre and the War Memorial and Museum at the other end. We renewed acquaintance with Sir Alastair Goodlad, our soon to depart High Commissioner who hosted a briefing dinner, accompanied us on some of our engagements in the Capital Territory and, with his wife Cecilia, gave us a splendid official dinner at the British Residence. It was good to meet them again in pastures new after our "whipping days" and he was clearly delighted that his four year appointment had been extended until after the forthcoming Election (Mr Blair did not want to risk a by-election).

We then adjourned to Sydney for the weekend. For years I had dreamed of visiting my namesake and was looking forward to doing so with mounting impatience. This clearly showed and the rest of the delegation were beginning to take the proverbial out of me as we were driven in from the airport. I like to think that honours were even when we entered the city under a banner which proclaimed: "Welcome to Sydney." I turned to the others and said with a pained expression: "Sorry they forgot to mention the rest of you." I was anxious to collect appropriate T-shirts and an informal contest was arranged to see who could find the best one. The obvious "I Love Sydney" was soon spotted, quickly followed by a more up-market variation which depicted the Opera House, Bridge and some tall buildings under which was written: "Sydney, Simply The Best." The winner of the competition (I was the sole judge) was Diana Meale. Some of us had taken a boat across the Bay to Manly, reputedly named by Captain Cook when he saw unclothed male aboriginees lined up on the beach looking at his galleon in wonder. Diana was searching around the clothes section in the local store and suddenly screamed: "I've found it," appearing with a white singlet on which was printed in two lines: "Manly Sydney." I wear it with pride. During the weekend I was able to meet my nephew Mark, who joined us for dinner and was now in the Australian Army. I appreciated his gesture in driving over two hundred miles to see me, then having to return to Queensland for a 7am appointment. A footnote on my namesake. The place was named after Lord Sydney, previously Thomas Townshend who was raised to the peerage by William Pitt the Younger when he became Foreign Secretary in 1783. In his excellent biography of Pitt, William Hague writes:

"Townshend earlier toyed with the title of Lord Sydenham, and his decision not to adopt that name was to be of lasting importance to the people in Australia, since a few year's later Sydney was to be named after him."

Onwards to Alice Springs at the heart of this vast country for three days of meetings which sadly (to the amazement of the Federal Minister of Tourism) precluded a trip to Ayres Rock (Uluru) four hundred miles away. The last leg of our visit was to Darwin, the principal objective of which was to study the workings of the governance of the Northern Territory and the relationship between its First Minister, the Legislature and the Administrator,

Ted Eagan, whose wife Nerys originally hailed from South Wales. She seemed to epitomise our Commonwealth of Nations: a British born lass now living in an important but distant outpost on the farthest flung continent. We had arrived in the Antipodes in their winter but Brisbane was like a hot summer's day in England and we had left it in the scorching climate of Darwin. It is the sheer vastness and relative emptiness of the country which amazed me: three million sq. miles with deserts and mountain ranges in an environment which stretched from the Snowy Mountains outside Canberra to the sub-tropical climate of Darwin. Only twenty million souls inhabit this land (fewer than live in the Tokyo-Yokohama conurbation) and 98 per cent of them live within sight of the surrounding oceans and seas. One of the Federal Parliamentary constituencies in Western Australia, Kalgoorlie, was the size of Western Europe (I hope its MP gets travelling expenses). The spirit of Australians is best expressed in the country's coat of arms which consists of the two animals unable to walk backwards: an emu and a kangaroo, with the motto: "Forward Australia."

Three weeks in Australia more than compensated for the loss of my annual holiday and August is usually the least frenetic month for MPs. Constituency correspondence falls (as it usually does over Christmastide) but there was still a mountain of mail to tackle. Parliamentary recesses broadly coincide with school holidays but with one exception - after the summer break schools return in early September but MPs only come back to Westminster after the Party Conference season has ended in mid-October. September is usually the busiest month for MPs in their constituencies when they have the opportunity to visit businesses, local groups and schools. And so it was that after catching up on my post bag, I scurried around my part of Barnet carrying out engagements on what was to be my last autumnal tour, but there was to be an exceptional event which was to be a timely reminder that retirement was beckoning.

22

FAREWELL TO POLITICS

An official from Barnet Council approached me with courteous diffidence but armed with a resolution in his hand to enquire if, in recognition of my twenty five years service as a Barnet MP, I would agree to have a road named after me. This honour had been instigated by Cllr Brian Coleman, chairman of the Borough's Environment Committee (who was also our directly elected member of the Greater London Assembly). I was greatly flattered but a sixth sense told me that something was wrong. I knew that, in law, every road had to have a name but there were no new roads being constructed in my area. I told him that I was extremely honoured, but surely there was a problem adding: "if you lived in Acacia Avenue, you would surely object to having it changed to Chapman Avenue – or whatever." "Ah", he said, "we've thought of that and found a road on which no one lives." There was indeed a road, fully one furlong long, which traversed Hadley Green and was called Hadley Green Slip Road. It now is officially called 'Sydney Chapman Way', the 'Way' being written on a second line all by itself. Graffitists were to have a field day; 'Sydney Chapman Way Out; Sydney Chapman No Way; and Sydney Chapman On Way Out' being some of the more family friendly descriptions. Rudi Vis (from next door Finchley) was one of a number of guests who attended the grand opening ceremony, even though my newly designated thoroughfare was one of my most distant roads from his constituency. He now affectionately refers to it as "Sydney's Back Passage."

I was determined to carry out my parliamentary and constituency duties until the last Division Bell of the Parliament and if the best advice to any new MP is

'start as you mean to continue' I was resolved to ensure that I finished as I had started. Little did I realise that this would turn out to be literally true. When the House returned in the autumn Michael Ancram approached me during the first Division to ask if I would like to be his Parliamentary Private Secretary. Why he should ask me still remains a mystery but I happily agreed, realising that my political career would start and end as a PPS. When in Opposition, only the Leader has a PPS, or so I thought, but Michael was our Deputy Leader (as well as Shadow Foreign and Defence spokesman) and was also entitled to a bag carrier. The irony of accepting this post was not lost on my contemporaries – an about to depart MP in his seventieth year serving the likeable and ten years younger deputy leader of his Party. My duties were performed at a more relaxed level than when first appointed with fewer meetings and a more laid back approach in the Chamber. I also had the opportunity to rcncw my acquaintance with David Howell who was now our Foreign Affairs spokesman in the Lords after holding a clutch of ministerial posts in Conservative Cabinets. The downside of helping Michael was that I had to resign from the Public Administration Select Committee (to which I had been appointed in 2001) and could not make speeches in the Chamber on Foreign and

Defence matters. I bore these restraints with fortitude but I did miss the Select Committee meetings under the outstanding chairmanship of Tony Wright.

I continued to play a part in Standing Committees and was again appointed to examine a Housing & Planning Bill, concerned *inter alia* with homes in multiple occupation and yet another attempt to speed up the planning process. The five Tory backbenchers could indulge themselves when the opportunity arose and the hours were spent in reasonably good humour by all, given the Government majority and the competent ease of the minister, Keith Hill. In one exchange I used my own parliamentary *pied-a-terre* in Battersea to query the extent and effect of a proposed Clause, describing its whereabouts as 'Batter-sear' (which I preferred to call 'South Chelsea') and referring to the minister's nearby constituency as 'St.Reatham.' Keith duly entered into the spirit of the occasion and was followed by one of his colleagues David Kidney who introduced himself as the Member for 'St.Afford.' One of my colleagues on this committee was John Randall who had a family Department Store which sold all types of furniture. He had explained to me that the reason he had held his seat in the first by-election of the previous Parliament (caused by the shock death of Michael Shersby who was about to be elected Deputy Speaker) was because half of his constituents slept in his beds. John was a keen amateur photographer and as he was speaking a particular species of bird flew past the Committee Room window. He suddenly stopped and said in an excited voice: "Mr Chairman, I've snapped many birds in my time but never got a shag."

Ever active at Question Time, in a supplementary to a Work & Pensions minister about encouraging people to make informed choices about their retirement, I averred:

"Speaking as a person who defines youth as anybody who is younger than a year older than I happen to be, do the Government intend to give advice to those of us who are voluntarily not seeking re-election about informed choices on retirement? If they do, may I suggest that it would be helpful to have confirmation that the next election will be held on Thursday 5 May?"

I received one of the best ministerial answers I have heard from the relatively new Minister Malcolm Wickes: "I have been told the date, but I have not brought my diary with me, so I aplogise to the hon.Gentleman. I cannot believe that he is even thinking of retiring. I urge him to be age positive, to have an active old age and to take part in voluntary activity – his local Labour party always needs some help."

Perhaps one of my better efforts in the Chamber was when I was called during a question to the Member answering for the Church Commissioners about insuring cathedrals. Normally Sir Stuart Bell, the Second Church Estates Commissioner, would answer but he was away so it fell to a junior minister, David Lammy, to answer. I asked him:

"Can the Minister tell the House whether the Church insures its buildings against acts of God? If it does, does that not show a certain lack of faith, and if it doesn't, does that not show a certain lack of acumen?"

Unfortunately I did not know beforehand that David would be replying (or indeed that I would be called by Mr. Speaker). If I had, I would have forewarned him and perhaps even suggested his reply might have been along the lines of "God only knows."

As departure time approached I suppose it was inevitable that I began to reflect on times past and the changes that had taken place since I first became an MP. The composition of the Chamber had certainly changed; only twenty one colleagues remained in the House from thirty-five years before (including some, like me, with broken service); our procedures and sittings had been dramatically altered; our influence had declined and our powers had been curtailed. Additionally, all the evidence suggested that respect for us from the public was evaporating. Some would say it was ever thus but in 2004 the Committee on Standards in Public Life undertook an in depth survey about your views of those in public life. On the question of trust, top of the list came family doctors and bottom were journalists on tabloid newspapers. MPs and government ministers were near the bottom, only fractionally above estate agents. What interested me was that whereas only just over one-quarter of the public trusted MPs to tell the truth, nearly one-half of all those asked thought their local MP was truthful. This would support a remark often made to me (and doubtless other colleagues) when constituents made disparaging remarks about our profession: "of course, you are different." Nevertheless it is a sobering thought for your legislators that one in five people think we take bribes; half of you think we use power for our own gain; and two in five see us as incompetent.

Our country has also changed significantly. In the more than a quarter of a century that I have represented Chipping Barnet, Britain's population has increased by four million but the number of households has also risen by that number. This underlines starkly the social trends that have taken place. Loneliness is more widespread today with the number of one parent families doubling and three in ten dwellings containing only one person. Correspondingly the proportion of households consisting of couples with children has declined from one in three to just over one in five. Whereas we used to think of a typical family as a couple with 2.4 children, today the figure is 1.6. With divorce and separations rising, perhaps we ought to be thinking of a typical family as a child with 2.4 parents. We are also an ageing population with life expectancy of men having risen from sixty-nine to seventy-six and of women from seventy-six to eighty-one years. Little wonder that the working age group in our country has declined from half the population to under 45 per cent. The UK's rising population has been fortified by significantly increased immigration and with smaller households the demand for extra housing has inevitably put pressure on our green and pleasant land.

My constituency has reflected all these changes with few significant exceptions. The inevitable spread of our towns into the countryside has not happened around Chipping Barnet, protected as it has been by the Metropolitan Green Belt which surrounds much of it. Set against this, overfilling in our suburbs has been rampant, as instanced by many large family homes being replaced with flats and their former gardens covered with tarmacadam for off-street parking. Mention parking and another visible change in our towns and countryside has been the growth of cars: from under two million to over twenty-seven million in my lifetime, with available on-street parking spaces at a premium. More vehicles have inevitably meant more pollution even though technology has lessened pollution per vehicle. Air travel has tripled in the last twenty-five years and with the need to dispose of more human waste, the assault on our environment has come from all directions. Throughout my political life, there has been at least one common thread: my deep interest in matters environmental and yet I will be found wanting by those who embrace the whole ecological agenda without question. My record will be judged for itself but I remain in favour of nuclear power as a contributor to our energy needs while supporting a much more rigorous energy conservation programme; and I am not against the growing of GM crops in Britain *per se*. In my view, the environment, like life and politics, is a question of balances – not absolutes.

The age structure of my constituents has been roughly in line with that in the country though we have a slightly higher proportion of over eighty-five year olds and, in a report published in 2004, I was pleased to read that Barnet was the healthiest Borough in Greater London, vying with the healthiest region, South-West England. Another exceptional feature of the Borough is the high

244

proportion of Jews - 24 per cent in Finchley, 23 per cent in Hendon and 10 per cent in Chipping Barnet – easily the greatest concentration in any local authority. With the exception of these differences and having a higher number of professionals and managers but fewer semi-skilled and unskilled workers, Chipping Barnet really is typical of middle England.

My last constituency chairman was to be David Miller, one of Baroness Miller of Hendon's three sons who, a few years before, had bought a house on a new housing estate in my patch. I had known his mother Doreen for many years. She was a bundle of political energy in the Greater London Conservatives, having been successively Treasurer, Chairman and President in the 1990s and she has ceaselessly campaigned for more women in public life. Shortly after going to the Lords she was appointed a junior minister in the last three years of the last Conservative Government.

Parallel to my political career has been my sister's service in local government. Christine's interest was first aroused when she took part in a survey and then joined a campaign for a new hospital in Mississauga, near Toronto when she and Peter were raising their family there. That town now has one of the largest hospitals in Canada. Upon returning to England in 1979 she joined the Parish Council of Wokingham Without, followed by South Ascot when she moved there. Since 1995 she has been a Borough Councillor in Windsor & Maidenhead, now a unitary authority, and was deputy leader of the Council. Christine was also Chairman of the East Berkshire Conservatives and following boundary changes Chairman of the Windsor constituency. It must be recorded that in our respective 1997 elections her majority was double mine in her Sunningdale Ward, with less than one-tenth of the number of voters in Chipping Barnet!

And so to my valedictory speech in the Commons. I judged that the appropriate occasion would be the debate on the Budget and decided to home in on the vast increase in public expenditure during my political career and to question whether we were getting value for money. After regretting that I had no financial interest to declare, I reminded the House that I had first fought a parliamentary election over forty years before when annual government expenditure was less than £13bn but had increased to £22bn by 1970. During the eighteen years of Conservative governments (1979-1997) it had grown from £87bn to £320bn and since then to nearly £500bn. Only during the previous Labour administration (1974-79) had public spending not grown significantly in real terms and it was absurd to suggest that spending would be cut under a future Conservative government.

Health expenditure had increased from £1bn in 1964 to £85bn in 2005, having quintupled during the eighteen years of the last Tory government and increased by nearly £40bn in the last eight years. I went on: "One feature of NHS spending worries me. Despite the huge increase in the last eight years, all the NHS Trusts around me complain of massive and increasing deficits... if all the increased spending is not getting to the sharp end, a lot must have leaked in the pipeline between the Government and the local trusts."

I then turned to the National Debt saying that it had increased from £30 billion to £450 billion in the last forty years and that the value of the pound had been reduced by 90 per cent since I first arrived in the House in 1970. I asserted the obvious: that we had to spend more because of inflation and an increasing population; and my thesis was that whereas yesteryear people were impressed with rising spending on the vital public services, now they were beginning to question whether the increases were being allocated effectively and efficiently. I complained that the Chancellor in his Budget statements was being "highly selective in the statistics he gives us" (are not we all?) then referred briefly to the fifty successive quarters of economic growth, Gordon Brown's timid tightening of public spending, the accumulating current deficits and the deterioration in private savings. I welcomed the doubling of the threshold before stamp duty was liable but complained that the liability should not apply to the whole purchase price after the new threshold of £120,000, when the current average house price in England was £190,000 and double that in Chipping Barnet. I finished on a personal note, referring to the diminishing power of the legislature vis-à-vis the Executive but asserting: "Members of Parliament still have a fundamental role and it has been a privilege to have been here for thirty years. The hours have been long and the job has been stressful but rewarding. I shall miss serving my constituents and the camaraderie and friendship that I have enjoyed throughout the House."

My final contribution on the floor of the House was not intended to set the place alight, nor did it, and my only worry was that it might have contained too many statistics but it was after all made in a Budget debate. Ken Clarke and Stephen Dorrell were good enough to stay to hear me after their contributions and subsequent speakers were complimentary, not least the Shadow Chancellor Oliver Letwin and Chief Secretary to the Treasury Paul Boateng who wound up the debate.

On the twenty-fifth anniversary of my first election in Chipping Barnet the year before, John Major was guest-of-honour at a special dinner and three months before my retirement Margaret Thatcher attended my final constituency fund raising 'Blue Ball' making her last public speech. It was at the Waldorf Hotel in The Aldwych, from where the Palm Court orchestra broadcast in pre-war days. It was an emotional evening and an historical one for my association. My only duty on the night was to propose a vote of thanks to her and after the standing ovation she received it would have been foolish of me not to have kept it short:

"Margaret, we salute you tonight not just because you were our neighbouring constituency MP and became Prime Minister; nor just because you have been our first woman Prime Minister,

John Major at the dinner to celebrate Sydney Chapman's
twenty-five years as the MP for Chipping Barnet

Margaret Thatcher at her last public speech in 2005

though all of that deserves recognition in itself. We salute you not just because you have been the longest serving Prime Minister in the 20th century though that is a matter for our heartiest congratulations. We salute you above all because you have turned our country around from being the sick man of Europe to one that is admired throughout the world. I was proud to be a humble foot soldier on your long march and we thank and salute you for your historic service to our nation."

I can say in all immodesty that it was one of the best received speeches I have made (probably because it was also one of the shortest) but I have to confess that the audience wasn't cheering me!

In my last week in the House I was told that William Hague had agreed to be the guest speaker at a retirement dinner to be held for me in Hatfield House after the Election. Just before the election was announced, I had accepted Michael Howard's invitation to oversee his correspondence unit during the campaign, signing hundreds of letters on his behalf while he was out and about the country. The battle commenced and I cleared my desk and left the Palace on my last day as an MP. The place was almost deserted; the building was like a vast mausoleum and I suddenly felt alone. With my no more to be produced Rover 75 (MG Rover had just become insolvent) full of books and files, I drove out of Carriage Gates in New Palace Yard for the last time. Unusually, a policeman on duty (whom I did not recognise) walked out into the road, stopped the traffic and came across to me. I wound down the window to thank him and he simply said: "Sir Sydney, I wish you a long and happy retirement."

As I turned the vehicle homewards, it wasn't the car that nearly broke down.

Lightning Source UK Ltd.
Milton Keynes UK
11 January 2010

148467UK00003B/2/P